The
Chains of
Protection

The Chains of Protection

THE JUDICIAL RESPONSE TO WOMEN'S LABOR LEGISLATION

Judith A. Baer

Contributions in Women's Studies, Number 1

 GREENWOOD PRESS
WESTPORT, CONNECTICUT · LONDON, ENGLAND

Library of Congress Cataloging in Publication Data

Baer, Judith A
    The chains of protection.

    (Contributions in women's studies ; no. 1
ISSN 0147-104X)
    Bibliography: p.
    Includes index.
    1. Discrimination in employment—Law and legislation—United States.
2. Women—Employment—United States. 3. Sex discrimination against
women—Law and legislation—United States. 4. Equal pay for equal work—
United States. I. Title. II. Series: Contributions in women's studies ; no. 1.
KF3467.B3   344'.73'014   77-82695
ISBN 0-8371-9785-6

Library of Congress Catalog Card Number: 77-82695
ISBN: 0-8371-9785-6
ISSN: 0147-104X

First published in 1978

Greenwood Press, Inc.
51 Riverside Avenue, Westport, Connecticut 06880

Printed in the United States of America

10 9 8 7 6 5 4 3 2 1

ACKNOWLEDGMENTS

The following material is reprinted by permission:

Excerpt from *The Politics of Aristotle,* translated by Sir Ernest Barker (1948). By permission of Oxford University Press.

Excerpt from Simone de Beauvior, *The Second Sex,* translated by H. M. Parshley. Copyright 1953. By permission of Alfred A. Knopf, Inc.

CONTENTS

PREFACE

This book is an effort to unite feminism and scholarship. It arose from my conviction that passionate commitment is compatible with dispassionate inquiry, and from my determination to explore the moral issue of sexual equality. It had its origins in my career as a graduate student in political science at the University of Chicago, where both the scholar and the feminist in me were nurtured: the former through a stimulating intellectual environment and through excellent teachers and fellow students, and the latter through the women's movement both on and off campus. Over several years, these influences—reading, classes, meetings, and always, discussion—combined to convince me both of the universality and injustice of male supremacy and of the ability of scholarship to illuminate problems which may be very personal in impact. I was struck by the absence of reason in many discussions of this issue, and became determined to bring my scholarly skills to bear on it.

As a specialist in public law, I have naturally been concerned with the role of law in this system of male domination. When I decided to write this book, the subject of "women and the law" came to mind. This topic soon proved to be of unmanageable complexity, and I recognized the need to narrow my focus. I selected women's labor legislation as a topic only after I had done extensive general reading in the field, enough to learn that this area of law provided not only much legal material to analyze and criticize, but also many opportunities to identify and discuss the moral questions involved. This is the result of that inquiry.

This work owes much to several members of the Political Science Department of the University of Chicago, Professors Herbert Storing, Susanne Hoeber Rudolph, and Gerhard Casper. Professor Storing in particular provided insightful, extensive criticism which immeasurably has improved the final product. Greenwood Press and its reviewer provided constructive criticism and advice which greatly assisted me in completing my book. I am also grateful to Toby Resnick, Betty Strom, and Ada Bradley, who typed the manuscript in various stages.

Finally, to paraphrase the Ninth Amendment, the enumeration here of certain individuals does not deny or disparage the help of many other friends, whom I gratefully acknowledge.

Judith A. Baer

The
Chains of
Protection

INTRODUCTION

The issue of sexual differences has received much attention in the last few years, but it is not a subject on which everything worth saying has been said. One crucial aspect of the problem which has not received due attention in contemporary literature is the set of moral questions involved. How *should* society, and law, treat men and women? Are the restraints imposed upon women in our society just or unjust? These problems have been neglected mainly because those who discussed the issue have not seen them as questions at all, but have usually assumed the truth of one answer or another. Writers have started from one or the other of two value positions, each of which includes assumptions which are uncritically accepted by the proponents of the position and which, they think, dictate certain conclusions.

Feminists assume that, despite the biological differences, the sexes are more alike than unlike; that, therefore, a life style desirable or undesirable for one sex would be equally so for the other; and, consequently, that all artificial sexual distinctions should be removed. Contemporary feminists have not tried to prove that women are oppressed, but have assumed it, and have devoted their efforts to illuminating various aspects of the alleged oppression.[1] Traditionalists assume that biological differences between the sexes dictate different life styles, and, therefore, justify many restrictions.[2] Each position includes not only assumptions about human nature which cannot be accepted without investigation, but also the less obvious and equally questionable assumption that the resolution of the moral questions depends on the discovery of facts about human nature which would confirm either set of psychological assumptions.[3] The two groups tend to talk past each other.

This, I think, represents an unfortunate gap in our thinking about sex equality. The major problem in examining the moral issues is how to limit the scope of an investigation into so complex a social phenomenon to reduce it to manageable size, while at the same time ranging widely enough and probing deeply enough to have grounds for drawing conclusions. One good place to look for arguments about justice (though not necessarily a place to look for good arguments about justice) and information about social attitudes is law, often in the text of statutes themselves, but particularly in the making of new laws and the defense of existing ones.

Although the law may in fact reflect only the balance of political power, we expect it to embody higher moral standards.[4] We agree that its role is not only to coerce but also (within limits) to teach by example. This expectation is revealed in the public discussion which surrounds the making and interpretation of laws, in which appeals are made not only to the needs of competing interests but also to the ideals of justice.

The area of law that I have chosen to examine is special labor legislation for women, usually called protective labor legislation. Some sort of protective legislation existed in every state before 1969, when the Equal Employment Opportunity Commission ruled that such laws conflicted with and were superseded by the Civil Rights Act of 1964, which prohibits sex discrimination in employment.[5] Until the early 1970s these special laws provided the basis of most of the opposition to the Equal Rights Amendment to the Constitution since it was first proposed in 1923.[6]

The drive for women's employment legislation was, of course, part of a larger reform movement, and cannot be studied in isolation from it. Since employment regulation is an exercise of police power, traditionally the domain of the states, we deal here mainly with state, not federal, law. However, in a sense this is a historical accident which has little to do with the labor movement itself, although it dictated strategy to some extent. The conditions which gave rise to labor legislation were not peculiar to each state, and many of the same groups were involved in the fight for these laws in different states. Therefore, I think it would have made little sense to restrict the study regionally. It seemed more valuable to concentrate on some aspect of labor legislation common to all states rather than all legislation in a few states.

One important part of this history is the judicial treatment of labor legislation. Briefs, arguments, and court decisions are a particularly abundant source of discussions of moral questions in relation to law. The difficulties which these laws encountered in the courts are well known. In the fifty years after the Civil War, several laws were invalidated in state[7] and federal[8] supreme courts. Many of these laws fell because the courts thought they infringed upon freedom of contract.[9] At the same time, nearly identical laws were being upheld in other jurisdictions.[10]

Initially, laws applying only to women had a similar erratic fate.[11] But in the landmark case of *Muller v. Oregon*[12] in 1908, the U.S. Supreme Court upheld a ten-hour law for women, and the state courts soon fell into line.[13] *Muller* has been considered a landmark case not for its relevance to sex discrimination but for its legitimization of economic regulation by the government. But it has been the controlling case in the former area as well as in the latter; the constitutionality of protective labor legislation for women has, until recently, been almost totally accepted by the courts.[14] Indeed, *Muller* has been cited as binding precedent in cases which have nothing to do with employment.[15]

Protective labor legislation was not questioned by the courts until the 1960s, after the passage of two federal laws which curtailed sex discrimination in employment. These laws were the Equal Pay Act of 1963, which amended the Fair Labor Standards Act of 1938 to forbid sex discrimination in payment for substantially equal work, and Title VII of the Civil Rights Act of 1964, which absolutely prohibited race discrimination in employment and imposed a more limited ban on discrimination based on sex, religion, or national origin. Title VII, in particular, produced much litigation from women who had been refused jobs which would have required them to work under conditions forbidden by state laws. In 1968, in *Rosenfeld v. Southern Pacific Company*,[16] a Federal District Judge ruled that California's wage, hours, and weight-lifting regulations for women violated Title VII and thus were nugatory. After the Equal Employment Opportunity Commission endorsed this decision, all federal courts which heard similar cases followed suit.[17]

This study analyzes the developments I have described. I have explored the process by which protective legislation became constitutionally legitimate, and the effect of its legitimization both on economic regulation and, more extensively, on women's rights. I have then examined the circumstances of its demolition, in order to discover what can be learned from these readings about protection, restriction, and equality.

This judicial history can be divided into four phases, three constitutional and one statutory. The three constitutional phases follow in chronological order, while the final, statutory, phase coincides with the last years of the third constitutional one. The first phase ends in 1908, with *Muller*. In this case, for the first time, reformers presented to a court substantial medical and sociological data, inaugurating the era of the "Brandeis brief," named after its creator. The second period runs from 1908 to 1937, by which time the courts considered the expansion of the *Muller*

principle to general labor regulation[18] and other kinds of special women's
labor legislation.[19] Nineteen thirty-seven marks the end of this period because of the decision that year in *West Coast Hotel v. Parrish,*[20] which
upheld a minimum-wage law for women while repudiating the doctrine
of freedom of contract which had been the foremost obstacle to economic regulation by government. In the third period, from 1937 to the present, we have seen the almost infinite expansion of the *Muller* principle
by the courts and, in the past six or seven years, the beginning of recon-
sideration. The fourth phase covers the adjudication of the Equal Pay
and Civil Rights Acts, from their enactment to the present.

My first chapter is devoted to a discussion of the historical background
of this legislation, without which no understanding of the decisions is possible. I have not attempted to formulate a radical reinterpretation of American labor history, but only to provide enough information to permit an
evaluation of the courts' performance. In the following four chapters I
trace the development of the law in the phases identified. I have tried to
assess the effects of the constraints imposed by the judicial context, examining the ways in which the arguments were transformed by the movement
of the conflict to the courts, and the sensitivity of the courts to external
factors. I explore the ways in which the judges' perceptions of these cases
changed over the wide time span studied, how the amount and quality of
the evidence needed to convince them waxed and waned, and how the
courts used statute and precedent. After analyzing the logical and constitutional validity of the decision and arguments, and trying to explain why
these questions were resolved as they were, I turn in the final chapters to
an exploration of the moral issues.

My exploration of the judicial history of women's labor legislation has
two purposes: to evaluate the courts' response to this particular issue and
to approach some of the normative questions involved in the law's treatment of the sexes. I am trying to resolve two problems: the limited one
of the constitutionality of special employment legislation for women, and
the broader question of the justice of differential treatment of the sexes in
general. My investigation has proved to be a fruitful way of approaching
the moral issues, because first, it revealed in microcosm many of the *a
priori* assumptions and logical fallacies which have characterized our
thinking about sex equality, and second, it involved a crucial political
problem—the tension between protection and restriction.

Any law which protects by requiring or forbidding certain actions
inevitably restricts individual freedom. The power to protect is the power

to control. We can see this clearly in areas which have nothing to do with women or employment. For example, parents cannot effectively protect their child from crossing the street without forbidding her to cross the street. A state cannot protect its citizens from pornography without forbidding them access to it. These rules could be made for either or both purposes. The hypothetical parents might forbid their child to cross the street to protect her, or simply for the pleasure of being boss. Obscenity laws may be motivated by a sincere desire to protect people from what are thought to be evil influences or by a wish to limit their pleasure. Public debate over this issue provides ample evidence of the existence, singly or in combination, of both motives (along with other motives which are interesting but irrelevant to this discussion).

Not only may the same rules be promulgated for either protective or restrictive purposes, but they may have either or both effects, depending not on the motives behind them but on the circumstances of the case. If the child in the first example were two years old, the rule against crossing the street would protect her; it would restrict her only in a formal sense. If she were twelve (assuming mental and physical normality), the rule would substantially curtail her freedom; the protection it afforded would be unnecessary. In my second hypothetical case, we can find advocates at either end of the spectrum and at all points in between. Some argue that obscenity laws protect no one from any real danger but only limit freedom of expression; others argue the very opposite. The effect of the regulation would vary, depending on who was denied access to what material.

One point in the preceding paragraph cannot be emphasized too strongly. The question of the *motives* of the proponents of a given regulation has to be separated from the question of the *effects* of the regulation. Good motives can produce bad laws and vice versa. One argument that I shall discuss is the contention that women's labor legislation has been designed, not to protect women from harm, but to prevent them from competing with men for jobs. There is indeed evidence that this motive existed among some supporters of these laws, but there is equally persuasive evidence that in the years when states began to enact this legislation, its most successful advocates were motivated by a sincere desire to protect women workers. However, this does not dispose of the question of whether the restrictions imposed on women workers have provided necessary protection or have unnecessarily curtailed their freedom, and to what extent at what time. However sincere the altruistic motives which produced these laws, the intentions of their proponents could not dictate their effects, either at the time of passage or in the intervening years.

If protection and restriction are inextricably joined, how can one evaluate a rule which is designed to protect? Two questions must be asked in order to determine the legitimacy of such a law. First, does the restriction help or hurt those directly affected by it? If it does help them, the policy is justified, at least from their point of view. If the restriction is harmful rather than helpful, a second question arises: are the adverse effects of the restriction on those affected by it outweighed by the benefits it gives to others?

In answering the first question, one crucial set of factors is, to borrow from free speech theory, the clarity, proximity, and gravity of the evil which the rule is designed to prevent. In the parent-child example, an automobile accident clearly is an evil grave enough to justify parental constraint. Why, then, is the rule against crossing the street protective for the two-year-old and overly restrictive for the twelve-year-old? Obviously, there is a second crucial variable: the extent to which the persons covered by a regulation need outside protection against the evil. A two-year-old does not have the capacity to understand or guard against the dangers of traffic, and, therefore, needs the prohibitory rule. A twelve-year-old, however, can interpret these dangers and, to a great extent, protect herself from them without parental guidance. The case would be more problematical if the child were five or eight, or if the activity were not crossing the street but walking in a large American city after dark.

A third factor is the extent to which personal freedom is actually curtailed by the restriction, or the extent to which freedom would be increased if the restriction were removed. It makes little sense to talk of a two-year-old's freedom in this example. She lacks the capacity to make intelligent and significant choices as to which side of the street she wants to be on. Our hypothetical twelve-year-old could make such choices, and her freedom would therefore be significantly curtailed. In order to decide whether a rule is justified, one would have to decide whether the need for protection justifies the extent to which freedom is abridged.

The situation becomes still more complex when we move from parental to governmental power. Laws, unlike family rules, affect a large number of people whom the legislators rarely know personally and who vary widely in circumstances and capacities. Any law is likely to have different effects on some of those covered by it than on others. In any single case we need to consider who is being deprived of how much of what value or values and to what extent by restriction, as well as who is gaining how much of what value or values by protection.

What sort of questions must one ask, then, in order to determine where a particular labor law for women falls on the protection-restriction continuum? One must assess the evils from which women are allegedly being protected. A law which keeps them from spending an additional four hours a day in a hot, unventilated factory filled with dangerous machinery is different from one which keeps them from another two hours in an air-conditioned office with no equipment more threatening than a typewriter. The second factor is, as I have suggested, the extent to which the rule is needed in order to afford the protection. Workers organized into recognized active unions may be able to bargain for reduction of hours; for unorganized and unorganizable workers, legislation may be the only means of ameliorating their situation. The third variable is, again, the extent to which the workers' freedom is actually limited by the rule, rather than by other factors. The opponents of labor legislation frequently argued that these laws abridged the workers' freedom to contract with their employers with respect to their labor. Therefore, it becomes relevant to ask whether the workers did enjoy such freedom in reality. In fact, they did not; in the absence of viable unions, workers accepted the terms offered, and, if not, there were plenty who would. If the factory working day was thirteen hours long, the individual either worked a thirteen-hour day or did not take the job. Legislation which reduced the working day to ten hours (assuming it was enforced) would not deprive workers of any freedom of choice they actually had. When women can choose whether to work during the day or night, laws against night work do deprive them of freedom.

When Oregon's ten-hour law was appealed to the U.S. Supreme Court, reformers searched for a lawyer to defend it. They first approached Joseph H. Choate, a leader of the Massachusetts bar. He refused the case, saying that he saw no reason "why a big husky Irishwoman could not work more than ten hours a day in a laundry if she and her employer so desired."[21] Conceding for the purposes of argument that the hypothetical laundress had such a choice, we must ask whether she could be allowed to exercise it without jeopardizing the interests of smaller and less husky women similarly situated. A similar problem is raised by the arguments of some proponents of special legislation, who frequently suggest that women need protection because of the hazards involved in working during pregnancy. Here, the question arises whether the freedom of all women workers can be curtailed because some of them are pregnant.

The fact that protective legislation has an element of restriction does not, of course, make all such laws unjust. As Justice Holmes remarked in a dissenting opinion I shall be examining, "pretty much all law consists in forbidding men to do some things they want to do."[22] The state frequently substitutes its judgment of our interests for our own, or decides there are other interests to which ours must be subordinated. What must be decided—not assumed—is precisely this: whether the control exercised over an individual or group by a regulation is balanced by the protection it affords its welfare, or that of others.

My thesis here is that the kinds of arguments presented to courts in favor of protective legislation, and the judges' need to reconcile their decisions with prevailing doctrines of constitutional interpretation, led the courts to reach humanitarian but misguided conclusions in early cases, and to ignore the effects of socioeconomic and technological changes in later ones. The courts have overlooked the impact of these changes on the appropriate answers to the first question I posed, and have frequently collapsed the second question into the first by assuming (along with the law's proponents) that women's interests are either included in, or properly subordinate to, those of others. The historical evidence indicates that much of the early legislation was justified by my three criteria, not because of permanent physical differences between the sexes or persistent differences in their social responsibilities, but by temporary social, political, economic, and technological conditions which made women's working conditions worse than men's and intensified the impact of permanent differences. But the defenders of the laws did not find it necessary to distinguish among these factors, and the arguments they presented to the courts were confused. The early courts, because of their adherence to an exaggerated notion of freedom of contract, felt forced to legitimize variations from this principle by reference to permanent sexual differences, and became fixed on that notion.

I suggest that this emphasis developed a life of its own as precedent which, combined with the rise and fall of freedom of contract, has had various results, of cumulative intensity, in the intervening years, which have been unfortunate for the courts' treatment of cases involving sex discrimination. One consistent effect of this body of precedent has been to give a strong presumption of legitimacy to any kind of employment discrimination which can be related to permanent diffences, a presumption which persisted even as conditions changed. Up to 1937, while freedom of contract still had shaky but persistent status as a fundamental right, another result was to cast doubt on the legitimacy of laws such as minimum wage legislation for women, which could not be justified by physical differences but were defensible as mitigations of economic disadvantage. After 1937, the virtual abandonment of any independent judicial review in cases involving economic regulation combined with the force of precedent on sex discrimination to produce judicial acquiescence in virtually all sex-based discrimination, with very little evidence of serious thought about the justifications of these laws either among their proponents or among judges. These developments left the states free to impose restrictions upon women which may hurt rather than help them, in order to benefit others—a public policy nowhere expressly or implicitly forbidden by the Constitution. Only in very recent years, with the emergence of the doctrine of suspect classification, and the passage of new laws, have courts begun to reconsider the legitimacy of sex-based discrimination.

In critically analyzing these decisions, I examine not only their approach to sex discrimination but also the doctrines which helped determine the results during the various constitutional phases. I argue that although these doctrines were overstated, they can be rephrased and improved, and that under the revised principles the laws I examine cannot stand up as protections of women. But they can pass muster as discriminations against women. Only new legislation and the recently developed doctrine of suspect classification could prohibit such discrimination. In evaluating these developments, I have been led to consider, first, the ways in which we can approach the question of sex equality, and second, examination of the evidence we have about the relationship between sex and ability. These problems lead to a discussion of the moral questions which compose one of the two foci of my study.

NOTES

1. See, e.g., Susan Brownmiller, *Against Our Will: Men, Women, and Rape* (New York: Simon & Schuster, 1975); Phyllis Chesler, *Women and Madness* (New York: Doubleday & Co., 1972); Phyllis Chesler and Emily Jane Goodman, *Women, Money, and Power* (New York: William Morrow and Co., 1976); Karen DeCrow,

Sexist Justice (New York: Random House, 1974); Eva Figes, *Patriarchal Attitudes* (New York: Stein & Day, 1970); Shulamith Firestone, *The Dialectic of Sex* (New York: Bantam Books, 1970); Ellen Frankfort, *Vaginal Politics* (New York: Bantam Books, 1973); Vivian Gornick and Barbara K. Moran, eds., *Woman in Sexist Society* (New York: Basic Books, 1971); Elizabeth Janeway, *Between Myth and Morning: Women Awakening* (New York: William Morrow & Co., 1974), and *Man's World, Woman's Place: A Study in Social Mythology* (New York: William Morrow & Co., 1971); Kate Millett, *Sexual Politics* (New York: Doubleday & Co., 1970); Juliet Mitchell, *Psychoanalysis and Feminism* (New York: Pantheon Books, 1974); Robin Morgan, ed., *Sisterhood Is Powerful* (New York: Random House, 1970); Letty Cottin Pogrebin, *Getting Yours* (New York: David McKay Co., 1975); Barbara Seaman, *Free and Female* (New York: Coward-McCann & Geoghegan, Inc., 1972). The subjects treated include employment, marriage, motherhood, sex, health care, psychology, and violence. This is by no means an exhaustive list either of recent feminist writings or of topics covered by them.

2. See, e.g., Midge Decter, *The New Chastity* (New York: Coward-McCann & Geoghegan, Inc., 1972); Norman Mailer, *The Prisoner of Sex* (Boston: Little, Brown & Co., 1971); Phyllis McGinley, *The Province of the Heart* (New York: Viking Press, 1959) and *Sixpence in Her Shoe* (New York: Macmillan & Co., 1964). One book which, rather than assuming psychological sexual differences, argues from some data that such diffences exist, is Lionel Tiger's *Men in Groups* (New York: Random House, 1969).

3. An important exception to this generalization is Judith Bardwick, *Psychology of Women* (New York: Harper & Row, 1971). On the basis of an extensive review of the literature, Bardwick takes a traditionalist position on sexual differences, but neither argues nor implies the need for differential coercive treatment.

4. For a cogent argument in support of this statement and a critique of some legal philosophies which would deny it, see Samuel E. Stumpf, *Morality and the Law* (Nashville: Vanderbilt University Press, 1966), especially chs. 1, 3, and 6.

5. U.S. Women's Bureau, *Handbook of Women Workers* Bulletin no. 294, (Washington, D.C.: U.S. Government Printing Office, 1969), pp. 261-80, 29 C.F.R. Sec. 1604.2 (b) (1) (1969).

6. Leo Kanowitz, *Women and the Law: The Unfinished Revolution* (Albuquerque, N.M.: University of New Mexico Press, 1967), ch. 6.

7. See Godcharles v. Wigeman, 113 Pa. St. 431 (1886); Millett v. People, 117 Ill. 294 (1886); *In re* Morgan, 26 Colo. 415 (1899); Low v. Rees Printing Co., 41 Neb. 127 (1894).

8. See Lochner v. New York, 198 U.S. 45 (1905).

9. See Ernst Freund, "Constitutional Limitations and Labor Legislation," *Illinois Law Review* 4 (April 1910): 610; George Gorham Groat, *Attitude of American Courts in Labor Cases: A Study in Social Legislation* (New York: Columbia University Studies in Economics and Political Science, 1911), pp. 281-333.

10. Cf., Holden v. Hardy, 169 U.S. 366 (1898) with *in re* Morgan, 26 Colo. 415 (1899).

11. See, e.g., Commonwealth v. Hamilton Mfg. Co., 120 Mass. 183 (1876); Commonwealth v. Beatty, 15 Pa. Super. 5 (1900); State v. Buchanan, 29 Wash. 602

(1902); Wenham v. State, 65 Neb. 394 (1902). But c.f., Matter of Maguire, 67 Cal. 604 (1881); and Ritchie v. People, 155 Ill. 98 (1895).

12. 208 U.S. 412.

13. Ritchie v. Wayman, 244 Ill. 509 (1910); *ex parte* Miller, 162 Cal. 687 (1912).

14. In the U.S. Supreme Court, see Riley v. Massachusetts, 232 U.S. 671 (1914) (posting of working hours); Stettler v. O'Hara, 243 U.S. 629 (1917) (minimum wage); Miller v. Wilson, 236 U.S. 373 (1915) (eight-hour law); Radice v. New York, 264 U.S. 292 (1924) (night work prohibition); Goesaert v. Cleary, 335 U.S. 464 (1948) (prohibition against women bartenders). The court did invalidate a minimum-wage law in Adkins v. Children's Hospital, 261 U.S. 525 (1923), but reversed itself in West Coast Hotel v. Parrish, 300 U.S. 379 (1937). In Sail'er Inn, Inc., v. Kirby, 5 Cal. 3rd 1 (1971), the California Supreme Court invalidated under the Equal Protection Clause a law prohibiting women bartenders. In Frontiero v. Richardson, 411 U.S. 677 (1973), a plurality of the justices accepted the argument that sex was an inherently suspect classification under the Equal Protection Clause.

15. See, e.g., Commonwealth v. Weloskey, 276 Mass. 398, *cert. den.* 284 U.S. 684 (1931) (jury exclusion); Allred v. Heaton, 336 S. W. 2d 251 (Tex. Civ. App. 1960) (exclusion from state-supported universities).

16. 293 F. Supp. 1219 (C.D. Cal. 1968).

17. See, e.g., Weeks v. Southern Bell, 408 F. 2d 228 (5th Cir. 1969) (weight-lifting restrictions); Caterpillar Tractor Co. v. Grabiec, 317 F. Supp. 1304 (S.D. Ill. 1970) (hours limitations); Sail'er Inn, Inc., v. Kirby, supra n. 14 (prohibitions on certain kinds of employment).

18. Bunting v. Oregon, 243 U.S. 426 (1917).

19. See supra, n. 14.

20. See supra, n. 14.

21 Alpheus Thomas Mason, *Brandeis: A Free Man's Life* (New York: Viking Press, 1956), p. 248.

22. Adkins v. Children's Hospital, 261 U.S. 525, 528 (1923).

1

THE HISTORICAL CONTEXT

It is a truism by now that court decisions cannot be fully understood out of historical context. Labor law, however, is one area in which this context is already well known. The Industrial Revolution and its manifestations, along with efforts to reform resultant conditions, are discussed at length in high-school textbooks in American history. For those whose curiosity is piqued rather than satisfied by this material, primary and secondary sources are voluminous and readily available. Child labor, sweatshops, and long working days are matters of common knowledge, as are unions, strikes, injunctions, and laws. Extensive recapitulation would be superfluous, and I shall not attempt it.

My historical review will be limited to an attempt to answer two questions which are central to my study: first, why women were singled out for special treatment, and second, why that special treatment took the form of legislation. This task may not involve extensive recapitulation, but it does require significant reinterpretation. The available material provides much insight into these questions, but they have not specifically been asked of the material.

The answer to the first question may seem obvious: women were singled out because of physical differences from men. But at least one alternative answer readily suggests itself: that male workers advocated restrictions as a means of protecting themselves from female competition. And examination of the evidence suggests still other explanations. The second question has no immediately obvious possible answer, but the reasons why legislation became the preferred method for improvement are not hard to discover.

The first important fact that we need to know about American industry in order to answer these questions is that a division of labor on the basis of sex has persisted throughout our history, surviving the change from agricultural to industrial society. This phenomenon is not, of course, unique to this country. Although the exact definition of men's work and women's work has frequently changed—for example, clerical work was originally a male, and is now a female occupation—there has always been a fairly sharp division between men's and women's work. Even when men and women have worked in the same industries, they nearly always worked in different jobs.[1]

The American Industrial Revolution began in New England and gradually moved southward and westward; industrial development was spurred by new inventions, population growth, rising per capita income, and abundant natural resources. Between 1815 and 1850, one task after another was taken out of the home and placed into the factory.[2] Goods and services which each family had provided for itself began to be provided by mass industries. Throughout this process, the sexual division of labor which had prevailed on family farms was maintained. Men became carpenters, printers, or shoemakers (or, if they felt unsuited for urban life, moved westward); women became weavers and spinners in textile mills, and later seamstresses, laundresses, and waitresses. As new occupations were developed which had no analogies in farm life, the division of labor was based loosely on physical capacities—men took the jobs that required muscular strength, and women those that demanded manual and digital dexterity—but sometimes the assignment seems purely arbitrary: for example, the displacement of women by men in the cigar-making trade, when the nature of the job had not changed.[3]

A second generalization which can be made from labor history is that most women who were gainfully employed worked under conditions much worse than those under which most men worked. Men's working conditions were bad enough by modern standards, but women's were worse.[4] Hours were even longer in women's jobs, rules were even stricter, and places of employment were even less safe or healthful. In the early nineteenth century, men worked from sunrise to sunset, just as women did, but they worked as carpenters, printers, mechanics, or shoemakers in their own or their employers' uncrowded shops, or outdoors in the building trades.[5] In those days, most employed women were found in the textile mills of New England. Primary and secondary source material about their working conditions exists in abundance.

One 1840s visitor to factories in Lowell and Manchester, Massachusetts, found women working thirteen hours a day in rooms which held about 500 looms each; a worker usually tended three looms, but some women could handle four.

"The din and clatter of these five hundred looms under full operation struck us as something frightful and infernal, for it seemed such an atrocious violation of one of the faculties of the human soul, the sense of hearing."[6] But the weavers evidently got used to it. The rooms were hot and close, and workers often fainted at their looms. The air was "charged with cotton filaments and dust, which, we were told, is very injurious to the lungs."[7] Tuberculosis was common, and after a few years many of the workers returned to their families in Vermont or New Hampshire to die.[8]

The regulations of the Hamilton Manufacturing Company in Lowell[9] reveal much about what factory work was like. All workers had to be at their places at all times; overseers might grant leaves of absence only when they had spare hands, "except in cases of dire necessity."[10] (What this regualtion often meant in practice was that women became ill at their looms because they could not get, or were too embarrassed to ask for, permission from male overseers to go to the lavatory.) The mill hands were under a twelve-month contract, and would be blacklisted by all factories if they left before the contract was up. The exploitation of the workers was accompanied, and frequently exacerbated, by a paternalistic, authoritarian attitude on the part of employers which left workers little freedom even after hours. Another clause stipulated that "the company will not employ anyone who is habitually absent from public worship on the Sabbath, or known to be guilty of immorality." The corporation boarding houses where the women were required to live[11] were not much improvement. Not only was there "no privacy, no retirement here"[12]—the workers slept two to a bed, six to a room—but there was a 10:00 P.M. curfew, and tenants could have no company at "unreasonable hours" (even if they had had the space or the energy), and were answerable for "improper conduct." The only regulation which softened the quasimilitary tone—and which was clearly necessary for pragmatic reasons—was a clause providing free smallpox vaccination "for such as wish it."

The differences between men's and women's working conditions became even greater as the nineteenth century progressed. Male workers had frequently won by the 1840s, 50s, and 60s the hours limitations which legislation began to win for women in the 70s, 80s and 90s.[13] Agitation for a ten-hour day for New England mechanics and working men began as early as 1825 and continued, usually unsuccessfully, through the 1830s,[14] but by 1840 the building trades had obtained a sixty-hour, six-day week in most of the United States and even shorter hours in some cities.[15] In that year, a ten-hour day for federal employees was established by order of President Van Buren. In the next fifty years, the labor movement succeeded in establishing a ten-hour day and a six-day week in most occupations except factory work, which still had most women employees and in which these women worked eleven to thirteen hours, sometimes seven days a week.[16] Some predominantly male industries, like cigar making, had less than *fifty* hours a week in at least fifteen states, and below fifty-three hours in most places.[17] Even in the steel industry, where improvements lagged behind other industries, the average working week was sixty-five to sixty-six hours—significantly less than for factory workers—and in the 1890s a sixty-hour week became the rule.[18] As late as 1910, Alice Henry, a labor organizer, reported that some women steam laundry workers had as long a day as *eighteen* hours in rush season.[19] The U.S. Senate report on women and child workers, published at about the same time, revealed that a similar pattern of long hours, hard labor, and dangerous conditions had persisted throughout the nineteenth century, and continued into the twentieth. Legislation did not reduce women's hours below men's, but brought them—at best—to that level.

This phenomenon is illustrated by a famous, tragic event which had enormous influence on the future of labor legislation: a fire at the Triangle Shirtwaist Company in New York City in 1911, in which over a hundred seamstresses were killed. They did not die because they were women, but because there were no fire escapes and only one staircase, and because too many people were crowded into rooms with sewing machines packed too closely together to permit escape. Any workers, male or female, would have been in danger under such conditions. But the lesson which the state drew from this incident was that special restrictions on women's employment were needed, as well as general safety regulations. When men had to work under conditions of comparable danger—in underground mines, for instance—special laws were frequently passed for their protection.

Why did women's industries lag so far behind men's? One reason is that usually only the poorest of women were permanent members of the labor force, and, like all poor people, they had a disproportionate share of the worst jobs. In the nineteenth century, women did not work outside the home on a permanent basis unless they had to, unless no one else could support them adequately. The women who did work were already

at the very bottom of the economic ladder, had little education or training, and therefore were concentrated in the jobs where conditions were
hardest. A further reason that women were concentrated in jobs such as
factory work, where things were bad, is that they frequently were suited,
both physically and temperamentally, for the work itself. Historians of the
Industrial Revolution in Britain reported that male factory workers were
replaced by females whenever possible, not only because the women were
—as they always were—cheaper, but also because they were found to be
both more amenable to the discipline and more likely to have the necessary dexterity.[20] And in England, as in the United States, it was in the
factories that the worst conditions prevailed. The industrial history of
the United States has not been studied as extensively as that of England,
but since the same sexual differences obtained here, and women also pre-
dominated in factory work in this country, there is no reason to assume
that similar factors were not operative.

Some American observers, however, thought that one reason for the
bad conditions was just the opposite: not that women were particularly
good workers in some industries, but that they were inferior workers in
any industry. This possibility is explored by Helen L. Sumner, who directed the preparation of the Senate Report:

> Usually, [women] have been employed, in the first in-
> stance, only in the least skilled and most poorly paid occu-
> pations, and have not competed directly with men. This has
> been due partly to custom and prejudice, perhaps, but pri-
> marily it has been due to lack of training and ambition, and
> to general irresponsibility.[21]

Sumner's argument is buttressed by the observations of Dorothy Richardson, a New York factory worker at the turn of the century:

> One may have no experience whatever in any line of work,
> yet one may know *how* to work—may understand the general
> principles of intelligent labor. These general principles a girl
> may learn equally well by means of normal-school training or
> through familiarity with, or participation in, the domestic
> labor of a well-organized household. The working girl in a
> great city does not have the advantage of either form of train-

ing. Her education, even at the best, is meager, and of housework she knows less than nothing.

Not having learned to work, either at school or at home,
she goes to the factory, to the workshop, or to the store,
crude, incompetent, and worst of all, with an instinctive an-
tagonism toward her task. *She cannot work, and she does not
work. . . . She is simply "worked."* The average working girl
puts neither heart nor mind into her labor, she is merely a
machine, though the comparison is a libel upon the functions
of first-class machinery.[22]

The validity of these observations is called into question, both by the
British studies and by the fact that neither Sumner nor Richardson studied
the way men work; for all we know, they may have been just as inefficient.
Furthermore, inefficiency hardly justifies thirteen-hour working days and
dangerous conditions. These observations are important, however, as evidence of how women workers viewed themselves, and how those dedicated
to improving their lot saw them.

Another reason for the differences between men's and women's working conditions was that unionization and collective bargaining, the major
alternative to legislation as a means of improvement, were rarely feasible
for women. Nearly all the gains which men won in the nineteenth century
were achieved by these means. But union organizers throughout that century reported frustration at their failure to organize women workers effectively.[23] Describing the "awakening period" of the labor movement
from 1820 to 1840, John R. Commons wrote:

Whatever may have been its origin in other countries, the
labor movement in America did not spring from factory conditions. It arose as a protest against the merchant-capitalist
system. The factories were as yet confined to one branch of
cotton textiles, employing mainly women and children.
These did not take part in the organized movement. The effort, indeed, of the New England Association of Farmers,
Mechanics, and Working Men to secure the cooperation of
the factory operatives, was distinctly a failure.[24]

Why were women workers so passive? Edith Abbott points to "the familiar fact that a labor movement is born only when a definite wage-earning

class is created which is concerned with the permanent improvement in the condition of that class and is willing to make sacrifices on its behalf."[25] None of these conditions prevailed among women workers before the Civil War. The situation of the first large group of women workers outside the home—the mill hands in the New England and Middle Atlantic states —is useful illustration. These operatives did not form a distinct working class; they came from, and usually married into, middle-class families. They were not, and did not expect to be, permanently employed in the mills. They expected to work only for a few years, and for most this expectation was realistic. After a few years the workers married or, less frequently, entered the women's academies of their day. Nearly all the mill workers from 1815 to 1860 were between the ages of sixteen and twenty-five.[26]

As bad as conditions were, these women had sturdy farm constitutions, and endured heat, monotony, and fatigue without apparent permanent injury. A worker whose health did fail was out of luck, but at least she could usually return home. Under these circumstances, it was easier to tolerate these conditions than to work to change them, especially since unionization might have led to loss of present jobs and future employability. Some women workers did, however, organize, as early as the 1830s. Strikes did occur, but rarely, and usually not to improve conditions but to prevent their worsening.[27]

The expectation that work would be only temporary persisted among women workers long after the heyday of the New England textile industry, even when it became much less realistic.[28] By the 1850s, as immigrant women began to displace native workers, the women represented not only two distinct classes but also separate groups of permanent and temporary workers. Even in the early period, two distinct types of factory organization existed which employed two distinct types of workers.

The Lowell system, which I have described, used frames and throstle spindles, and employed mostly women, as both weavers and spinners. This system prevailed throughout northern Massachusetts and New Hampshire. Adult males formed a large minority of the operatives at times; in Lowell in 1833, slightly less than one-fourth were male.[29] The second type, the Fall River system, was in force in southern Massachusetts, Rhode Island, New York, Pennsylvania, New Jersey, and Maryland. Here mule spindles were used, and the factories employed men as spinners, and women and children as weavers. Entire families, often recent immigrants, worked in the same mill. The women continued at the mills after marriage, during pregnancy, and as soon as possible after childbirth. Wages were even lower, and hours longer, in these mills than in the Lowell system.[30] In both systems, the men endured the same conditions as did the women; and, as we shall find, they were to welcome women's hours legislation because its effect was to shorten their own hours as well.

Even in the Lowell system, the factory population changed after 1860. In fact, as early as 1848, refugees from the Irish famine began appearing in the mills. Because they would work for any wages they could get, they tended to displace the native workers. Later the Civil War drew many of the educated women from the mills, both by causing a prolonged depression in the cotton industry and by increasing the demand for nurses and for teachers and clerks to replace men going into the army. After the war, most of the native-born operatives had entered other fields, married, or moved westward, and were replaced by immigrant women—first Irish, then French-Canadians, and eventually Armenians, Portuguese, and Poles. By 1900, 95 percent of the operatives in Massachusetts were foreign-born or of foreign parentage.[31] Whether married or single, these women needed to work to support themselves and often to help support their families.[32] This same pattern developed in other occupations in the nineteenth century. Women worked not only as factory hands, but also as waitresses, store clerks, and laundresses. These jobs were frequently taken by immigrants but also, eventually, by their children and grandchildren. The long hours and unhealthy conditions persisted, but they were no longer mitigated by the voluntary and temporary nature of the work. After the Civil War, many women worked as a matter of necessity, and an increasing proportion were permanently in the labor force.[33]

How do we know this? The Senate report on women and children in industry showed that nearly all the store and factory workers studied either lived alone and had to support themselves, or with their families (either parental or marital) and had to help support them. Most of these women had been in the labor force since their mid-teens. In the seven cities studied, the average age of store workers living with parents or siblings was 22.5, and that of factory workers 21.1, well within the age bracket in which the early mill workers had been concentrated, but the average age of those workers *not* at home (i.e., in any other situation) was, respectively, 28.2 and 27.7. Whether married or unmarried, women who remained in the labor force that long (between 13 and 35 percent of all working women) had, the report suggests, little realistic hope of ever being able to quit.[34]

Census figures bear this out. Between 1870 and 1920, only between 25 and 30 percent of all women workers were sixteen to twenty-five; about 43 percent were between twenty-five and forty-four; and approximately 20 percent were forty-five to sixty-four. Employment outside the home clearly was no longer simply a temporary occupation for young women until marriage. And the census figures for those years do not show the pattern we have come to expect in recent years: a decrease in the proportion of women employed during the most common childbearing years followed by an increase after, say, forty. In 1920, the percentage of married women who worked outside the home consistently declined with age, but by no more than six points.[35] These statistics indicate that for women who never married or who, for whatever reasons, did not follow the then-prevailing social pattern of leaving the labor force at marriage, work outside the home was a permanent condition.

Not only did bad conditions persist as the wage-earning class changed from a temporary to a permanent one, but so did the workers' passivity. By the 1870s, Abbott's first condition existed, but the other two conditions had only sporadic existence. Realistically or not, women workers often entertained the hope that they would either be able to leave the labor force through an upward-mobile marriage or be able to find a better-paid occupation. The first hope was rarely fulfilled. After all, fourteen-hour days in hot, filthy rooms, living in boarding houses or tenements, and wages too low to provide any but the most meager wardrobes, probably could not have been conducive to ambitious husband-hunting. Since the same conditions all but precluded the training and education necessary to qualify women for better jobs—no time for classes, no quiet and privacy for study, and no money for tuition and books—the second hope seems, in retrospect, to have been equally vain. There was not even much hope for advancement on the job; less than 2 percent of women employees in stores were buyers, and about the same percentage in factories were forewomen.[36] But however vain these hopes were, they persisted.

Another reason for the workers' passivity may have been that the conditions of their lives were so bad that all their energy was consumed by coping with them, and there was none left for promoting change. It should not surprise us that those at or near the bottom of the socioeconomic ladder fail to protest or revolt. Social movements and revolutions tend to originate either with the relatively fortunate members of a group or among outsiders acting in their conception of the group's interests. American history alone provides several examples of this phenomenon, well and fully described by social scientists. One example is, of course, the contemporary feminist movement, against which the observation about the status of its members is frequently made in the nature of an accusation. Students of social movements should know better.

In short, the history of American industry reveals several reasons why women's industries lagged behind men's in improvements: mainly the concentration of women in the worst industries, partly because of their particular suitability for such work, and partly because usually only the least fortunate women were permanent workers; and also the lack of strong labor organizations among women workers, which in turn was due to a variety of complex causes. These factors and other aspects of women's situation are important in understanding the history of the movement for legislation.

SEX DIFFERENCES AND EMPLOYMENT: A RECAPITULATION

I have now identified several factors which could provide support for arguments for special labor legislation for women. These factors can be divided into four groups. First, there are the *physical* characteristics which distinguish women from men. Second, there are *social* differences in the responsibilities of the sexes. Third, there are *economic* conditions: women's inferior working conditions, and the need perceived by male workers to protect themselves from female competition. Fourth, there are the *political* conditions, notably the lack of strong labor organizations which included women.

The physical distinctions are rather well known, and lengthy discussion of them may appear to insult the reader's intelligence. But these facts are so frequently misstated and misinterpreted that it is necessary to clarify them. Interestingly, the arguments for discrimination usually are not based on the factors which distinguish all men from all women, and vice versa. No one seriously argues, for instance, that testicles are a requirement for executive jobs or ovaries for clerical ones. Menstruation does sometimes become a possible basis for differential treatment, but most arguments do not rely nearly as much on it as they do on two phenomena which are common only to some men or to some women: physical strength and childbearing.

Sexual differences in physical strength are usually described by the following generalization or its equivalent in nineteenth-century style: "Men are stronger than women" (or, if preferred, "women are weaker than men"). This generalization is misleading when it is worded in the same way that generalizations about organs common to all men or all women are. On the average, men are superior to women in gross muscular strength, primarily because they have greater muscle mass but also partly because on the average males tend to get more exercise than females. *Most* men can run faster, hit harder, lift heavier weights, and perform these tasks longer than *most* women. However, *some* women are stronger in these respects than *some* men. There is a considerable degree of overlap. When considering an individual man or an individual woman, one knows that in all but an infinitesimal number of cases the man will have testicles and the woman ovaries, and that—outside of medical grotesqueries—the man will not have ovaries nor the woman testicles. But one cannot predict with any certainty that the man will be stronger in the ways described than the woman. Plato noted this fact long ago, and the situation has not changed since.[37]

Sexual differences in reproductive function are usually expressed by some variation of the following: "Women bear children." But this, too, is an overgeneralization. It would be more accurate to say, "Women are capable of bearing children," or, "*Only* women are capable of bearing children." Virtually all women have the *capacity* to bear children, but some women never bear children, and very few women bear children all the time. Pregnancy does not occur automatically, even among sexually active women, the way menstruation occurs among women of childbearing age, or lactation among women who have just delivered. When considering an individual woman somewhere between puberty and menopause, one knows that in all but a tiny number of cases, she will menstruate. But one cannot predict with any certainty that she will ever bear, or know that she has borne, a child. The generalization is even more misleading if it is interpreted as meaning that "Woman's *primary function* is to bear children." That frequently drawn conclusion is a statement about social responsibility, *not* physiological fact. And the social conclusion does not follow, at least as a matter of logic, from childbearing capacity. It is not *disproven* either by logic or by empirical evidence that not all women bear children, but its validity is at least highly questionable. This is a crucial point for understanding this whole issue.

However overstated the common generalizations about sexual differences are, they have been effective weapons in the struggle for protective legislation. The argument has been made that women's relative weakness and childbearing function make working conditions which men can tolerate dangerous for them, and that, therefore, restrictions are necessary. And considering that reformers were responding to a situation in which all working women were exposed to conditions which perhaps only especially husky women could endure, this is understandable.

A second distinction between the sexes which is pertinent here is a social one: the greater responsibility of women, especially married women, for housework and child care. As we shall see, reformers frequently used this situation as the basis for arguments for legislation.[38] The third set of factors I have identified are economic ones, some of these pertaining to the employment of men as well as women. As Florence Kelley, an eminent reformer in this field, wrote:

> Statutes restricting the hours of labor of women and children, while enacted in the interests of health and morality, have often been urged by persons animated by two other motives as well. In many cases, men who found their own occupations threatened by unwelcome competitors, demanded restrictions upon the hours of work of those competitors for the purpose of rendering women less desirable as employees. In other cases, men who wished reduced hours of work for themselves, which the courts denied them, obtained the desired statutory reduction by the indirect method of restrictions upon the hours of labor of the women and children whose work interlocked with their own.[39]

The first motive is discussed by Commons, writing about the 1830s:

> . . . The factory system was almost entirely outside the labor movement, and the competition of women and children showed itself most keenly when organized labor attempted to advance its wages or shorten its hours by strikes. Factory legislation was therefore for the first time seriously broached, and the beginning was made of that agitation that took the leading place in the following decade.[40]

Further evidence of the existence of this motive is provided by a passage from the 1879 annual report of Adolph Strasser, the president of the Cigar Makers International Union, whose members had been seriously threatened by female competition:

> We cannot drive the females out of the trade, but we
> can restrict their daily quota of labor through factory
> laws. No girl under eighteen should be employed more
> than eight hours per day; all overwork should be prohibi-
> ted; white [sic] married women should be kept out of the
> factories at least six weeks before and six weeks after con-
> finement.[41]

The second goal Kelley discusses is illustrated by the twenty-year struggle in Massachusetts for a law to reduce hours of labor in the textile mills. By 1867, when the law was finally passed, its proposed coverage was restricted to women and children in the hope, which was realized, that this would facilitate its passage. However, "It was realized that the preponderance of these groups in the textile labor force would necessitate a general reduction of hours in the mills. Thus in Massachusetts as in England, the men employed in the textile industry decided to 'fight the battle from behind the women's petticoats.' "[42]

The particularly bad conditions under which women worked also could provide support for arguments for protective legislation. The position could be taken that women needed special restrictions not because they fare worse than men under identical conditions, but because they had to endure worse ones in the limited occupations open to them. This argument is frequently made by proponents of minimum-wage legislation in the second constitutional phase. The final set of conditions I identified —the lack of political strength, especially in the form of unions, among women workers—made it difficult for them to make any improvements in their own situation. Legislation was viewed as the most effective alternative means of change. But if most of the workers subjected to bad conditions were women, legislation which applied to all workers, regardless of sex, would have achieved the desired results. The goals of the reformers thus could have been met without any discrimination on the basis of sex. Working conditions did not justify the broad, discriminatory legislation which was adopted.

It may be useful at this point to arrange our knowledge in another way, and to classify all of these conditions according to the extent to which they have persisted to the present. Obviously, the physical distinctions, at least within our present technological capacities, are permanent. However, the analysis of them cannot stop here. Justice Brewer's reference in the *Muller* opinion to "the burdens of motherhood"[43] was to conditions far more onerous than those facing any American woman today. In the nineteenth century, pregnancy and childbirth were frequent for sexually active women, and they were disabling and dangerous. By 1908, they were safer, but still frequent and burdensome. Modern science has made it easier both to avoid and to endure them. Contraceptive devices still are not as safe, reliable, and convenient, or as universally and readily available, as they might be, but the situation has greatly improved. Death in childbirth, which to the contemporary middle-class American woman seems, and is, as remote a possibility as death from smallpox, was a real danger to their nineteenth-century counterparts, and even more so to working-class women. Even affluent women with access to the best available medical care left accounts of the extraordinary depth of their fear and dislike of pregnancy and childbirth.[44]

It is questionable whether the legislators who were becoming increasingly more willing to pass special labor legislation for women were really doing all they could to make motherhood less burdensome. At this time, most states still had, and frequently enforced, laws which prohibited the dissemination of contraceptive devices or information; reformers like Margaret Sanger met with consistent governmental opposition in their efforts to spread this knowledge. The idea of restricting women's freedom to work outside the home so that they might better cope with their responsibilities within it gained political acceptance much earlier than did the idea of increasing women's freedom to control their fertility.

Another burden of motherhood which was greater than it is now was that of breast feeding. Although nursing bottles were available by 1908, not all substitutes for breast milk were equally suitable for infants. Working mothers who had to leave their babies at home either had to give up nursing or to combine it with other methods. Overall infant mortality was higher among the children of working mothers than children whose mothers stayed at home.[45] However, the causal connection between maternal employment and infant mortality was indirect and tenuous. A study included in the Senate report of infant mortality in Fall River,

Massachusetts, in 1908 showed, first, that in only 8 percent of their cases did a mother stop nursing because she returned to work, and second, that babies fed appropriate substitutes did as well as breast-fed babies.[46] It concluded: "The causes of excessive infant mortality in Fall River may be summed up in a sentence as the mother's ignorance of proper feeding, of proper care, and of proper hygiene. To this all other causes must be regarded as secondary."[47] At present, of course, there are well known, readily available alternatives to breast feeding which permit the growth of healthy babies.

Another exclusively female function related to both childbirth and employment is, of course, menstruation. There are references to menstrual difficulties among working women in some of the literature on women's employment. But menstruation was a subject on which the amount of misinformation and misunderstanding prevalent in nineteenth-century England and America is almost unbelievable;[48] it is difficult for medicine to alleviate what it does not understand. And this function, too, is less disabling now than it once could be. Symptoms the source of which is known, and the temporary nature of which is recognized, usually can be coped with. "Furthermore, to the extent that menstrual disorders are treatable and that males control and withhold medical knowledge, and therefore the implements of cure, it is a profoundly immoral act for men to point to menstrual troubles which in fact exist as support for the proposition that females are biologically less fit than males."[49]

Women still perform all these functions, but the functions themselves are simply not as demanding of time and energy as they were during the movement for protective legislation. But the discussion of women's reproductive functions cannot stop with the physical facts. Society continues to use these facts as a basis for drawing conclusions about appropriate sex roles. Arguments about woman's (not women's, note) "nature" and "primary functions" and "proper place" are as common as they once were. And these arguments, too, become justifications for special treatment. But women's greater responsibility for housework and child care, like the burdens of reproduction itself, has less impact now that technological advances have made these tasks less arduous.

The other important physical distinction between the sexes—men's relative superiority in muscular strength—persists, but its impact, too, has been lessened by technological advances. Outside the home as well as inside, work is not as fatiguing; increased automation has made it possible to perform most tasks without over-exertion. Few men or women workers do anything today as exhausting as workers did in the nineteenth and early twentieth centuries. Neither sex has to use its strength to its full capacity. One can see, then, that the sexual distinctions which have persisted—the physical and social ones—do not have the same impact as they once did.

The economic distinctions between the sexes as workers have varied in persistence. Conditions of women's work—and men's, too, of course— are nowhere near as bad as they once were. This is partly due to legislation, but also to the advances I have discussed. The need felt by male workers to be protected from female competition is, potentially at least, as great as it ever was. It is always possible for workers to feel threatened by competition. The related phenomenon—the "riding on the women's petticoats" effect—is less potent now that collective bargaining has achieved so many of the gains fought for in the nineteenth century.

To elaborate on perhaps the most important point in the preceding paragraph, working women are not locked into the kinds of conditions they once endured. The range of opportunities open to them, while still limited, has greatly increased. It is now possible for a few women to choose *voluntarily* to expose themselves to working conditions which might be harmful to most women—as miners, steelworkers, or football players, for instance—without forcing other women into these occupations. The removal of restrictions against such choices would mean, and has meant, a significant increase in the amount of freedom which women actually enjoy.

Political conditions have changed. Not only can women vote, make contracts, and control their earnings, but they can effectively be, and frequently have been, unionized. The most persistent factor, and the one most invariant in its force, of this whole long list is the possibility of female competition with males.

THE MOVEMENT FOR LEGISLATION

There are three ways of improving working conditions. One is through technological changes which make work less onerous. This means of change is extremely effective but of limited usefulness in bringing about immediate reform. One cannot, at least not from a relatively powerless position, simply go out and order someone to find an easier way of doing something. A second method is through collective bargaining between employers and employees. This method requires organization. Not only was it difficult to organize women workers, as we have seen, but unionization efforts on the part of *any* workers were extremely risky activities until 1935, when the National Labor Relations Act insured this right to workers. The third means of change is through governmental intervention into employer-employee relations, usually through legislation. This method has the not inconsiderable advantage of settling, for a time, the question of which side the government is on. It also can be used to protect the interests of workers who, for whatever reasons, cannot protect their own. And, unlike striking, it is a useful method even in periods of depression, so frequent throughout the nineteenth century, which made strikes virtually futile.[50] The great disadvantage of legislation as a means of improving working conditions is that it has to be enforced by the government, and, for reasons we shall explore, this can be difficult. The powerful labor unions of the nineteenth century were sensitive to this problem, and felt themselves competent to protect their own interests; although they vacillated on the issue, they tended to prefer collective bargaining to legislation as a means of reform. (Perhaps there is a fourth method of change—voluntary action on the part of employers. As even the most casual student of American labor history knows, that rarely happens.)

E. E. Schattschneider suggested that "private conflicts are taken into the public arena precisely because someone wants to make certain that the power ratio among the private interests most immediately involved shall not prevail."[51] The history of industrial conflict is marked by repeated efforts by both sides to politicize the conflict. Employers, faced with the threat of strikes which might force them to make concessions, summoned the police or sought injunctions; this process began as early as 1806.[52] Employees, when their bargaining position was weak, sought legislation to achieve their goals.

Frequently, legislation was sought not by the workers it would cover, but by others. The first labor laws passed in the United States regulated child labor. They were advocated primarily by the labor organizations, which were composed, as we have seen, of adult males, not children. As early as 1813, Connecticut had passed a law relating to the education of employed children. The first maximum-hours law for children was enacted by Massachusetts in 1842, and by 1879, seven states had fixed a minimum age for employment, and twelve had set maximum hours. The first labor inspectors appointed in any states—in Massachusetts in 1867 and Connecticut in 1869—were appointed to enforce child labor laws.

A type of regulation which early unions frequently advocated in their own interests was a general limitation on hours of work, generally known as a declaratory law. This type of statute, usually applying to all adult laborers other than farm or domestic workers, made eight or ten hours the legal working day in the absence of a contract to the contrary, and was, therefore, useless.[53]

Up to the Civil War, eight states—New Hampshire, Maine, Pennsylvania, New Jersey, Ohio, California, Rhode Island, and Connecticut—had passed ten-hour laws of this sort.[54] After the war, the drive for declaratory laws intensified under the leadership of Ira Steward, an advocate of the universal eight-hour day. By 1896, eleven more states had enacted such laws, most of them for eight rather than ten hours. "[These laws] are significant chiefly as a monument to a belief now largely obsolete; namely, that state action in the interest of workers should not curtail individual liberty to contract, but could be effective without so doing."[55] Several states also limited hours of labor on public works, but most of these laws were similarly ineffective.

Before 1908, special regulations for women usually took one of two forms. The more common was hours regulation, either establishing a maximum number of hours women could work or prohibiting them from working during certain hours, typically at night. Twenty-one states had passed maximum hours laws by 1908; one—New York—had such a law applying only to women under twenty-one; and four had night work laws.[56] The latter type of regulation was proposed not only as a means of protecting safety and preserving family life, but in the hope that it would act as an aid to the enforcement of maximum-hours laws. As Josephine Goldmark, an authority in this area who will figure prominently in Chapters 3 and 4, pointed out, it is difficult to prove that women at work in the evening have been employed beyond the maximum number of hours unless employment after a normal closing hour is made illegal.[57]

The second common type of women's legislation was the prohibition of women from entering certain occupations at all. The occupations most frequently forbidden were mining and smelting; another frequently prohibited activity was working in places where liquor was served. A few laws prohibited women from cleaning moving machinery. By 1908, fourteen states had passed this sort of law. Illinois deserves special mention here for a unique demonstration of the belief that a foolish consistency is the hobgoblin of small minds. In 1872, this state enacted one law prohibiting women from working in coal mines and another providing that no person should be barred from any occupation except military service on the basis of sex.[58]

The progress of this kind of legislation was nearly as slow as that of child labor laws. The first women's hours law was a ten-hour regulation passed by Ohio in 1852. In the next twenty-five years, two more states (Minnesota and Massachusetts) and one territory (Dakota) passed ten-hour laws, and Illinois, an eight-hour law.[59] Between 1877 and 1908, the Ohio law was repealed, the Illinois law was declared unconstitutional, and only eight more states passed maximum hours laws, while five passed night work laws.[60] The trend was very gradual, with no peak years.

Most of these laws were virtually unenforceable. The earliest women's hours laws provided only that women could not be "compelled" to work more than the specified hours, or established penalties only for "willful" violations by employers. Even the statutes which did not contain such qualifications usually had no workable means for enforcement; in order to instigate a prosecution, a worker or observer had to complain.[61] Only five states—Illinois, Maine, Massachusetts, Wisconsin, and New Jersey—had factory inspectors before 1908, and the Illinois law had been struck down in 1895. Wisconsin's law was unenforceable because of its use of the verb "compelling."[62] Out of the twenty-six maximum-hours and night work laws in twenty-five states, then, only four—the Massachusetts ten-hour and night work laws, the Maine ten-hour law, and the New Jersey eleven-hour law—could be enforced with any regularity or predictability.

The first women's hours laws were the product of agitation by labor organizations, including the few women's unions. The men's unions which fought for such laws were not very vulnerable to the charge that their primary concern was to eliminate competition. This motive was present, as the quotations from Kelley, Commons, and Strasser show. But as we shall see, the legislation was not primarily intended to have, nor, apparently, did it have, the effect of removing female competition. Some skilled unions found better ways to keep women out of the trades: one was to demand strict observance of apprenticeship rules,[63] and another, paradoxically, was to demand equal pay for the women who did get jobs, so they could not drive the men out by accepting lower wages.[64] But not all skilled unions were hostile to women workers. The International Typographical Union, for example, not only had a long-standing equal pay regulation, but amended its constitution in 1869 to prohibit sex-based discrimination in subordinate unions.[65]

Up to 1890, the unions were the chief proponents of legislation. After that time, this role was assumed by middle-class reformist organizations, the most influential of which was the National Consumers' League, under the leadership of women like Kelley and the Goldmark sisters, Josephine and Pauline. The League and similar organizations led the fight for labor legislation from then until the New Deal, lobbying for bill after bill and instigating lawsuit after lawsuit. The leading labor organizations, first the Knights of Labor and then the American Federation of Labor, supported this legislation, but with neither the commitment nor the effect of the reformist groups. (Women's suffrage groups neither supported nor opposed these laws actively, although the reformist groups supported women's suffrage.)[66]

One must be careful to separate consideration of the *motives* which produced the drive for this legislation from consideration of its *effects*. The fact that few of the supporters of protective legislation were motivated by male fear of female competition does not necessarily mean that the laws did not have the effect of removing this threat. It is difficult to determine what the effects of the legislation were, since in making a judgment like that one is trying to decide what *would* have happened *if* certain conditions had not prevailed. As late as 1928, the U.S. Women's Bureau concluded that legislation had almost never restricted women's employment opportunities, because occupations were so rigidly segregated by sex that women's opportunities were effectively limited without legislation.[67] The laws, they concluded, took no opportunities from women that they would have had in their absence. These investigators found only two instances of protective legislation being used to limit opportunities, and in one instance the women affected won an eight-year battle for an exemption.[68]

This evidence is corroborated by other sources.[69] The conclusions are, however, open to question. They amount to an assertion that without legislation, no one would have hired women for work usually performed by men, anyway. But there are instances of the displacement of one sex by another in an occupation—clerical work and cigar-making, for example—and, since women usually could be paid less than men, it is equally plausible that em-

ployers might have tried to replace men with women in the absence of legislation. Furthermore, the Women's Bureau conclusions have to be called into
question because of the way the advisory committee which wrote its report was set up. Violent disagreement among its original members forced
the representative of the Woman's Party—a group of feminists which had
already begun to question the legitimacy of protective legislation—to re-
sign, leaving on the committee representatives of the AFL, the National
Women's Trade Union League, and the League of Women Voters, groups
which had consistently supported protective legislation.[70] Thus, the people predisposed toward finding evidence of discrimination against women
in employment, caused by legislation, were not represented while those
predisposed toward viewing the effects of legislation favorably remained.

The motives of the labor organizations and the reformist groups were
quite similar. Although there were occasional suggestions like Strasser's,
most of the evidence indicates that unions were motivated by a sincere
desire to improve the lot of women workers as well as their own. However,
in the minds of labor leaders these motives frequently were fused, or
confused.

The following excerpt from the Report of the Committee on Female
Labor of the 1836 convention of the National Trades Union is a particularly eloquent plea for protection:

> The physical organization, the natural responsibilities, and
> the moral sensibility of women, prove conclusively that her
> labors should be only of a domestic nature. The health of
> the young female, in the majority of cases, is injured by the
> unnatural restraint and confinement, and deprived of the qual-
> ities essentially necessary in the culture and bearing of healthy
> children. Their morals frequently depart before their health, in
> consequence of being often crowded in such large numbers,
> with all characters and all sexes; and what evil example thus
> fails to do, necessity too often urges and palliates; and this one
> part of the subject, above all others, should arouse the jealous
> responsibilities of every moral man, and more particularly of
> every parent. These evils themselves are great, and call loudly
> for a speedy cure; but still another objection of the system
> arises, which, if possible, is productive of the other evils,
> namely, the ruinous competition brought in active opposi-

tion to male labor, actually producing a revision of the very good intended to do the guardian or parent, causing the destruction of the end which it aims to benefit; because, when the employer finds, as he surely will, that female assistance will compress his ends, of course the workman is discharged, or reduced to a corresponding rate of wages with the female operative. By these means the parent, the husband, or the brother is deprived of a sufficient subsistence to support himself and family, when without the auxiliary aid of the female, by his own labor alone he might have supported himself and family in decency, and kept his wife or relative at home, to perform the duties of the household.

[In manual labor] the female in a short time becomes so expert as to supercede [sic] to the necessity of the male; and this fact is apparent to everyone, that, when females are found capable of performing duty generally performed by the men as a natural consequence, from the cheapness of their habits and dependent situation, they acquire complete control of that particular branch of labor.

[It] must be apparent to every female. . . that her efforts to sustain herself and family, are actually the same as tying a stone around the neck of her natural protector, Man, and destroying him with the weight she has brought to his assistance.[71]

It is hard to interpret this document as a statement that a conflict of interests exists between male and female workers, and that male interests must prevail. Instead, the interests of men, women, and, implicitly, children, are seen identical; female labor outside the home is regarded as destructive to everyone's interests. This report suggests that men and women are designed by nature to fulfill distinct, complementary functions. In order for women to play their roles properly, certain moral qualities must be inculcated in them; these are threatened, if not destroyed, by outside work. (This concern for morality was echoed by the supporters of prohibitory employment laws. Although it seems logical that exclusion of women from mines would be defended on the grounds of safety, this legislation was usually designed for the same purpose as were prohibitions against work in bars: the protection of morality in the relations between the sexes.)[72] Furthermore, the argument continues, when women assume a role different from their natural one, they handicap men in the performance of their natural role. Limitations on women's employment, therefore, serve the interests of both men and women.

It is instructive to compare the NTU statement with one made as late as 1910 by Annie MacLean, a reformist of the Kelley-Goldmark sort. She wrote that

> the prime function of women in society is not "speeding up" on a machine; it is not turning out so many dozen gross of buttons or cans in one day; it is not making the heaviest sale of notions, or tending the greatest number of looms. . .
>
> The prime function of women must ever be the perpetuation of the race. If these other occupations render her unfit physically or morally for the discharge of this larger social duty, then woe to the generations that not only permit but encourage such wanton prostitution of function. The woman is worth more to society in dollars and cents as the mother of healthy children than as the swiftest labeller of cans . . .
>
> It would appear from this that the plain duty of society is to have care for its increasing throng of working girls. They must be protected. Desirable legislation should be obtained, and, moreover, maintained, regardless of constitutional quibble. A shorter working day and a higher wage should be advocated, and all types of organizations working for industrial betterment should cooperate in the effort to make America's wage-earning young women fit daughters of the country's noblest traditions and fit mothers for her sons.[73]

Both of these statements articulate ideas which are implied in many of the briefs and opinions I shall examine, and help explain the preference for sex-specific over sex-neutral legislation. These statements emphasize the permanent rather than the temporary aspects of women's situations. They insist that women need special protection not because they are exposed to particularly harmful conditions, but because of their physical (and sometimes psychological) characteristics. Arguments for labor legislation easily became arguments in defense of traditional sex roles.

Both writers share a particular view of the primary functions of men and women in society. MacLean differs from the committee members in one significant respect, however. She does not sound so sure that the interests of men, women, and children—perhaps the three principal classes of humankind, if seen in relation not to the means of production but to the means of reproduction—are all served by the same social arrangements. She is concerned with woman's function, not her nature. There is a discernible tone of moralistic discipline, a suggestion that, whatever people might like to do, their function is to serve society. We can interpret MacLean's remarks as identifying the interests of women with those of "the race," but that is not the only possible inference. The passage can, with equal validity, be interpreted as insisting that whatever the interests of women are, they must be subordinated to other interests. If interpreted that way, her argument is twin not to the NTU statement but to one made years later by Phyllis McGinley:

> By and large; . . . the world runs better when men and women keep in their own spheres. I do not say that women are better off, but society in general is. And that is, after all, the mysterious honor and obligation of women—to keep this planet in orbit. We are the self-immolators, the sacrificers, the givers, not the eaters-up of life. To say to us arbitrarily . . . that it is our *duty* to be busy elsewhere than at home is pretentious nonsense. Few jobs are worth disrupting family life for unless the family profits by it rather than the housewife herself.[74]

These latter two arguments, then, may share not only a view of what "woman's place" is, but a view of women as being peculiarly interestless. According to this view, women have no legitimate interests separate from those of men, children, "the race," or society. If a conflict of claims does occur, it is resolved either by insisting that women's claims, or perceived interests, do not represent their "true" interests (as the 1836 statement implies), or by insisting that (as the 1910 statement implies) women's claims, whether or not they represent their "true" interests, must yield to other "true" interests (though not necessarily to other claims: female workers' demands for a shorter working day are not properly subordinated to male employers' demands for a longer working day).

The possibility of conflicts of interests did not usually arise in the minds of those who supported restrictions on women's employment. Insofar as they were willing to restrict women's opportunities in the interests of male workers, they insisted that this restriction was also in the interests of women (although women workers might claim the opposite). The first commentator to attempt to deal with the possibility of conflict was the economist Sophonisba Preston Breckenridge. Writing in 1906, she warned:

> Such legislation is usually called "protective legislation" and the women workers are characterized as a "protected class." But it is obviously not the women who are protected. For them, some of this legislation may be a distinct limitation. For example, the prohibition against work in mines or against night work may very well limit the opportunities of women to find employment as to result in increased congestion and decreased wages in such other occupations as are open to them. Because of the smaller number of women industrially employed, and because of the survival in present-day notions of the medieval idea that where unsuitable conditions of intercourse between the sexes exist it is the woman whose presence is the disturbing factor, for those two reasons it is not unnatural and may be most desirable to exclude women from these forms of employment. But no one should lose sight of the fact that such legislation is not enacted exclusively, or even primarily, for the benefit of the women themselves. [75]

Trade unionists, usually male, and middle-class social workers, frequently female, argued for restrictions according to their views of the women workers' interests. Manufacturing and business interests, opposed to these laws, insisted that they violated these workers' rights to freedom of contract. On neither side of the controversy did women workers regularly speak for themselves; on both sides, others spoke for them. The women were given little chance to determine what it was that they themselves might want.

The representative arguments we have examined make three basic assumptions: first, that the conditions which justified special laws for women were permanent rather than temporary ones; second, that women's reproductive function implied a commitment to childrearing and homemaking; and third, that women's interests were either identical with or properly subordinate to those of families and of society. The arguments imply that the primary evil against which women workers must be protected is not the unhealthy conditions which could, theoretically at least, be ameliorated, but a "wanton prostitution of function" which prevents women from properly fulfilling their natural role. The reformers' fusion of the interests of women with those of others obscured the possibility of conflict of interests which Breckenridge saw. These assumptions were generally accepted without question, and, as we shall see, they enter into court decisions as well. It is necessary now to move from review of the historical context of protective legislation to examination of its fate in the courts, in order to learn how these issues and arguments were translated into the judicial context.

NOTES

1. The best sources on women workers are Edith Abbott, *Women in Industry* (New York: Appleton & Co., 1909); Elizabeth Faulkner Baker, *Technology and Women's Work* (rev. ed.; New York: Columbia University Press, 1964); Robert W. Smuts, *Women and Work in America* (New York: Columbia University Press, 1959).

2. See, e.g., Witt Bowden, *The Industrial Revolution* (New York: F. S. Crofts & Co., 1928), chs. 4-7; Y.S. Brenner, *A Short History of Economic Progress* (New York: Augustus M. Kelley, 1969), ch. 4; Harold U. Faulkner, *American Economic History* (8th ed.; New York: Harper & Row, 1959), ch. 22; Ellen L. Osgood, *A History of Industry* (rev. ed.; Boston: Ginn & Co., 1935), ch. 17.

3. John R. Commons et al., *History of Labor in the United States* (4 vols.; New York: Macmillan, 1936), 1:343.

4. The most complete source on American labor history is Commons, *History of Labor*. Other sources are Bowden, *Industrial History;* Foster Rhea Dulles, *Labor in America* (3rd ed.; New York: Thomas Y. Crowell & Co., 1966); Richard T. Ely, *The Labor Movement in America* (rev. ed.; New York: Thomas Y. Crowell & Co., 1890); Susan Kingsbury, *Labor Laws and Their Enforcement* (New York: Longmans, Green, & Co., 1911); George E. McNeill, ed., *The Labor Movement* (Boston: A. M. Bridgman & Co., 1887). On women specifically, in addition to the material cited, supra n. 1, see Helen L. Sumner, "The Historical Development of Women's Work in the United States," in Academy of Political Science, ed., *The Economic Position of Women* (New York: Academy of Political Science, Columbia University, 1910), pp. 1-23; U.S. Congress, Senate, 61st Cong. 2nd Sess.; 62nd Cong., 1st and 2nd Sess., Doc. No. 645, *Report on the Condition of Women and Child Wage-Earners in the United States* (19 vols.; Washington, D.C.: U.S. Government Printing Office, 1910-1915), esp. vol. 5.

5. Commons, *History of Labor*, vol. 1, Part I, chs. 1-4; Dulles, *Labor*, pp. 30-34.

6. John R. Commons et al., eds., *Documentary History of American Industrial Society* (10 vols.; New York: Macmillan, 1936), 7:134.

7. Ibid.

8. Sumner, "Women's Work," p. 21.

9. Commons, *Documentary History*, 7:135-36.

10. Ibid., p. 135.

11. Abbott, *Women*, pp. 114-15; Commons, *History of Labor*, 1:173.

12. Commons, *Documentary History*, 7:135.

13. McNeill, *Labor Movement*, chs. 4, 5, 7.

14. Commons, *History of Labor*, 1:302-25; 3:97.

15. Ibid., 3:96.

16. Ibid., pp. 97-99.

17. Ibid., p. 99.

18. Ibid., pp. 97-103; McNeill, *Labor Movement*, chs. 4-5.

19. "Women in the Trade Union Movement," in Academy of Political Science, *Women*, p. 111.

20. E. P. Thompson, *The Making of the English Working Class* (New York: Random House, 1964), pp. 248, 308-09, 328-29.

21. "Historical Development," p. 15.

22. "The Long Day" (1905), in William L. O'Neill, ed., *Women at Work* (Chicago: Quadrangle Books, 1972), pp. 227-29. Emphasis in the original.

23. See, e.g., Alice Henry, *Women in the Labor Movement* (New York: George H. Doran Co., 1923); Eleanor Flexner, *Century of Struggle* (New York: Atheneum, 1971), chs. 13, 14, 15, 17; U.S. Senate Report, *Women and Child Wage-Earners*, vol. 10, ch. 5.

24. *Documentary History*, 5:23.

25. *Women*, p. 131.

26. Ibid., p. 121.

27. Baker, *Technology*, chs. 2-5; Commons, *History of Labor*, vol. 1, ch. 5; Commons, *Documentary History*, 8:222-30; U.S. Senate Report, *Women and Child Wage-Earners*, vol. 10.

28. See Flexner, *Struggle*, chs. 13, 14, 15, 17.

29. Commons, *History of Labor*, 1:173.

30. Ibid., 1:169-75.

31. Abbott, *Women*, p. 145.

32. U.S. Senate Report, *Women and Child Wage-Earners*, vol. 5, ch. 1.

33. Ibid., ch. 2.

34. Ibid., pp. 9-19; 23-25.

35. U.S. Bureau of the Census, Monograph No. 9, *Women in Gainful Occupations, 1870 to 1920* (Washington, D.C.: U.S. Government Printing Office, 1929), pp. 23-25, 79.

36. U.S. Senate Report, *Women and Child Wage-Earners*, vol. 5, ch. 2.

37. *The Republic*, in *Great Dialogues of Plato*, trans. by W. D. Rouse (New York: Mentor Books, 1956), Book V, p. 253.

38. See infra, pp. 34-38.

39. *Some Ethical Gains Through Legislation* (2nd ed.; New York: Macmillan, 1910), p. 134.

40. *Documentary History*, 5:35.

41. U.S. Senate Report, *Women and Child Wage-Earners*, 10:94.

42. Commons, *History of Labor*, 3:462.

43. 208 U.S. 412, 421 (1908).

44. See, e.g., Anne Firor Scott, *The Southern Lady* (Chicago: University of Chicago Press, 1970), ch. 2; Elizabeth Longford, *Queen Victoria: Born to Succeed* (New York: Harper & Row, 1965), pp. 154, 234, 270, 271, 373, 377.

45. Josephine Goldmark, *Fatigue and Efficiency* (New York: Charities Publications Industries, 1912), Part II, pp. 269-76.

46. U.S. Senate Report, *Women and Child Wage-Earners*, vol. 13, Part II, ch. 3.

47. Ibid., 13:169.

48. See Ronald Piersall, *The Worm in the Bud* (London: Weidenfeld & Nicolson, 1969), pp. 205-13.

49. Aleta Wallach and Larry Rubin, "The Premenstrual Syndrome and Criminal Responsibility," *UCLA Law Review* 19 (December 1971):211.

50. See Commons, *Documentary History*, 5:190ff.

51. *The Semisovereign People* (New York: Holt, Rinehart, & Winston, 1960), p. 38.

52. See Commons, *History of Labor*, vol. 1 and *Documentary History*, vol. 1.

53. Commons, *History of Labor*, vol. 3, "Labor Legislation," ch. 2.

54. Ibid.

55. Ibid., p. 541.

56. Ibid., ch. 3.

57. Ibid., p. 473; Goldmark, *Fatigue*, ch. 8.

58. U.S. Women's Bureau, Bulletin No. 66-II, *Chronological Development of Labor Legislation for Women in the United States* (rev. ed.; Washington, D.C.: U.S. Government Printing Office, 1935), esp. p. 33.

59. Ibid., pp. 53, 65, 105, 112. The Dakota law continued in effect in both North and South Dakota when the territory became two states in 1889.

60. Commons, *History of Labor*, 3:457-500.

61. Ibid., p. 630.

62. Ibid., p. 631.

63. Ibid., 1:104.

64. Commons, *Documentary History*, vol. 8, passim.

65. McNeill, *Labor Movement*, p. 187.

66. See J. Stanley Lemons, *The Woman Citizen: Social Feminism in the 1920s* (Urbana: University of Illinois Press, 1973).

67. Bulletin No. 65, *Effects of Labor Legislation on Employment Opportunities for Women* (Washington, D.C.: U.S. Government Printing Office, 1928).

68. Ibid.

69. See Elizabeth Faulkner Baker, *Protective Labor Legislation* (rev. ed., New York: AMS Press, 1969), pp. 424-28, 432; Lemons, *Citizen*, pp. 22-25, 194-95.

70. E. Pendleton Herring, *Public Administration and the Public Interest* (New York: McGraw-Hill, 1936), pp. 358-59.

71. Commons, *Documentary History*, 6:281-84.

72. See Sophonisba P. Breckenridge, "Legislative Control of Women's Work," *Journal of Political Economy* 14 (January 1906): 107-09.

73. *Wage-Earning Women* (New York: Macmillan, 1910), pp. 177-78.

74. *Sixpence in Her Shoe*, p. 47.

75. "Legislative Control," pp. 107-08.

2

THE LEGITIMATION OF PROTECTIVE LEGISLATION, 1876-1908

Just as there was a substantial time lag between the development of labor problems and the enactment of legislation designed to mitigate them, there was a lag between the legislation and its judicial interpretation. It was not until 1876 that one of these protective laws was challenged in a supreme court, and not until the late 1880s that laws regulating labor conditions began reaching the courts with any regularity. One reason for this lag was, of course, the nugatory character of much early legislation. But after the Civil War, as the pace of industrial development quickened and was accompanied by the concentration and subsequent, if not consequent, abuse of economic power, reformers began to see the need for enforceable restrictions on this power. These restrictions can be divided into two general categories: laws designed to benefit workers, and those designed to retard the concentration of wealth and power. I will naturally be concerned primarily with the first category, but will draw from the second when helpful.

THE CONSTITUTIONAL CONTEXT: CONTRACTS, CLASSIFICATION, AND CREATIVITY

The business interests which had fought this legislation did not regard its enactment as a final defeat. They had another arena left—the courts—and lost little time getting into it. In the closing years of the nineteenth century, American courts were inundated with these cases.

Law may be too important a matter to be left to the lawyers, but its defense and interpretation are frequently left to the legal profession. Appreciation of the character of that profession at a particular time is an asset in understanding the performance of the judiciary. .

The growth of big business had a profound effect on the legal profession in the nineteenth century. By the 1880s the independent practitioner was no longer the law's dominant figure. Lawyers and businessmen had become increasingly interdependent. The postwar era

> saw the emergence of the specialist, first in commercial law as a whole, and then in the various aspects of it. Soon men devoted their entire careers to trusts or estates or receiverships or stock issues. Since big business needed all these skills, the result was the growth of large offices, staffed with any number of specialists and subordinates, all working on corporate problems.
>
> . . . Very few lawyers could see beyond their little niche to advise on larger problems. The earlier generalists had been admired as men of affairs; the specialists were not expected to know anything outside their narrow enclaves. Businessmen might seek their skills for specific problems, but not necessarily their advice on questions of overall policy. Soon industrial leaders stopped asking "what should I do?" with all its moral implications and started demanding "tell me the way to do this." Lawyers thus abdicated their responsibility as moral instructors and confined their activity to devising the best way for corporate clients to effect certain ends, some of them of questionable legality.[1]

This type of lawyer was well described by one magnate (the remark has been attributed variously to Gould, Morgan, and Harriman) about his lawyer, Elihu Root: "I have had lawyers who have told me what I cannot do. Root is the only lawyer who tells me how to do what I *want* to do."[2] And lawyers like Root were at the top of the profession.

Not all lawyers were corporation lawyers, of course, but the ones who argued cases for corporations, naturally enough, tended to be. And, since these became the most prestigious jobs in the profession, big business provided a disproportionate share of the appellate court judges. Corporation lawyers displayed considerable ingenuity in thinking up arguments which would support the positions of their employers, and they took their pro-business attitudes onto the bench with them. Business also found useful friends among the jurisprudents of the period, most notably Supreme Court Justice Stephen Field[3] and Professors Thomas M. Cooley and Christopher Tiedeman.

Not only was the legal profession biased because of the source of its income, but at the same time the country was being exposed to intellectual influences which predisposed well-informed people to sympathy with business. The dominant themes in nineteenth-century Western social thought combined to discourage governmental intervention in economic and social affairs. College students in the years after the Civil War were exposed to the writings of classical liberals who advocated laissez-faire, social Darwinists who applied the principle of natural selection to human society, and sociologists like William Graham Sumner and his disciples who argued that "folkways" were impervious to governmental change.[4] These ideas found their way into law schools as well, as the following quotation from Tiedeman's *State and Federal Control of Persons and Property,* a curious hybrid of Spencer and Sumner, indicates:

> . . . Between adults, employer and employed, since all men are free and equal, and are entitled to equal protection of the law, neither party can be compelled to enter into business relations with the other, except upon his own terms, voluntarily and free from any coercion whatsoever. The State has no right to interfere in a private employment and stipulate the terms upon which the services are to be rendered.
>
> Ordinarily, this proposition will be readily conceded; particularly, if one considers the question in its bearings upon his own affairs. A feeling of indignation arises within us at the contemplation of state interference to determine the wages we shall pay to our domestic servants. But insofar as the question is removed from its relation to our own affairs, so that it becomes less and less influenced by our prejudice and self-interest, the contemplation of the social inequalities of life, and the truly heartless, if not iniquitous, oppression which is afforded by reason of these inequalities; when we see, more and more clearly each day, that the tendency of the present process of civilization is to concentrate social power into the hands of a few, who, unless restrained in

some way, are able to dictate terms of employment to the masses, who must either accept them or remain idle; when at best they are barely enabled to provide for themselves and their families, while their employees are, at least apparently, accumulating wealth to an enormous extent. When all this injustice exists, or seems to exist, the impulse of a generous nature is to call loudly for the intervention of the law to protect the poor wage-earner from the grasping cupidity of the employer.

[But he] has acquired this superior position. . . through the exertion of his powers; he is above, and can to some extent dictate terms to, his employees, because his natural powers are greater, either intellectually or morally; and the profits, which naturally flow from this superiority, are but just regards of his own endeavors. At any rate, no law can successfully cope with these natural forces.

. . . Law can never create social forces. Law, on the contrary, is the result of social forces.[5]

As dominant as these ideas became in academic circles, they did not go unopposed in political life. The years immediately following the Civil War saw an unprecedented effort to use law to create and restrain social forces. But ironically, one result of this effort was to strengthen the position of business by attaching great importance to personal liberty and property. As Edward S. Corwin wrote, "The whole tendency . . . of the effort succeeding the Civil War to put the negro on a parity with the white race was, in the first place, to enlarge very greatly the significance of both these terms, and, secondly, by investing civil rights with the sanctity of property rights, to merge them and thus to confer upon property something of the broad connotation that it bears in the pages of Locke."[6] And in a strictly pragmatic way, the nineteenth-century civil rights movement provided the grounds for the arguments made by corporation lawyers by getting the Fourteenth Amendment enacted.

The conservative judicial reaction to business regulation was slow to develop—some initial decisions were friendly to it[7]—but when it came, it was pervasive and powerful. Lawyers and judges developed two major conceptual weapons in their attack on these laws: the doctrines of freedom of contract and of class legislation. The former doctrine became the most effective one, as courts piled dubious precedent upon dubious precedent to create a structure solid enough to endure without cracking for nearly thirty years. Beginning in 1886, with two cases—one from Illinois[8] and one from Pennsylvania[9] —involving the regulation of the manner of payment of workers, the state and federal courts interpreted the Due Process Clause of the Fourteenth Amendment to protect the rights of employer and employee to contract freely with respect to labor. These courts ruled that the states' police power did enable them to protect the citizens' health, safety, welfare, or morals, but not at the expense of this fundamental right (which made it a more precious right than, say, freedom of expression in that era). The statement of Judge Gordon of the Pennsylvania Supreme Court in *Godcharles v. Wigeman* is typical:

> [These sections of an act prohibiting payment of workers in "truck" or "scrip" negotiable only at corporation stores] are utterly unconstitutional and void, inasmuch as by them an attempt has been made by the legislature to do what, in this country, cannot be done; that is, to prevent persons who are *sui juris* from making their own contracts. The act is an infringement alike of the rights of the employer and the employee. More than this, it is an insulting attempt to put the laborer under a legislative tutelage, which is not only degrading to his manhood, but subversive of his rights as a citizen of the United States. He may sell his labor for what he thinks best, whether money or goods, just as his employer may sell his iron or coal; and any and every law that proposed to prevent him from so doing is an infringement of his constitutional privileges, and subsequently vicious and void.[10]

To tell a worker in 1886 that "he may sell his labor for what he thinks best" to a large corporation made very little sense. In law, the freedom might exist, but in fact, the power to use that freedom is totally lacking. It is unnecessary to belabor this point. Another point, which is often overlooked, is that this is not even good legal history; it is as wrong an interpretation of law as of fact. Writing after the doctrine had held sway for over twenty years, Roscoe Pound expressed this idea cogently:

> . . . one cannot read the cases in detail without feeling that a great majority of the decisions are simply wrong, not only

in constitutional law, but from the standpoint of the common law, and even from that of a sane individualism. Looking at them upon common-law principles, we must first of all recognize that there never has been at common law any such freedom of contract as they postulate. From the time that promises not under seal have been enforced at all, equity has interfered with contract in the interests of weak, necessitous, or unfortunate promisors. . . . Not only did equity grant to a debtor the right of redemption for which he did not stipulate but it would not and will not let him contract it away in advance. . . . It refused and refuses to grant specific performance of hard bargains, simply because they are hard, leaving promisees to confessedly inadequate and nugatory actions for damages. But there are no "natural incapacities" here! Courts of equity have simply recognized the facts of human intercourse, and have not suffered jural notions of equality to blind them thereto. . . . It has been said that the common law will not help a fool. But equity exists to help and protect him. It is because there are fools to be defrauded and imposed upon, and unfortunates to meet with accidents and careless to make mistakes, that we have courts of equity. Surely what equity has done to abridge freedom of contract, legislation may do likewise.[11]

Freedom of contract was never an unabridgeable right in any branch of law. But it was accepted by a bench, bar, and academy predisposed to sympathy for business. It might be argued here that what our ancestors did is not always the best guide to what principles they held; the fact that censorship was frequent in the eighteenth century has not led to the conclusion that courts must be lenient about it now. But there, at least, arguments have been made that wide latitude for expression of ideas is in line with fundamental principles rooted deeply in American traditions. No such effort is made in these decisions with freedom of contract; its nature is simply asserted.

Law after law—regulating method of payment,[12] hours of work,[13] various kinds of conditions[14]—fell under this doctrine in appellate courts. The doctrine did not convince all judges. Counterexamples can be found, not only in dissents, like Holmes' tart reminder that "the Fourteenth Amendment does not enact Mr. Herbert Spencer's *Social Statics,*"[15] but

in majority opinions upholding labor regulations, like the New York
Court of Appeals' sensible statement that "It is to the interest of the
state to have strong, robust, healthy citizens" and that "laws to effect
this purpose by protecting the citizen from overwork, and requiring a
general day of rest to restore his strength and preserve his health, have
an obvious connection with the public welfare."[16] But the conservative
arguments convinced enough judges to make the future of any economic regulation precarious indeed.

The other concept which became a powerful conservative weapon
was that of class legislation. The term is a sloppy and inaccurate one;
it carries a negative connotation which it does not fully deserve. Classification was legitimate if it was reasonably related to a valid state purpose.
"Class legislation" became shorthand for legislation which classifies arbitrarily and unreasonably. The constitutions of all the states contain
some sort of prohibition of arbitrary discrimination, and the Equal Protection Clause of the Fourteenth Amendment has been interpreted to
prohibit this kind of legislation. Classic examples of arbitrary discrimination are laws singling out people for special treatment for a reason un-
related to any rational goal, such as, placing special restrictions on red-
haired or blue-eyed people. Of course, real laws passed by real legislators
are not that simple. The trouble began when the courts had to decide
what constituted an arbitrary classification.

Laws which in retrospect seem to make thoroughly reasonable discriminations were struck down. A law which provided that a state would
pay attorneys' fees for persons who sued railroads for damages but left
railroads to pay their own fees was arbitrary.[17] A law which regulated
the activities of stockyards was arbitrary because it set a minimum number of cattle per year which yards had to receive before they were covered
by it.[18] A law which prohibited trusts in business was arbitrary because
it exempted trusts in agriculture.[19] And the laws which fell under the doctrine of freedom of contract were usually also discredited as establishing
an arbitrary classification. Laws which applied only to workers in certain
named activities (as most laws did) were declared unconstitutional for
two reasons: both because they infringed freedom of contract and because they established unjustifiable classifications in the opinion of the
judges.[20]

This discussion has not exhausted the theories which can be found in
these cases involving labor and business practices. Another common ground

for invalidation was the argument that the laws bore no reasonable relation to the proper subjects of police power. Courts insisted either that there was no relation between, say, the hours a person worked and his health—for example, "It would be absurd to argue that, while the process ifself is continuous, limiting the hours of those laboring in a smelter in any wise conduces to preserve the health of any portion of the public"[21] (apparently not even that portion employed in smelting)—or that the laws were designed not to preserve the health of the general public but a particular segment of it (it being assumed that the citizens have no legitimate interests in the health of groups of their fellow citizens; a "one man's death does not diminish me" attitude on the parts of nineteenth-century judges). Courts usually found several reasons to overturn these laws which were clearly so odious to them.

Judges did not invariably refuse to make exceptions from the general rule of noninterference with freedom of contract. For example, laws which restricted working hours in occupations thought to be particularly dangerous were frequently, though not always, upheld.[22] The decision with the greatest precedential impact was the United States Supreme Court's affirmance of a Utah ten-hour law for miners in *Holden v. Hardy* in 1898.[23] The Court did not emphasize the character of the occupation, but the decision we are about to examine indicated that it had regarded this point as crucial.

One of the most famous, and best, examples of the typical reasoning employed in these cases is the Supreme Court's opinion in *Lochner v. New York* in 1905, voiding that state's ten-hour law for bakers. Because of the importance of the decision, I quote at length from Justice Peckham's opinion for the Court.

> The question of whether this act is valid as a labor law, pure and simple, may be dismissed in a few words. There is no reasonable ground for interfering with the liberty of person or the right of free contract, by determining the hours of labor, in the occupation of a baker. There is no contention that bakers as a class are not equal in intelligence and capacity to men in other trades or manual occupations, or that they are not able to assert their rights and care for themselves without the protecting arm of the state, interfering with their independence of

judgment and of action. They are in no sense wards of
the state. Viewed in the light of a purely labor law, with
no reference whatever to the question of health, we
think that a law like the one before us involves neither
the safety, the morals, nor the welfare, of the public, and
that the interest of the public is not in the slightest degree affected by such an act.

We think the limit of the police power has been reached and
passed in this case. There is, in our judgment, no reasonable
foundation for holding this to be necessary and appropriate as
a health law to safeguard the public health. . . .

We think that there can be no fair doubt that the trade
of baker, in and of itself, is not an unhealthy one to that
degree which would authorize the legislature to interfere
with the right to labor, and with the right of free contract
on the part of the individual, either as employer or employee; . . . There must be more than the mere fact of the
possible existence of some small amount of unhealthiness
to warrant legislative interference with liberty. . . .

The act is not, within any fair meaning of the term, a
health law, but is an illegal interference with the rights of
individuals, both employers and employees, to make contracts regarding labor upon such terms as they may think
best, or which they may agree upon with the other parties
to such contracts. Statutes of the nature of that under review limiting the hours in which grown and intelligent
men may earn their living, are mere meddlesome interferences with the rights of the individual, and they are not
saved from condemnation by the claim that they are
passed in the exercise of the police power and upon the subject of the health of the individual whose rights are interfered with, unless there be some fair ground, reasonable
in and of itself, to say that there is a material danger to
the public health, or to the health of the employees, if
the hours of labor are not curtailed.[24]

It should be pointed out that these courts were rarely presented with
powerful arguments in favor of the laws. Lawyers on each side simply re-

viewed—or merely listed—the precedents which supported their position;[25] and here the corporations were sure to win. That does not excuse the abandonment of the presumption of constitutionality, but it makes it more understandable. And it took reformers twenty years to realize that it might be facts, not precedent, that judges needed in order to be convinced of the legitimacy of these laws and to assume the burden of furnishing these facts. It is fascinating to speculate on how American constitutional history might be different if reformers had assumed this burden three years earlier than they actually did, in *Lochner* rather than *Muller.*

WOMEN'S LEGISLATION AND THE COURTS, 1876-1908

In order for a law applying only to women workers to withstand assault, judges who accepted the prevailing doctrines would have had to take one or both of the following steps. First, they might insist that women, like children and unlike adult males, were not persons *sui juris* and, therefore, were not capable of making their own contracts. Second, they might agree that classification by sex was reasonably related to a legitimate governmental purpose, like the preservation of morality, the protection of the general public welfare, or the protection of a particularly vulnerable segment of the population. Considering the conceptual world in which judges operated, the fate of women's legislation was anybody's guess. And examination of the cases up to 1908 reveals an erratic performance.

Two kinds of women's laws received judicial attention in these years: hours limitation and prohibitions from certain occupations. The second type was of relatively minor importance, since it presented little challenge to the new doctrines, and can be disposed of briefly. This was the first kind of women's legislation to reach the highest court of a state, in *Blair v. Kilpatrick*[26] in 1872. At issue was an Indiana statute allowing "white males only" to become licensed bartenders. The court avoided the race issue, but upheld the sex discrimination. Unfortunately, the opinion is so clumsily written that it is almost impossible either to discern the facts or disentangle the arguments. We never learn *why* Blair's suit, which challenged the award of a liquor license to Kilpatrick, was brought in the first place, or what the suit had to do with the race and sex limitations. Both Kilpatrick (who kept his license) and Blair were white males.

Several similar laws or ordinances were reviewed by the courts in this phase.[27] All were upheld except a San Francisco ordinance in 1881, and the California Supreme Court reversed itself in 1893, upholding a new ordinance from the same city. In the earlier case, the court relied on an article of the state constitution which read, "No person shall on account of sex be disqualified from entering upon or pursuing any lawful business, vocation, or profession."[28] That clause was still in force in 1893 (and, indeed, remains in force today), but in the *Hayes* case the judges had no difficulty reconciling the constitution with the ordinance. They simply said in a unanimous opinion that the antidiscrimination clause did not "operate as a limitation upon the power of the state or of its municipalities to prescribe the conditions upon which the business of retailing intoxicating liquors shall be permitted to be carried on."[29] The apparent contradiction may not seem so easily resolvable to the reader, but, at any rate, California was not alone. Both Washington and Illinois combined prohibitory laws of this type with antidiscrimination provisions and Illinois even passed both of these in the same year.[30]

The other decisions resolved the cases simply by referring to the state's power over the liquor trade; with one exception, they did not even refer to "morality." The exception was a Federal District Court ruling upholding the Washington law. The court wrote, ". . . the intent of the legislature was manifestly to check the tendency towards immorality of the association of the sexes in places of resort where intoxicating beverages are sold and where the worst passions are aroused."[31] It is questionable whether "immorality," without further elaboration, is an evil grave enough to justify restriction at all. But even if one assumes that it is, the opinion does not explain why it is permissible to restrict only one sex in the interests of morality. One could just as plausibly argue that men should have been prohibited from working in bars. The court, however, simply accepts the state's assumption that it is women who must be restricted in the interests of sexual morality.

The adjudication of hours laws provided more significant—and erratic—precedents. The first such law to be challenged was upheld, but not on the basis of sexual distinctions. It was the first hours law in the United States with any teeth in it, the Massachusetts law discussed in Chapter 1. Passed in 1867 and amended in 1874, it applied to women and children under eighteen. A complaint was filed against the Hamilton Manufacturing Company for violating this law. In 1876—which, it should be remembered, was ten years before the first freedom of contract decisions—the Supreme

Judicial Court ruled unanimously in favor of the statute, apparently mis-
reading the law in the process. Judge Lord wrote that the law did not restrict the hours any person might work: ". . . it merely prohibits her being
employed continuously in the same service more than a certain number
of hours per day or week."[32] He continued: [The law] merely provides
that in an employment, which the Legislature has evidently deemed to
some extent dangerous to health, no person shall be engaged in labor
more than ten hours a day or sixty hours a week. There can be no doubt
that such legislation may be maintained as a health or police regulation."[33]
The fact that the law applied not to all persons, but only to two categories
of persons, did not strike the court as relevant (perhaps understandably in
terms of the law's effect). *Hamilton* illustrates the ease with which judges
could reconcile themselves to economic regulation when not saturated with
exaggerated doctrines. Later courts would find considerable doubt that police power encompassed such regulation. In each of the three cases decided
before 1908 in which acceptance of the law was based on sexual differences,
the state court was confronted with a decision, binding in its jurisdiction,
which had rejected general hours legislation.[34] Judges felt forced to legitimize exceptions from the general rule they had established, and focused
on the most obvious differences between general hours laws and women's
hours laws: the differences between the persons covered by the regulations.

We must recognize the fact that these judges were reasoning within a box
they had gotten themselves into. With the exception of the Oregon Supreme
Court in 1906, the year after *Lochner,* they were not forced to accept the
principle of freedom of contract or to apply it to hours legislation. As I
have suggested, not all judges shared the prevailing ideas, and they were
not always accepted by a majority within every court. In New York,[35]
Minnesota,[36] and West Virginia,[37] laws regulating labor conditions were
upheld against the charge that they violated freedom of contract. There
is no reason why other courts could not have done the same. Until *Lochner,*
state courts were never forced either by precedent or by unanimity of professional opinion to invalidate labor laws. Those courts which did so were
exercising considerable freedom of choice.

After *Hamilton,* no women's hours law reached a state supreme court
for nearly twenty years. By then—1895—twelve states had such laws. The
Illinois Supreme Court overturned an eight-hour law for women in factories or workshops under both the Due Process and Equal Protection Clauses.
Ritchie v. People[38] was decided the year after the Pullman strike; it proba-

bly would have been a bad year for any labor law in Illinois. The court insisted that women were entitled to the same liberty of contract as men, regardless of differences of "sex and physique."[39] The legislature, it declared, "has sought to impose an unreasonable and unnecessary burden
upon . . . one citizen or class of citizens."[40] The arguments and the result
would have been satisfying only, perhaps, to a feminist who was also a
judicial conservative. The *Ritchie* decision probably discouraged enactment of women's hours laws in other states. Between 1896 and 1908,
nevertheless, nine states passed such laws.[41]

Comparatively speaking, 1902 was a bumper year for this adjudication:
two cases were decided, both favorably. Their geography is indicative of
industry's westward spread; they came from Nebraska and Washington.
At issue were two almost identical laws establishing a ten-hour day for
women in "manufacturing, mechanical and mercantile establishments,
hotels, and restaurants." The Nebraska Supreme Court wrote as follows:

> Women and children have always to a certain extent been
> wards of the state. Women in recent years have been partly
> emancipated from their common-law disabilities. But they
> have no voice in the enactment of the laws by which they
> are governed, and can take no part in municipal affairs. They
> are unable, by reason of their physical limitations, to endure
> the same hours of exhaustive labor as may be endured by
> adult males. Certain kinds of work, which may be performed
> by men without injury to their health, would wreck the con-
> stitutions and destroy the health of women, and render them
> incapable of bearing their share of the burdens of the family
> and the home. The state must be accorded the right to guard
> and protect women as a class, against such a condition; and
> the law in question, to that extent, conserves the public health
> and welfare.[42]

A few pages later, the court again takes up this theme:

> The employer and the [adult male] laborer are practical-
> ly on an equal footing, but these observations do not apply
> to women and children. Of the many vocations in this coun-
> try, comparatively few are open to women. Their field of

remunerative labor is restricted. Competition for places
therein is necessarily great. The desire for place, and in many
instances the necessity of obtaining employment, would subject them to hardships and exactions which they would not
otherwise endure. The employer who seeks to obtain the
most hours of labor for the least wages, has such an advantage
over them that the wisdom of the law, for their protection,
cannot well be questioned.[43]

These two passages from *Wenham v. State* mention nearly all the distinguishing features of women's employment which I identified in Chapter 1. The opinion does not attempt to rank-order them, or even to organize them according to type. Physical, economic, and political features
are mentioned. The court does not suggest that any of these conditions
by itself would be sufficient to justify special legislation, but neither does
it foreclose that possibility. And, like the statements I analyzed earlier,
it implicitly fuses the interests of women with the "public health and
welfare." The law is justifiable both to protect the health of women and
to enable them to bear their share of family burdens. All women are assumed to have the same burdens; no distinctions are made on the basis
of marital or parental status.

Two months later, the Supreme Court of Washington decided *State
v. Buchanan*.[44] It did not cite *Wenham*, but did cite *Hamilton*, concluding: "It is a matter of universal knowledge to all reasonably intelligent
people of the present age that continuous standing on the feet by women
for a great many continuous hours is deleterious to their health. It must
logically follow that that which would deleteriously affect any great number of women, who are the mothers of succeeding generations, must necessarily affect the public welfare and the public morals."[45] Thus working
women were distinguished from working men, whose hours could not be
limited even in public employment.[46] This decision represents a clear
shift in emphasis from *Wenham*. Instead of basing its ruling on a variety
of undifferentiated factors of the situation of working women, the Washington Court has clearly chosen to emphasize physical and quasi-permanent, rather than socioeconomic and situation-bound, factors.

The next case was *State v. Muller*,[47] in 1906. This involved Oregon's
ten-hour law, passed in 1903, similar to the Nebraska and Washington
ones. With *Lochner* very much on its mind, the Oregon Supreme Court

depended almost entirely on sexual differences in upholding the law. The opinion consists almost wholly of quotations from *Wenham* and *Buchanan;* the only new feature was a rejection of *Ritchie* as "borne down by the weight of authority and sound reason."[48] Curt Muller, the owner of a Multonomah County laundry who had been convicted of violating the law, went a step farther than his predecessors. He appealed to the U.S. Supreme Court.

As the case wound its way up, reformers got two setbacks. In *People v. Williams,*[49] the New York Court of Appeals considered a night-work prohibition for women and children under eighteen. A factory inspector had found women at work beyond the permitted hours in a New York City bookbinding establishment; the proprietor was tried and convicted. Both the intermediate and the final appellate courts reversed the conviction. The Court of Appeals did not (appropriately) reach the question of hours limitation, but it did cite approvingly the opinion of the Supreme Court's Appellate Division: "In order to sustain the reasonableness of the provision we must find that owing to some physical or nervous differences, it is more harmful for a woman to work at night than for a man to do so. We are not aware of any such difference, and in all the discussions that have taken place none such have been pointed out."[50] This was quite true. Although the state's brief contained references to the "well-known" fact that "women are physically weaker than men" and to their role as "mothers of the race," these distinctions were never shown to have any relationship to night work. The second adverse decision, the Colorado case of *People v. Burcher,* invalidated an eight-hour law for women in "any mill, factory, manufacturing establishment, shop or store" on a technicality.[51]

By January 1908, with oral argument in *Muller* scheduled for that month, seven cases involving women's hours laws had been decided by state supreme courts over a period of thirty-two years. Four laws had been upheld, and three overturned. Of the successful four, one, *Hamilton,* had been decided on the basis of arguments decisively rejected in *Lochner.* The decisions formed no discernible pattern, chronological, geographic, or theoretical. The weight of precedent fell on neither side. The states had provided the Supreme Court with little guidance. *Lochner* indicated strong disapproval of hours legislation, but in 1898 in *Holden v. Hardy*[52] the Court had indicated willingness to sustain limitations in special circumstances. The *Muller* case could go either way, and the result would be crucial.

The law's supporters were determined to win, not only to sustain protective legislation for women but also to mount a successful attack on "the highest bastion of legal conservatism."[53] The fact that the law at issue pertained only to women was to some extent an accident. The major goal was to establish "a factual connection between the law and the conditions of life which had provoked it."[54] Reformers developed a startlingly innovative strategy. Instead of emphasizing legal precedents, they marshalled empirical evidence to convince the Court of the law's wisdom.

It was not the State of Oregon, but the National Consumers' League, which originally assumed this task. The League approached Louis Brandeis, the brother-in-law of its publications secretary Josephine Goldmark. Brandeis had distinguished himself from his colleagues at the bar by his sympathy to reform. The League asked him to represent it as *amicus curiae.* Brandeis refused to take the case unless he was hired as special counsel for the State of Oregon. This was agreed to, and the lawyer, the League, and the state joined forces. Josephine Goldmark supervised the collection of data, and she and Brandeis organized it into a brief which was filed before the Supreme Court.

This was the first Brandeis brief, and it made the term "brief" seem a misnomer. It may have been the longest the Court had ever seen, but it would not hold that record for long. In the opinion, Justice Brewer referred to Brandeis' "very copious collection of all these matters."[55] In comparison with later Brandeis briefs, which could run over a thousand pages, "copious" seems a gross exaggeration. The *Muller* brief was 113 pages long. Two pages were devoted to precedent and legal argument, thirteen to a list of all the hours laws enacted so far anywhere in the world, one to a conclusion, and the remaining eighty-seven to empirical evidence.

It is usually a risky business to persuade any group out of a position it took as recently as three years previous, especially a court. Here, that might have been possible. The *Lochner* vote had been five to four, and one of the justices in the majority had since retired. But it is much safer to try to persuade people that the circumstances of a present case are distinguishable from those of an earlier one, and therefore not controlled by it. That was the tack Brandeis took, both in the brief and in oral argument. The obvious difference between the New York law and the Oregon one was that the former applied to all adults in a certain occupation and the latter only to women. So Brandeis was naturally encouraged to emphasize sexual differences, which he did.

A good way to indicate the range of topics covered and the relative emphasis given to each is simply to reproduce the relevant parts of the Table of Contents.

One feature of the brief (also characteristic of later Brandeis briefs) is the amount of space devoted to proving that this law does not subvert the interests of employers: almost one-fourth of the brief. This indicates the extent to which Brandeis and Goldmark had assumed the task of furnishing the Court with the relevant facts.

What kinds of data does the brief contain? One kind it does *not* contain is arguments about women's "primary role" or "inherent nature." Views like these are sometimes implied, but they are not stated. The brief sticks to observable conditions. Most of the data are anecdotal rather than statistical, consisting of selections from reports of factory or health inspectors both in the United States and in foreign countries; testimony before legislative investigating committees of witnesses such as physicians or social workers; quotes from medical texts and journal articles; and similar sources. There are a few examples of questionable data such as Havelock Ellis' statement that women's muscles and blood had more water in them than men's,[57] but for the most part the brief contains presumably accurate reports of witnesses about conditions they observed.

The methodological sophistication of the reports, however, is not very great. The experts did not seem to realize that a report of injury and illness among workers does not suggest, let alone prove, a causal relationship between working conditions and health unless it is accompanied by statistics which show that the incidence of pathology is significantly greater among workers than in the general population. Even if such controls are available, no causal connection would be proved. Intervening variables might still be controlling, as in the matter of maternal employment and infant mortality. (The data available to Brandeis, Goldmark, Felix Frankfurter, and Mary Dewson for later briefs is better in this respect).

In these pages, we find report after report of a high incidence of tuberculosis, lead-poisoning, menstrual problems, miscarriages, deformed joints, and general ill health among women workers, with occasional pointed references to ill health among men workers. But there are few attempts at finding a control group. There are three exceptions to this generalization—the testimony of a British physician on sterility among working women but not among nonworkers in the same family,[58] the report of two other doctors that in one town, women operatives had far more digestive problems than women in general,[59] and a statement that infant mortality was highest in industrial areas[60] —but even these are very small, contain no statistics, and are not duplicated elsewhere.

The data provide convincing evidence that women factory and laundry workers are subject to disease and injury, and that fatigue tends to increase accidents, but does not prove that women are more vulnerable than men are. Most of the reports were of shops, factories, or laundries where all or most of the employees were women. There was little evidence that men would have withstood the same conditions better. There are exceptions here, too, such as a report from Massachusetts compositors that women, unlike men, could not stand at the "case" and therefore suffered from muscle pain, menstrual difficulties, and general weakness.[61] But most of the evidence does not prove that women suffered because of their physical characteristics any more than the Triangle Fire did.

The part of the brief which discusses the effect of shorter hours is more persuasive as evidence of causal relationships; we find testimony that when hours were reduced, health improved. Whether or not long hours caused injury, disease, alcoholism, or infant mortality, amelioration of these conditions frequently followed reduction of hours. The evidence here is as anecdotal as that in the rest of the brief, but here there is, at least, a control group, with conditions before hours were reduced compared with conditions after reduction.

The portions of the brief which deal with the health of infants and children contain many references to the "puny, sickly, partly developed

children"[62] of factory workers, but they do not indicate a causal relationship between the employment of the mother and such pathology.
We have already discussed the problem of infant mortality, prominent
in the brief. And many of the children described as puny and sickly were
themselves factory workers, and would probably have been weak no matter what their mothers did. Presumably, malnutrition was also a factor,
but it is not suggested that, after weaning, this is caused by maternal employment.

One set of conditions which is ignored in the brief are the political
ones. Brandeis makes no effort to argue that women need the protection
of the state because they lack the political power to protect themselves.
Throughout the brief we find not only a failure to prove causal connections between long hours and ill health (probably not Brandeis' and
Goldmark's fault, considering the data available to them), but failure to
distinguish physical causes from economic ones. The brief permits either
of two conclusions: that working women suffer because of their physical
structure, or that they suffer because the only jobs open to them are particularly dangerous and unpleasant.

The Supreme Court records of the *Muller* case contain no brief for the
plaintiff, although the headnote to the opinion states that one was filed.
Its argument is summarized here. The attorneys not only insisted that
freedom of contract was protected by the Fourteenth Amendment, but
that "women . . . as persons and citizens are entitled to all the privileges
and immunities provided, and are as competent to contract with reference
to their labor as are men."[63] It cited the usual long string of precedents
on the former point, and *Ritchie, Williams,* and, mystifyingly, *Wenham*
on the latter.

THE DECISION: WOMAN IN A CLASS BY HERSELF

The case decided by the Supreme Court on February 24, 1908, became a landmark case not for its relevance to women's rights, but for its
implications for economic regulation. It put a crack in the *Lochner* doctrine, and paved the way for "shift[ing] the emphasis from the fact that
they are *women* to the fact that it is *industry* and relation of industry to
the community that is regulated."[64] The decision is not usually analyzed
as I shall analyze it here, with an emphasis on the discussion of women.
Even contemporary feminist scholars do not spend much time on it. They
may, like Kate Millett, deplore its "patronizing air of concessions made

to the physically inferior"[65] or, like Leo Kanowitz, criticize its "male supremacist notions"[66]—and these are valid and necessary criticisms—but no writer that I know of has yet examined in detail precisely what the opinion has to say about women.

The opinion for a unanimous Court was written by Justice David Brewer, a leading judicial conservative who had concurred in *Lochner* and dissented in *Holden v. Hardy*. It is short, only seven pages. Brewer wrote:

> That woman's physical structure and the performance of maternal functions place her at a disadvantage in the struggle for existence is obvious. This is especially true when the burdens of motherhood are upon her. Even when they are not, by abundant testimony of the medical fraternity, continuance for a long time on her feet at work, repeating this from day to day, tends to injurious effects upon the body, and, as healthy mothers are essential to vigorous offspring, the physical well-being of women becomes an object of public interest and care in order to preserve the strength and vigor of the race. Still again, history discloses the fact that woman has always been dependent upon man. He established his control at the outset by superior physical strength, and this control in various forms, and with diminishing intensity, has continued to the present. As minors, though not to the same extent, she has been looked upon in the courts as needing especial care that her rights be preserved. Education was long denied her, and while now the doors of the schoolroom are opened and her opportunities for acquiring knowledge are great, yet even with that and the consequent increase of capacity for business affairs it is still true that in the struggle for subsistence she is not an equal competitor with her brother. Though limitations upon personal and contractual rights may be removed by legislation, there is that in her disposition and habits of life which will operate against a full assertion of those rights. She will still be where some legislation to protect her seems necessary to secure a real equality of rights . . . looking at it from the viewpoint of the effort to maintain an independent position in life, she is not upon an equality. Differentiated by these matters

from the other sex, she is properly placed in a class by herself, and legislation designed for her protection may be sustained, even when like legislation is not necessary for men,
and could not be sustained. It is impossible to close one's
eyes to the fact that she still looks to her brother and depends
upon him. Even if all restrictions on political, personal, and
contractual rights were taken away, and she stood, so far as
statutes are concerned, upon an absolutely equal plane with
him, it would still be true that she will rest upon and look to
him for protection; that her physical structure and a proper
discharge of her maternal functions—having in view not merely her own health, but the well-being of the race—justify legislation to protect her from the greed as well as the passion
of man. The limitations which this statute places upon her
contractual powers, upon her right to agree with her employer as to the time she shall labor, are imposed not only for
her benefit, but also largely for the benefit of all. . . . The
two sexes differ in structure of the body, in the amount of
physical strength, in the capacity for long-continued labor,
the influence of vigorous health upon the future well-being
of the race, the self-reliance which enables one to assert full
rights, and in the capacity to maintain the struggle for subsistence. This difference justifies a difference in legislation.
. . . We have not referred in this discussion to the denial
of the elective franchise in the state of Oregon, for while
that may disclose a lack of political equality in all things
with her brother, that is not of itself decisive. The reason
runs deeper, and rests in the inherent differences between
the two sexes, and the different functions in life which they
perform.[67]

Brewer has weighed most of the distinguishing features of the situation
of working women, and has chosen to emphasize those which are physical
and, in his view, unalterable in impact. He does not mention the economic
conditions which might place women "at a disadvantage in the struggle for
existence."[68] He does discuss women's social and political disadvantages,
but suggests that in the present case they are rather beside the point. He
insists that even if these disabilities were removed, and the need for some
kinds of special regulations perhaps eliminated thereby, women's physical

and, perhaps, psychological nature ("disposition and habits of life")[69] would still necessitate some special protection. Labor legislation based on women's physical characteristics is ruled permissible and advisable not only now, but for all time.

The assignment of this opinion to a judge who held to the principle of freedom of contract even more rigidly than most of his colleagues did probably had significant influence on the reasoning employed, and thus on the development of American constitutional law in the area of sex equality. (It is fascinating to speculate what the decision would have said if Justice Holmes, say, had written it instead). Considering Brewer's constitutional views, his choice of emphasis is understandable. If he had stressed the social and economic disabilities, he would have left the door open for later conclusion that any workers who suffered such disabilities could claim governmental protection—a conclusion contrary to his entire philosophy. He was on safer ground arguing as he did. "Grown and intelligent men"[70] might someday be at a disadvantage in the struggle for subsistence, but they would surely never bear children.

Brewer makes the assumption, unsupported here by evidence, that the sexes differ psychologically as well as physically. This assumption bolsters his argument, but is not essential to it and is not, therefore, a very important part of it. Positing psychological differences makes it easier to identify the interests of women, as he *explicitly* does, with those of "the race." Surely, if women were psychologically constructed as men are, they would not yield willingly to limitations on their contractual rights. But Brewer does not need to, and indeed does not, dwell on this point. He emphasizes known physical facts rather than engaging in theorizing about female psychology.

That kind of theorizing would not have been unprecedented for Supreme Court opinions. Thirty-six years earlier, Justice Bradley, concurring in the affirmance of Illinois' denial of bar admission to a woman, had waxed eloquent in a manner very similar to the National Trades Union's 1836 report. Bradley had written of the "natural and proper timidity and delicacy which belongs to the female sex," unfitting it for many coarse occupations in favor of its "paramount design and mission . . . to fulfill the noble and benign offices of wife and mother."[71] He had even gone so far as to refer to "the law of the Creator."[72] Neither Brewer nor the justices who reviewed later employment laws produced anything like this. Given their evident views, they did not have to.

If one believes that freedom of contract is a constitutional right, which workers actually enjoy, the limitation of this freedom for women can be defended only if one agrees that women should have less freedom under the Constitution than men. The opinion does not flinch from this necessity. It declares that women may be denied rights which men enjoy, both for what the state views as their own benefit and in the interests of the larger society. Of course, any law which limits the working hours of a particular group of workers—miners, for example—curtails their freedom of contract relative to other workers. Viewed in this light, *Muller* would not seem startling—until we remember that it is possible to choose to be, or cease to be a miner; but one does not choose to be, or cease to be a woman.

Brewer has made the problem fairly easy to solve with his assumption that the interests of women coincide nicely with societal interests. Fusion of these two sets of interests obscures the possibility of conflict between them, conflict which, I have suggested, is a crucial problem in determining the legitimacy of a restriction. In this case, the assumption the Court has made appears reasonable. When one must stand all day in a hot, crowded factory, interest in one's own health demands shorter hours, which would also further society's interest in the production of healthy children.

But it is easy to envision situations in which these interests would conflict, as anyone informed on the abortion controversy knows. All steps which could be taken in the interests of women would not necessarily also protect actual or potential children. Indeed, one good way to help safeguard the health of women would be to discourage them from having children at all. This argument is, admittedly, extreme, but it is not therefore groundless. Despite medical advances, pregnancy and childbirth can be hazardous to health. The risk of death from pregnancy is statistically higher than the risk of death from any form of contraception,[73] and even without death, pregnancy carries an appreciable risk of attendant dangerous, disabling complications. But anyone who suggests, as Shulamith Firestone does, that "Childbirth HURTS. And it isn't good for you,"[74] and draws the obvious conclusion from this statement, is ignored.

When we turn from specific considerations of physical health to more general considerations of interests, it is even easier to see the possibility of conflict, unless we accept the Court's tentatively articulated, and empirically unsupported belief about the nature of women. Women who are free to select occupations which involve considerable physical exertion might be willing to jeopardize their childbearing capacities. Women who enjoy working for long periods of time, or at unorthodox times of the day, might want to minimize domestic tasks. To make things even

more complicated, some women might want one kind of life, and some
another. The *Muller* ruling implicitly places the balance overwhelmingly
on the side of "societal" interests, identified with family interests.

The opinion is fascinating not only as constitutional law, but as an
interpretation of history. In three pages, Brewer has advanced two conflicting interpretations of the origin of the inequality of women, without
resolving the apparent contradiction. First, he informs us that man "established his control at the outset by superior physical strength." The
stronger dominated the weaker. There was apparently initial reluctance,
if superior physical strength was needed. But a few lines later, Brewer
discusses how woman "looks to her brother and depends upon him"
for protection. This suggests that women voluntarily submitted to male
dominance because of their own recognized need for protection.

We do not expect judges to be either historians or anthropologists.
Indeed, considering some of their efforts in the former area, many of
us might prefer that they stay out of the latter. But when they do venture
into these disciplines, they invite, and usually deserve criticism. Brewer
presents no evidence whatsoever for either of his contradictory conclusions. His historio-anthropological excursion is not crucial to his conclusion, but it is significant for its implications and applications. Men establish control over women, but women seek the protection of men. Somehow
protection is inextricably intertwined with domination—a point which will
become increasingly important as the need for protection decreases and
men struggle to maintain their dominant position.

In *Muller,* the Court was presented with much evidence that people
who worked in the kind of occupations in which women were usually
employed needed shorter hours. But the conclusion that the Court drew
from this evidence was that women could not work as many hours per
day as men could. As I have suggested, this choice of emphasis was probably dictated in large part by the justices' need to reconcile the principle
of freedom of contract with the need for some kind of regulation, a need
powerfully argued by the Brandeis brief. The easiest way to make that
reconciliation was to stress the most obvious and most persistent differences between women and "grown and intelligent men": not the economic and social differences, but the physical ones.

As precedent, *Muller* was able to become even more controlling in the
area of sex equality than in the area of economic regulation. For more than
sixty years, courts upheld nearly all cases of sex discrimination, citing this
case as binding precedent, following its lead in emphasizing permanent

rather than temporary, physical rather than economic or social, aspects of women's condition. Indeed, the one important deviant case seemed to be the product of judicial inability to believe that any factors other than permanent physical differences could justify special legislation. The slavish following of the *Muller* precedent was to persist long after technological advances had ameliorated the conditions which had made restrictions necessary.

The emphasis on sex differences in *Muller* and the decisions leading up to it were necessitated in part by a highly artificial set of circumstances, such as the creation of the exaggerated doctrine of freedom of contract and the traducing of the principle of reasonable classification. In the next thirty years the courts would abandon these doctrines, thus legitimizing governmental regulation over economic activity, and completely overturning the principle that "like legislation for men . . . could not be sustained." But the courts did not rethink their position on sex discrimination, finding it as valid in the modern constitutional era as it had been before.

NOTES

1. Melvin I. Urofsky, *A Mind of One Piece: Brandeis and American Reform* (New York: Charles Scribner's Sons, 1971), pp. 20-21. Other good discussions of lawyers' attitudes in this era are Arnold M. Paul, *Conservative Crisis and the Rule of Law* (rev. ed.; New York: Harper & Row, 1969), and Benjamin R. Twiss, *Lawyers and the Constitution* (Princeton, N.J.: Princeton University Press, 1942).

2. Joseph C. Gouldner, review of Paul Hoffman's *Lions in the Street* in *New York Times Book Review* (July 8, 1973), p. 10.

3. See Robert G. McCloskey, *American Conservatism in the Age of Enterprise, 1865-1910* (2nd ed.; New York: Harper & Row, 1964), ch. 4.

4. See Sidney Fine, *Laissez-Faire and the General-Welfare State,* (Ann Arbor, Michigan: University of Michigan Press, 1956), chs. 2, 3, 4.

5. (St. Louis: F. H. Thomas Law Book Co., 1900), pp. 940, 942.

6. "The Supreme Court and the Fourteenth Amendment," *Michigan Law Review* 7 (June 1909): 664.

7. See, e.g., Munn v. Illinois, 94 U.S. 113 (1877); Slaughter-House Cases, 16 Wall. (83 U.S.) 36 (1873).

8. Millett v. People, 117 Ill. 294.

9. Godcharles v. Wigeman, 113 Pa. St. 431, 6 A.354.

10. 6 A. 354, 356.

11. "Liberty of Contract," *Yale Law Journal* 18 (May 1909): 454-487, 482-483.

12. Millett v. People, 117 Ill. 294 (1886); Godcharles v. Wigeman, 113 Pa. St. 431, 6 A. 354 (1886); Frorer v. People, 141 Ill. 171 (1892); Ramsey v. People,

142 Ill. 500 (1892); Braceville Coal Co. v. People, 142 Ill. 66 (1893). Contra, State v. Peel Splint Coal Co., 136 W. Va. 802 (1906).

13. Low v. Rees Printing Co., 41 Neb. 127 (1894); *ex parte* Jentzsch, 44 Pac. 803 (1896); Seattle v. Smyth, 22 Wash. 327 (1900).

14. *In re* Jacobs, 98 N.Y. 98 (1885).

15. Lochner v. New York, 198 U.S. 45, 75 (1905).

16. People v. Havnor, 149 N.Y. 195, 435 N.E. 541, 544 (1896).

17. Gulf v. Ellis, 165 U.S. 150 (1897).

18. Cotting v. Godard, 183 U.S. 79 (1901).

19. Connolly v. Union Sewer Pipe Co., 184 U.S. 540 (1902).

20. See, e.g., State v. Petit, 74 Minn. 376 (1895); *ex parte* Jentzsch, 44 Pac. 803 (1896); *in re* Morgan, 26 Colo. 415 (1899).

21. *In re* Morgan, 26 Colo. 415 (1899).

22. See, e.g., Holden v. Hardy, 121 Utah 71 (1896); *ex parte* Boyce, 27 Nev. 299 (1904); State v. Cantwell, 179 Mo. 245 (1904); *ex parte* Kair, 28 Nev. 127 and 425 (1905). But cf., *in re* Morgan, 26 Colo. 415 (1899).

23. 169 U.S. 366.

24. 198 U.S. 45, 57, 59, 61.

25. See, e.g., Low v. Rees Printing Co. 41 Neb. 127 (1899); State v. Cantwell, 179 Mo. 245 (1904); U.S. Supreme Court, Briefs and Records, Holden v. Hardy, 169 U.S. 366 (1898); U.S. Supreme Court, Briefs and Records, Lochner v. New York, 198 U.S. 45 (1905).

26. 40 Ind. 312.

27. *In re* Maguire, 57 Cal. 604 (1881); Bergman v. Cleveland, 39 Ohio 651 (1884); *ex parte* Hayes, 98 Cal. 555, 33 P. 337 (1893); People v. Ewer, 141 N.Y. 32 (1894); State v. Considine, 16 Wash. 358 (1897); *in re* Considine, 83 Fed. 157 (1897).

28. Calif. Const. Art. XX, Sec. 18.

29. *Ex parte* Hayes, 98 Cal. 555, 33 P. 337, 338 (1893).

30. U.S. Women's Bureau, Bulletin No. 66-II, *Labor Legislation,* pp. 17, 33, 149.

31. *In re* Considine, 83 Fed. 157, 158 (1897).

32. Commonwealth v. Hamilton Manufacturing Co., 120 Mass. 383, 385.

33. Ibid., p. 384.

34. Cf., Low v. Rees Printing Co., 41 Neb. 127 (1894), and State v. Wenham, 65 Neb. 394 (1902); Seattle v. Smyth, 22 Wash. 327 (1900) and State v. Buchanan, 29 Wash. 602 (1902); Lochner v. New York, 198 U.S. 45 (1905) and State v. Muller, 48 Ore. 252 (1906).

35. People v. Havnor, 149 N.Y. 195 (1896); People v. Lochner, 177 N.Y. 145 (1904).

36. State v. Petit, 74 Minn. 376 (1896).

37. State v. Peel Splint Coal Co., 136 W.Va. 802 (1906).

38. 155 Ill. 98 (1895).

39. Ibid., p. 111.

40. Ibid., p. 108.

41. Commons, *History of Labor,* 3:465-67.

42. Wenham v. State, 65 Neb. 394, 400.

43. Ibid., p. 405.

44. 29 Wash. 602.

45. Ibid., p. 610.

46. Seattle v. Smyth, 22 Wash. 327 (1900).

47. 48 Ore. 252 (1906).

48. Ibid., p. 257.

49. 189 N.Y. 131 (1906).

50. People v. Williams, 101 N.Y.S. 562, 563.

51. 41 Colo. 495 (1907). The Colorado Supreme Court ruled that the law was invalid because the subject matter of the portion of the law (Sess. Laws 1903, c. 138, sec. 3) quoted in the text of the chapter was not clearly expressed in the title of the law ("An act to prescribe and regulate the hours of employment for women and children in mills, factories, manufacturing establishments, shops, stores, or any other occupation which may be deemed unhealthful and dangerous"), as required by Colo. Const., Art. V, sec. 21. The opinion argued that neither the occupations listed in the law nor the laundry business, the subject of this particular case, had clearly been determined unhealthful and dangerous by the legislature. Ibid., p. 500.

52. 169 U.S. 366 (1898). The Court emphasized the fact that the occupation regulated, mining, was universally considered dangerous and unhealthy.

53. Urofsky, *Mind*, p. 40.

54. Ibid., p. 34.

55. Muller v. Oregon, 208 U.S. 412, 419.

56. Brief for Defendant in Error, Table of Contents, Muller v. Oregon, 208 U.S. 412 (1908).

57. Ibid., p. 21.

58. Ibid., p. 37.

59. Ibid.

60. Ibid., pp. 54-55.

61. Ibid., pp. 20, 38-39.

62. Ibid., pp. 51-55.

63. 208 U.S. 412, 415.

64. Felix Frankfurter, "Hours of Labor and Realism in Constitutional Law," *Harvard Law Review* 29 (February 1916):367.

65. *Sexual Politics*, p. 44.

66. *Women and the Law*, p. 153.

67. 208 U.S. 412, 421-23.

68. Ibid., p. 421.

69. Ibid.

70. Lochner v. New York, 198 U.S. 45, 61 (1905).

71. Bradwell v. Illinois, 16 Wall. (83 U.S.) 130, 141 (1872).

72. Ibid. I challenge the reader to find a similar religious reference in a Supreme Court opinion.

73. Boston Women's Health Collective, *Our Bodies, Ourselves* (New York: Simon & Schuster, 1973), p. 114.

74. *Dialectic*, p. 198.

3

THE SECOND CONSTITUTIONAL PHASE: FROM *MULLER* TO *PARRISH*

The middle phase of the constitutional history of women's labor legislation began with the decision which made women an exception to a general rule and ended, not quite thirty years later, with the abandonment of that rule. Each of these cases—*Muller v. Oregon* and *West Coast Hotel v. Parrish*[1] —upheld a law applying only to women, but had precedential impact far beyond its holding. *Muller* represented a tentative step toward judicial acceptance of economic regulation by government. It was followed by other steps in that direction, punctuated by steps backward. The movement was jerky, sporadic, and inconsistent. This period saw the development of three trends in judicial decision-making which influenced the courts' treatment of labor legislation: greater willingness to accept sex discrimination, increasing reluctance to make independent judgments on legislation, and gradual abandonment of the doctrine of freedom of contract. These trends culminated in *Parrish,* which represented total judicial capitulation to governmental power in economic regulation; since that decision, the Court has almost never invalidated such regulation.[2] After *Parrish,* it was no longer necessary to use sex distinctions to justify restrictions on freedom of contract.

In these years, while the courts struggled out of the contradictions they had gotten themselves into, more legislation involving working women was enacted and tested. Not only did numerous variations on the theme of hours legislation appear, but after 1912 a new type of regulation—the establishment of minimum wages for women—provided material for court cases. With two important exceptions, these laws were upheld. This phase saw the development of a persistent judicial habit: the interpretation of *Muller* as establishing the general principle that women were different from men, and thus justifying any and all types of sex discrimination.

The language of *Muller* does permit this interpretation, but that portion of the opinion is merely dicta; the decision itself established only the constitutionality of hours limitations in employment. Furthermore, the opinion spoke only to laws designed for the *protection* of women. But judges continued to rely on this decision even though we find that some laws become more restrictive than protective; the courts show no sensitivity to these effects.

WOMEN, LABOR, AND HISTORY, 1908-1937

The first four decades of the twentieth century saw technological advances which created changes in everyday life of a nature little short of revolutionary. The discovery of electricity had paved the way for development of machines which made work less arduous both inside and outside the home, and frequently created new jobs even as they made others obsolete. The increased use of the automobile and the telephone also created new jobs for men and women, as transportation and communication became huge industries. Safe, inexpensive methods of birth control enabled women to take the initiative in limiting family size; the steady decline in the rate of population increase from 1910 to 1940, even during periods of heavy immigration, indicated that where access to these devices was possible, women did not hesitate to take advantage of this opportunity.[3] Other advances reduced the dangers of pregnancy and childbirth, and made safe alternatives to breast feeding available. Not only were the burdens of motherhood reduced, but so were the burdens of industry, of housework, and of life itself.

In addition to technological advances, the period encompasses a war —which brought more women into the labor force; a decade of economic prosperity—which encouraged more technological advance, increased employment, raised the general standard of living and level of expectation; and, finally, the Crash and the Depression—which encouraged, or compelled radical rethinking of the relationship of the individual to government.

In 1908, of course, these changes had barely begun to affect the quality of life. The women who were reached by hours legislation were those in "sweated" industries, or in department stores, restaurants, or laundries who worked long, tedious hours, often for near-starvation wages, under the kinds of conditions described in Chapter 1. Two events—a U.S. Senate investigation and an accident—focused public attention on the situation of women workers in the first two decades of the twentieth century. In 1907, at the request of President Theodore Roosevelt, Congress had appropriated money to investigate conditions of working women and children. The nineteen-volume U.S. Senate Report on the Condition of Women and Child Wage Earners was published between 1910 and 1915, providing copious information for those sufficiently interested to read government reports.[4]

The second event, which received even more publicity, was the fire in the Triangle Shirtwaist Company in New York City on March 25, 1911, which I have already discussed in Chapter 1. A widespread demand for government action led to the appointment of a state Factory Investigating Committee which issued thirteen volumes of reports between 1912 and 1916, confirming the evidence of the Senate Report, and a revision of the entire state labor code, with thirty-six new laws passed between 1912 and 1914. Other states, spurred by these events as well as by the *Muller* decision, took action. Between 1909 and 1917, nineteen states passed their first hours laws and twenty other states tightened their existing laws. The years 1911 and 1913 were peak years; twenty-four of the thirty-nine laws were passed in that period.[5]

The federal and state investigators had spotlighted another distressing feature of the situation: the low wages which too many working women received. Women have always gotten, and continue to get, less money than men do for their labors. As Caroline Bird has written, "The fact is that women simply do not get hold of as much money that they can legally call their own as do the men in their lives."[6] It is not simply that women receive unequal pay for "equal work"—whatever that means, and whoever determines it—since men and women have nearly always had different occupations. The problem is that our society, like most societies, has always valued more highly the abilities which men are more likely to possess and the work that they do, and has rewarded men accordingly.[7] This situation has not changed much in the last seventy years. What has changed is that now most working women at least earn enough money to support themselves and their dependents (though many cannot; women are over-represented on welfare rolls and in the lower income brackets). Early in the twentieth century, this was not as widely possible. The Senate Report and similar documents tell a depressing story of women who simply did not earn living wages.[8] In 1915, experts agreed that the minimum living wage for women in American

cities was eight dollars a week; however, studies concluded that 75 percent of women workers earned less, with 50 percent getting less than six
dollars.[9] The 1900 census had exploded the "pin money" theory of
women's work by showing that virtually all women workers either lived
alone and supported themselves, were heads of families, or contributed
most of their earnings to their families.[10] All available later findings
supported this one.[11] Women could not earn enough to provide for themselves or their families. The reports give instances, several of which found
their way into Brandeis briefs, of women who skipped meals on the pretext that they were dieting, though "the evidence was pathetically against
the need thereof,"[12] of the pride and dignity which most of the inter-
viewed workers displayed as long as they could, and of those who finally
resorted to the support of "men friends" or to prostitution.[13] (The com-
mentators were always concerned about problems of sexual behavior,
but never seemed to worry about—and certainly never investigated—
theft, which would appear to be another possible resort.)

The arguments for special wage regulation for women were not strictly analogous to those for hours limitation. Reformers never insisted that
women needed *more* money than men, as they had sometimes suggested
that women needed shorter working days than men. (Such an argument
with respect to wages would have undercut the entire economic structure
of the United States, where it was, and still is a ubiquitous fact of life
that men earn more than women.) Advocates of minimum-wage laws
simply pointed out that women got less money than men. With hours
legislation, no one had consistently separated the argument that women
could not work as long as men from the fact that they frequently worked
longer hours in worse circumstances. The physical distinctions between
the sexes made the argument for shorter hours plausible enough, although,
as we have seen, the evidence did not really prove that women needed
shorter hours. But there is no equally obvious connection between sexual
differences and a minimum cost of living, and the reformers did not try
to establish one. The desired effects could have been achieved by minimum-
wage laws applicable to both sexes. As one judge later remarked, "That
adult male employees of equal efficiency can be obtained at less than the
minimum wage fixed for women and minors is contrary to common knowledge."[14] Sex discrimination was neither more necessary nor more justifiable in minimum-wage legislation than in hours legislation.

As women's economic disadvantages became widely known, some re-

formers began to agitate for minimum-wage legislation for women and
minors. This legislation typically provided for the establishment of a
board or commission empowered to investigate conditions and fix minimum wages by order. Usually, these were defined as wages "sufficient to
enable such employee to maintain himself or herself under conditions
consistent with his or her welfare." The single worker was taken as the
standard (not the female female family head, who was probably in the
worst shape). This type of law had first been tried in Australia and New
Zealand in the 1890s, where it had been successful enough to be re-enacted several times; a similar law was passed in England in 1909. Massachusetts was the first state to pass a minimum-wage law, in 1912. In the same
year, Ohio adopted a constitutional amendment giving the legislature the
power to set minimum wages for all workers. In the next two years, ten
more states passed minimum wage laws, usually for women and/or minors.
Two states, Utah and Arkansas, fixed a minimum wage by law; the others
established variously titled boards and commissions.[15]

Based on the three criteria I set out in the introduction, the restrictions
on workers' freedom established by these laws seem in retrospect to have
been clearly and legitimately protective. The evils of inadequate wages are
obvious, and grave; and they were documented, as we have seen, by the
Senate Report. The necessity of enforced wage regulation as a method of
raising wages, in the absence of unionization or voluntary action by employers on a large scale, is also fairly clear. My final criterion—the extent
to which freedom was actually abridged by the restriction—did provide
the basis for some arguments against the minimum wage. Although such
laws might seem only to limit one's "constitutional right to starve," as
was later suggested, employers frequently did argue that incompetent
women workers who were deprived of the opportunity to work at low
wages would be fired, and therefore lose their freedom to work at all.[16]
Proponents of the laws, however, insisted that these workers would be
benefited by being forced to secure jobs which they could perform adequately, and that whatever unemployment and loss of opportunity resulted would be counterbalanced by the benefits to most workers from
increased wages.[17] As we shall see, the preponderance of evidence indicates that the reformers were probably right.

This was by no means the only criticism levied against minimum-wage
regulations. These laws were extremely controversial; they were attacked
not only as interferences with freedom of contract but also because some

experts insisted that the minimum wage could become the maximum wage, and because employers insisted that some laborers did not *earn* a living wage and therefore had no right to receive one. It is true that most minimum-wage laws of the period did not provide that the value of the services rendered by the employee be taken into account in setting the wage. (This factor was, however, given implicit recognition in the exemptions established by the laws for learners, apprentices, or "defective" workers. These exemptions depart from the general "cost of living" standard established for wage regulation. Living expenses are not lessened by apprentice status, and it is arguable that for many handicapped workers they are greater, not less.) This argument against minimum wage is still heard—it has been made recently by Edward Banfield, for instance[18]— but the market value of an employee's labor is determined by so many variables, some of which are largely arbitrary factors, that it seems almost meaningless to say that a worker is not "worth" eight dollars a week.

The defenders of minimum wage laws could not do much more with this objection than point out the factors which I have just discussed,[19] but they did make an effort to refute other objections. The Brandeis briefs filed in these cases followed the practice of the earlier briefs of trying to persuade the opposition that such laws did, in fact, serve their long-range interests. Pages were devoted to data which indicated that minimum wages promoted efficiency because well-paid employees worked better,[20] that commerce prospered under such regulations,[21] and that industrial peace was improved by these laws.[22]

HOURS, NIGHT WORK, PROTECTION, AND RESTRICTION: FROM THE LAUNDRESSES OF OREGON TO THE NIGHT WORKERS OF NEW YORK

As I have suggested, the Supreme Court's favorable decision in *Muller* was one of several factors which encouraged the states to enact labor legislation for women. Few of these laws were ever appealed to the state courts; when they were, these courts had little difficulty in complying with the *Muller* precedent. When they bothered to elaborate their reasoning, they followed the U.S. Supreme Court's lead and emphasized the permanent rather than the temporary conditions, building up a body of precedent which indicated the permanent constitutional acceptability of protective labor legislation.[23] Not only did these courts dispose of the issue of freedom of contract, but they were equally unreceptive to the Equal Protection Clause challenge that the laws created arbitrary discriminations among women workers in various occupations. Occasionally, the judges tried to find reasons for the discrimination,[24] but usually— with a modesty lacking in earlier cases but becoming more characteristic of the judiciary[25]—they simply insisted that this was a matter for legislative and not judicial determination.

The state courts apparently did not require Brandeis briefs to convince them of the constitutionality of these laws; most went to the appellate courts accompanied only by the traditional kind of brief. But the National Consumers' League did not assume that, after *Muller*, its job had been done. Between 1908 and 1924, it was hired by state governments in six cases involving hours and night work, and three involving minimum wage. Brandeis acted as counsel in these cases until his appointment to the Supreme Court in 1916, when the task was assumed by Felix Frankfurter. The last Brandeis brief was filed in the case of *Radice v. New York* in 1924.

In the later hours cases,[26] the briefs did not differ materially from that in *Muller*. Josephine Goldmark simply added new evidence as it became available. The new data were of the same character and displayed the same methodological deficiencies as the old; both statistical and anecdotal information was given, but causal connections were not fully explored. The substance of the four briefs was published by Goldmark under the title *Fatigue and Efficiency* in 1912.

The opposition in these cases never seemed to know what hit them. Counsel for employers (or, rarely, employees) did not gather evidence to refute the Brandeis briefs nor, with one exception, did they challenge the causal inferences drawn therein. Many of these briefs are no longer available; no one sought to gather and publish them. The nature of these briefs, coupled with the fact that many of these laws never reached any appellate court, suggests either that employers were able to cope with the restrictions or, perhaps, that some laws were seldom enforced. Certainly, the laws did not prevent economic growth; and, as the Brandeis briefs indicated, productivity often increased with shorter hours.[27]

After the second women's hours law reached the Supreme Court, in the case of *Hawley v. Walker*, and was decided *per curiam* with no opinion, states rarely hired the League in cases like this. The Court unanimously upheld two more similar statutes—a Massachusetts law requiring the posting of times of starting and stopping work,[28] and a California eight-hour law[29]—in very short opinions which added almost nothing to *Muller*.

Hawley was the first women's hours case in which the law was challenged by an employee as well as an employer, but one must question whether the employee acted on her own initiative. Stephen Wood's comments about the complainants in the federal child labor case are apposite: "The irony of the petition apparently struck few persons at the time. A prayer to preserve the work opportunities of an obviously poor man's minor sons was presented by a distinguished group of nationally known corporation lawyers, the payment of whose fees would have necessitated the labor, practically in perpetuity, of the two cotton mill operatives supposedly concerned."[30]

The *Bosley* case is more problematical. One plaintiff here was Ethel Nelson, a female pharmacist working in a hospital who argued that the extension of the California law to hospital workers would deprive her of her job.[31] She was not a factory worker or a laundress standing on her feet in a hot, close room all day, but a trained professional working in an environment described as "not an unhealthful or unsanitary place."[32] The effect of the law on Nelson may well have been more restrictive than protective; the evil from which she was guarded may have been illusory. But *Muller* did not admit of such a possibility, and, following precedent uncritically as usual, neither did the courts in this case.

Two of the cases decided after 1908 which were accompanied by Brandeis briefs merit careful examination because they overturned earlier decisions of the same court on similar laws which were re-enacted after *Muller*. In *Ritchie v. Wayman*,[33] the Illinois Supreme Court upheld a ten-hour law passed in 1909. Five years later, New York's Court of Appeals decided *People v. Charles Schweinler Press*.[34] Each court carefully distinguished the present case from the earlier one, but they did not reason in the same way.

In the second *Ritchie* case, the Illinois court made an interesting effort to distinguish the 1893 law which had been overturned from the 1909 law which was now upheld. The opinion pointed out, first, that the purpose of the new law was stated in its title, whereas nothing in the old law indicated its purpose[35]—an objection which seems a mere formality—and, second, that a ten-hour law could be said to be a reasonable restriction

whereas an eight-hour law could not—which, at a time when working days
were being decreased to eight hours through union agreements, seems
specious indeed. But throughout most of the opinion, which is over twenty
pages long, the court sounds as if the first *Ritchie* decision had never existed.

The state of Illinois, through Brandeis and Goldmark, had provided
the judges with over 500 pages of data, but the opinion did not refer to
it. Repetitiously, the court stated:

> It is known to all men (and what we know as men we can-
> not profess to be ignorant of as judges) that woman's physi-
> cal structure and the performance of maternal functions
> place her at a great disadvantage in the battle for life: that
> while a man can work standing on his feet for more than ten
> hours a day, day after day, without injury to himself, a wom-
> an cannot, and that to require a woman to stand on her
> feet for more than ten hours in any one day and perform
> severe manual labor while thus standing, day after day, has
> the effect to impair her health, and that as weakly and sick-
> ly women cannot be the mothers of vigorous children, it is
> of the greatest importance to the public that the state take
> such measures as may be necessary to protect its women from
> the consequences induced by long, continuous manual labor
> in those occupations which break them down physically. . . .
> We think that the general consensus of opinion, not only
> in this country but in the civilized countries of Europe, is
> that a working day of not more than ten hours for women
> is justified for the following reasons: (1) the physical orga-
> nization of women; (2) their maternal functions; (3) the rear-
> ing and education of children; (4) the maintenance of the
> home; and these conditions are so far matters of general
> knowledge that the courts will take judicial cognizance of
> their existence.[36]

The court does not make clear why these well known facts were
any less well known in 1895—not, apparently, because of the brief,
which is never mentioned. Nor is it made clear why women's structure
and function justify limitations on the freedom of contract which the

court had valued so highly in the first *Ritchie* case. What does emerge with clarity from these decisions is that the Illinois court had to back down in order to perform its constitutional duty, and was trying to save as much face as possible while fulfilling its task. Whether the Illinois judges were reluctantly performing an unpleasant task or whether they had been convinced of the error of the earlier decision cannot be determined at this late date.

The New York reversal was both more graceful and better reasoned. The quality of the reasoning may have been improved by the fact that, for the first time, a court had before it both a Brandeis brief for the state and an attempted refutation of that brief from the employer. Brandeis and Goldmark followed the pattern established in the hours cases, gathering evidence from the same type of sources on physical dangers such as the deprivation of sunlight,[37] the difficulties of getting sufficient sleep in the daytime,[38] the effects of night work on family life,[39] and the dangers of traveling on city streets at night.[40] Much of the information presented is irrelevant to the specific problem of night work, such as the higher death rate among female factory operatives than in the general population,[41] or the incidence of infant mortality among children of working mothers.[42] Similarly, statements like "there is no doubt that the employment of married women at night naturally entails some neglect of the household duties during the day,"[43] while possibly true, are unpersuasive as arguments against night work. The daytime employment of married women would seem to entail even greater neglect of their household duties during the day.

Much of the evidence pertains to the harmful effects of night work on both sexes, and does not indicate that women are more injured than men. One intriguing passage is a quotation from an Italian physician to the effect that "the procreative power of men is diminished or impaired" by nightwork.[44] This statement clearly permits more than one interpretation, but if any of these is correct, it would seem vital for the state to restrict night work for men in order to insure the continuance of the human race whose welfare it is trying to protect.

Similar considerations are suggested by the data in the Brandeis briefs filed in the men's hours case.[45] The experts cited here describe men exhausted by long working days[46] whose first stop after work was the saloon, where they "sought relief from the strain of work in alcoholic stimulants."[47] Neither fatigue nor alcohol separately, let alone in combination, is a stimulus to "procreative power," as authorities as diverse as Shake-speare and Dr. David Reuben have pointed out, and one wonders again whether regulation of men's working conditions might also be necessary for the future of humanity.

Once more, Brandeis and Goldmark display their distressing tendency to assume rather than to prove causal connections. The brief quotes a study done by the Factory Investigating Committee which found a high incidence of backache, anemia, menstrual problems, and nursing difficul-ties among these workers.[48] However, no control group either of day workers or of the general population was examined. Since the briefs con-tain abundant data on the incidence of these problems among all women factory workers, it seems doubtful that they are traceable to night work. But this factor did not occur to the authors.

The brief for Schweinler makes an interesting attempt to answer some of these allegations; it makes some telling points, and is written in a delight-fully sardonic style. It deserves lengthy quotation:

> A case of this kind always presents the opportunity to appeal to sentiment and passion, and some heartbreaking in-cident is used as an illustration of conditions when it is no illustration at all, but only a rare exception. For many years thousands of dollars was collected by a charity organization in this city on an appeal made for funds for children and the plan of operation that brought out this very large amount of money was a picture of a boy strapped to a board and en-titled "Poor Little Joe." There was very little reflection upon the fact that in this great City there are not very many boys who are carried about strapped on boards.
>
> In the brief of the District Attorney before the Appellate Division, that very appeal to sentiment and passion was done and the shocking conditions in one factory in Auburn was set forth and a woman found that worked nineteen and three-quarter hours in one day. A moment's reflection would make it clear that such an illustration had nothing whatever to do with this case. This is not a question of the number of hours of work that a woman may perform or has performed, but whether she can work at all during certain hours.[49]

Undoubtedly, the lawyer has a valid point. Reasoning by horrible example, especially by horrible example of dubious relevance, is a useful persuasive tool but does not go all the way to establishing truth. However, such examples may be a legitimate way of showing just how far conditions can deteriorate under a prevailing policy.

Further on the brief argues:

> "Facts of Knowledge" [the title of the state's brief] seems to have one very serious objection which makes it worthless, namely the "Facts" are not up to date. It concerns itself in the main with old conditions. It is a well known and notorious fact that the conditions under which people labor have been tremendously improved during the last five or six years. The question before this Court is not what happened in Great Britain (see p. 302) in 1834, and so on through the years, but what the conditions are today under which women labor. There is no reference in the "Facts of Knowledge" to the present Labor Law of this state [which established new requirements for light, sanitation, and ventilation], and it is not fair to consider one without the other. It will be found that the place of work now is vastly different from that place of work under the conditions set forth in the "Facts of Knowledge."[50]

The charge of obsolescence is hardly fair; many of the facts come from two very recent investigations. But again the brief has raised a provocative question: whether changing conditions of labor might eventually obviate the need to protect women from long hours of work or work at specific times. This possibility is, as we have seen, denied by the *Muller* line of cases, but, given our knowledge of labor history, it seems a very real one.

With respect to the 1913 Factory Investigating Committee investigation quoted in the "Facts of Knowledge," the *Schweinler* brief for the appellee quite appropriately points out that, unless one controls one's experiment, the personal reports of one hundred workers are a poor basis for any conclusions.[51] It also disposes of the familiar Goldmark thesis that night work prohibitions are necessary in order to enforce hours laws by questioning "how a limitation of sixteen hours of labor in order to enforce a nine hours law would act as a strict enforcement of the nine-hour law."[52]

The brief also addressed itself to the effects of night work on family life:

> As the information reads, it would almost indicate that there was a statute which prohibited only married women from working at night. There may be very good reasons why a married woman living with her husband and having children should not work at night, but however good these reasons might be, they would not be any reasons whatever for the thousands of single women who support themselves and those dependent on them; of the other thousands who are married and whose husbands have deserted them and who have no children and of the many thousands who are so unfortunate as to be left widows, with or without children.[53]

This suggests that one of the purposes of the law could have been fulfilled by a more narrowly drawn statute, perhaps limiting the ban on night work to married women or to mothers of children under a certain age. Whenever the validity of women's legislation is made to depend on their childbearing function and/or role in family life, it is important to remember that not all women are wives and mothers, and to ask whether a narrower law could fulfill the desired purpose. In cases where it is argued that particular working conditions impair women's ability to bear healthy children, for example, the answer to that question is probably no; we cannot, with any degree of accuracy, separate out the potential mothers in the labor force. But we can distinguish the actual mothers—the form that the state of Illinois mails to prospective jurors does this by asking a single question—and, therefore, a regulation which purports to allow women to fulfill their family responsibilities could fulfill its purpose—whatever its legitimacy—if confined only to certain women. On its face, easing the burdens of working mothers by restricting all women workers is no more defensible than a law which purports to discourage extramarital sexual activity by prohibiting the use of contraceptives to all residents, married or unmarried,[54] or an effort to prevent subversive activity by American citizens in foreign countries by denying passports to all members of the Communist party, regardless of the degree of commitment of the member or the purpose of the trip.[55] Basing restrictions applicable to all women on the evidence that some of them are mothers implies either that the protection of this group is so vital that it outweighs the interests of other women, or that all women really *should* be childbearers and homemakers, and legislation should be designed mainly for the benefit of those in these roles.

The Court of Appeals did uphold the law, finding both the brief and the FIC Report more persuasive than the opposing argument. After the usual reference to women's need for protection, the court had little difficulty in distinguishing this case from *Williams:*

> That statute bore on its face no clear evidence that it was passed for the prospect of protecting the health and welfare of women working in factories. I feel that we should give serious consideration and great weight to the fact that the present legislation is based upon and sustained by an investigation by the Legislature deliberately and carefully made through an agency of its creation, the present factory investigating commission.[56]

This opinion suggests that all a court needs to sustain a law is some hard evidence that the law bears a reasonable relation to a legitimate legislative purpose—evidence not presented in *Williams,* and perhaps, not even here. The principle enunciated in *Schweinler* seems to be sound, but the court does not follow the principle it sets out. The demand for evidence seems to me to be entirely reasonable. Once a law has been challenged in a court—demonstrating that someone is unhappy with it— I cannot see that presenting some evidence of its reasonableness should put an intolerable burden on a state government. Presumption of constitutionality need not stretch so far as to remove any need for a state to defend its laws. Once the law's reasonable relation to a legitimate purpose is established, if it cannot be shown to violate some constitutional provision, then, surely, the *Schweinler* court is correct in concluding that the advisability of the law is a question for the legislature, not the court.[57] But in the area of women's labor legislation, this became a minority view. Courts continued to uphold these laws on the basis of "matters of knowledge." The pattern of the second *Ritchie* case, not of *Schweinler,* became and remained the prevailing one.

Schweinler, like *Bosley,* presents a new problem: the existence of women covered by the law who considered the new regulation a curtailment

of their freedom. In the former case, the appellant's brief pointed out
that the woman whom Schweinler had permitted to work after hours
was "a strong, healthy woman . . . [who] rather flippantly drew the attention of the Court to the fact that her health had not been impaired
by this work and also remarked to the District Attorney that if she lost
her place by reason of this prosecution, the people who were back of
this proceeding would not get her another job."[58] Both briefs alluded to
the statements of many women workers, including wives and mothers, that
that they preferred night work and that neither they nor their families
suffered any ill effects.[59]

The Brandeis brief tried to dispose of this point by quoting the FIC
Report's comment that "only a few of the women seemed to realize that
this combination might prove disastrous. . . . Ignorant women can scarcely be expected to realize the dangers not only to their own health but to
that of the next generation from such inhuman usage."[60]

The reader is again struck by the fact that women workers rarely spoke
for themselves. Both sides presumed to speak for them: the employers who
wished to exploit them, and the reformers who wished to "protect" them.
Without questioning the worthy motives of the latter group, one wonders
whether this dismissal of the desires even of "ignorant" women is justifiable. It is true that people do not always know their own interests, but that
does not imply that others know better. We all ought to be suspicious of
those who tell us what we really want, or should want. Even in cases like
this where a discernible selfish motive is lacking among the proponents
of a restriction, the question remains whether the judgment of mothers
who prefer night work is so irrational as to be totally discreditable.

Speculation suggests several reasons why a mother might choose to
work at night. Her husband, or other family members, might be home
to look after the children while she is at work; she could take over after
she returned in the early morning (after all, most people do not go to
bed for several hours after returning from work); and she could sleep
when some other adult returned home. If her children were in school,
it would be even simpler. She could sleep after they left, and there would
be time for the family to spend several hours together before she left for
work. It may well be true that most people do not easily adjust to day-
time sleeping patterns,[61] but, as anyone who has lived in a college dor-
mitory knows, a large minority can thrive this way. The brief really contains very little evidence that night work is significantly more dangerous

or more disruptive than day work. The resulting patterns of family life
may be somewhat unorthodox, but that perhaps is really not the state's
business. It is significant that the FIC Report mentioned not only women
who liked night work, but several who found it too disruptive of family
life and switched to days, indicating that the women had free choice of
when they would work. The evidence in the brief simply does not demand the conclusion that the reformers' judgment is superior to that of
the workers.

The data presented to the court in *Schweinler* leave considerable doubt
whether the night work law is a necessary protective measure or whether
its main effect is to restrict women's freedom of choice. The court may
be right in stating that that question is a matter for the legislature, but
that sort of modesty was not characteristic of courts at that time when
freedom of contract was involved. The attitude of courts in such cases
was very similar to what it is now in cases involving Bill of Rights guarantees: to shift from a presumption of constitutionality. But in cases involving women, that is abandoned. However objectionable the prevailing
doctrine of freedom of contract was, one would expect the courts to
have employed it consistently. But they did not.

The criteria I set out in the Introduction for measuring the effects of
restrictions provide little justification for this law. The evils which the
law is designed to prevent—ill health, interference with home life, and
exposure to crime—are, to borrow again from free-speech theory, substantive evils. But they are not shown to be particularly severe for wom-
en. The brief also does not show that these evils are caused, wholly
or in part, by the activity proscribed; therefore, it fails to demonstrate
that the prohibition of night work is necessary to remove any of these
dangers. Finally, no suggestion is made—and there is no external evidence
—that any woman's employment opportunities are confined to the evening hours; as far as one can tell, in the absence of regulation the women
would be as free to work during the day as at night. The brief implies
that the restriction might be necessary not for the women night workers
themselves but for their families, but, as I have suggested, a prohibition
reaching all women workers is not necessary to achieve these ends, whatever their legitimacy.

Schweinler appealed to the Supreme Court, but the case was thrown
out on a technicality. After 1915, opponents of hours and night work
restrictions seemed to have gotten the message that they would receive

no solace from the courts. No cases of this kind were decided for nine years, and the case heard then was the last. It involved an amendment to the law challenged in *Schweinler*. In 1917, the New York legislature had brought most women restaurant workers under the coverage of the nine-hour limitation and the night work provision. There is very little historical material on this law. Pay was higher and tips were better at night,[62] which suggests that the motives of the advocates of the law might have been to protect men's jobs rather than women's health, but the fact that the law was amended eight months after the United States' entry into World War I, when men were being drafted, casts doubt on the validity of that inter-pretation. So does the testimony of one restaurant owner that male waiters were impossible to find and that this law would force him out of business.[63]

In 1921, Joseph Radice, a Buffalo restaurant owner, was tried and con-victed of violating the night work provision. The conviction was upheld in the state appellate courts without opinions; then it went to the Supreme Court. *Radice v. New York*[64] brought to the Court the last Brandeis brief it ever saw, perhaps to its collective relief. (I have often wondered whether the justices actually read them, and if so, which justices, and how thorough-ly. I suspect that Justice Holmes, who often said that he hated facts, may never have read them at all, but if so, he did not mention it in his published correspondence.) The brief was the old *Schweinler* brief, with some new data added; it suffered from the same old defects, and some of the new evidence made the need for the amendment even more questionable than the need for the original law.

Scattered through the court records were references not only to the fact that night work was more lucrative, but that the restaurants were clean and sanitary,[65] that the waitresses' health was good,[66] that the work was light and easy,[67] and that, again, many workers found night work more compatible with their family responsibilities than day work.[68] Before the law was amended only four percent of the waitresses worked at night,[69] and several women switched to days because of family responsibilities[70] or because they had been frightened by the murder of a night worker.[71] One is left with the impression that some waitresses worked at night be-cause they wanted to, and that they had valid reasons for making this choice. The relationship of night work to health and safety hazards seems even more tenuous, and the degree of freedom of choice even greater, in 1924 than in 1915. This law seems to have afforded little protection against real dangers, and restricted women's opportunities significantly.

Incidentally, by 1924 significant opposition to protective legislation had developed among feminists.[72] In that year, women printers in New York finally won an eight-year battle to gain an exemption from the night-work law, after they had proved that it deprived them of their livelihoods.[73] The Supreme Court did not consider any of this.

The defendant had been given hope by the decision the year before in *Adkins v. Children's Hospital*,[74] in which a minimum-wage statute was invalidated, and the primacy of freedom of contract affirmed. But Justice Sutherland, speaking for the Court again as in *Adkins*, distinguished that "wage-fixing law, pure and simple"[75] from night work and hours limitations:

> The legislature had a mass of information from which it concluded that night work is substantially and especially detrimental to the health of women. We cannot say that the conclusion is without warrant. The loss of restful night's sleep cannot be fully made up by sleep in the day time, especially in busy cities, subject to the disturbances incident to modern life. The injurious consequences were thought by the legislature to bear more heavily against women than men, and considering their more delicate organism, there would seem to be good reason for so thinking. . . . Where the constitutional validity of a statute depends on the existence of facts, courts must be cautious about reaching a conclusion respecting them contrary to that reached by the legislature; and if the question of what the facts establish be a fairly debatable one, it is not permissible for the judge to set up his opinion in respect of it against the opinion of the lawmaker.[76]

This was the strongest expression of a philosophy of judicial restraint yet heard in one of these cases, but the deference to legislative judgment which is expresses had become evident in other decisions of the Court.[77] Although *Muller* is cited as controlling precedent, the reasoning employed here is significantly different from that of the 1908 case. The holding in *Muller* can be summarized as, "The physical differences between the sexes justify special limitations for women." The *Radice* holding, however, says, "Legislatures may conclude that physical differences between the sexes require special limitations for women." In *Muller* the Court was expressing wholehearted agreement with the conclusion reached by the lawmakers; in *Radice,* while suggesting its approval, it is more concerned with affirming the state's power to reach its conclusion. The Court has gone a long way toward abandoning the function of independent trier of fact which it had long ago assumed, and toward leaving legislatures free to discriminate on the basis of sexual differences as they chose.

Another feature of the *Radice* opinion is especially striking when read in the light of *Adkins,* which I shall discuss at length. The Court emphasizes physical differences between the sexes rather than two additional points emphasized by the state: the dangers of city streets at night and the effect of night work on women's domestic duties. The opinion does refer both to "the dangers and menaces incident to life in large cities" and to women's "peculiar and natural functions,"[78] but concentrates on the issue of health. (At any rate, it does seem to be stretching a bit to call house work a "peculiar and natural function.") This emphasis on physical, permanent characteristics as a basis for legislation is very much in tune with the opinion, written by the same justice, in the minimum-wage case.

GENERAL HOURS LAWS: BUNTING V. OREGON

We have already seen[79] that the earliest hours laws were generally declaratory statutes which covered adults of both sexes and were virtually impossible to enforce. Throughout the first constitutional phase, many states passed various hours laws for adult males in particular occupations. The most common of these were public works laws, mining laws, and railroad laws. The power of the government to limit the length of the working day of those in its own employ was finally upheld by the Supreme Court in 1903,[80] after a series of conflicting decisions in state courts. Although mining might seem so dangerous an occupation that the police power would easily extend to its regulation, courts did not always see it that way, even after the Supreme Court upheld a Utah law of that sort.[81] Laws limiting working hours on railroads gained easy acceptance as being essential to the general welfare; no one questioned the relationship of excessive working hours to railroad accidents.[82] But *Lochner* had effectively discouraged any attempt to establish general hours limitations or even to extend protection to establishments less patently dangerous than mines or moving trains. At the same time, *Lochner* also contained an implicit me sage to reformers that their most realistic strategy was to concentrate on laws applying to women, since these still had at least a chance of surviving judicial scrutiny. After 1905 there were sound practical reasons for restricting the scope of labor legislation, even though its aims could still have been achieved by sex-neutral laws in the absence of decisions like *Lochner.*

Even without *Lochner,* there might not have been much general hours legislation; organized labor was by no means united in its favor. Although the American Federation of Labor—by then the strongest national labor organization in the country—formally supported the enactment of general eight-hour laws, it did little actively to further their passage. Frequently this position was attacked as demonstrating a selfish refusal on the part of the skilled trades which dominated the AFL to help the unskilled and unorganized workers attain the benefits they themselves had achieved, but it may also have reflected a realization "that statutes limiting hours are of all labor laws the most difficult to enforce; that inspection in this field has rarely proved an entirely effective instrument; that workers (lured by overtime pay) are altogether too apt to connive with employers in violating hours laws."[83] (In that case, one is entitled to wonder about the AFL's consistent endorsement of eight-hour laws for women and children.)

The one general hours law was passed in Oregon in 1913, establishing a ten-hour day for men employed in all manufacturing industries and providing for up to three hours' overtime at time and a half (which no women's hours law did.) Not surprisingly, this law, which directly contravened the *Lochner* decision, reached the Supreme Court, where it was argued twice. It progressed through the judicial system in close company with the Oregon minimum-wage law. Brandeis, Goldmark, and the National Consumers' League were again hired by the state in both cases. When President Woodrow Wilson appointed Brandeis to the Supreme Court in the middle of the proceedings, Felix Frankfurter assumed his responsibilities as counsel.

The brief in *Bunting v. Oregon*[84] was the longest yet, running over 1,000 pages. It provides some interesting points of comparison with the cumulative brief submitted in women's hours cases and published in *Fatigue and Efficiency.* Of course, the *Bunting* brief contained no references to menstruation, miscarriages or nursing, but the differences go beyond that. First, we notice that the group which had heretofore concentrated its energies on proving that long hours were particularly harmful to women had no difficulty in compiling an even larger body of evidence on their general ill effects, even on the sex that had emerged from the early discussions as towers of strength. This data, going as far back as the 1830s, displayed a recognition that, in spite of what opinions such as the second *Ritchie* might suggest, "men are not the physical giants that failure to give them protection would seem to assume."[85] Secondly, the League's beliefs on the value and the use of time away from work varied interestingly according to which sex it was discussing. The *Bunting* brief devotes over 100 pages to the value of leisure and recreation and the benefits of short hours to citizenship. This is supplemented by several discussion in other parts of the record.[86] The brief quotes economists, social reformers and other authorities who argue that short hours are beneficial to individuals and society because workers can then educate themselves by going to libraries, night schools, university extension courses, and public lectures.[87] It is also argued that such education is necessary for good citizenship and the intelligent use of the vote.[88]

The combined briefs in *Muller, Ritchie, Elerding,* and *Hawley* do not place such emphasis on education for women. They devote only fifteen pages to "the benefit to leisure, recreation, family life and education"— much of this is taken up with references to domestic duties, a subject already covered.[89] One gains the impression that, while men are released to educate and improve themselves, women are released to perform household duties; at least, it does not strike Brandeis or Goldmark as very important that women have time to read and learn (even for the single workers—80 percent of the female work force in 1910[90]—who did not have primary responsibility for the maintenance of a home and for whom this would have been a realistic goal). It is true that at the time most women did not have the burden of the intelligent exercise of the vote, but good citizenship requires knowledge even for nonvoters, and Brandeis and Goldmark supported women's suffrage at any rate. The difference in emphasis reveals suppositions about the respective roles of men and women which will bear examining.

On rehearing, the Supreme Court upheld the Oregon law by a vote of five to three, with Brandeis not participating. The opinion of Justice McKenna touched on none of the issues raised by the brief. It found no difficulty in sustaining the law as a valid exercise of police power, and cited neither *Muller* nor *Lochner* (which, of course, it flatly contradicted). In his short opinion McKenna concentrated on showing that the overtime provision did not turn the law into a wage regulation (one of which the Court was about to uphold anyway) rather than an hours law;[91] he also cited data on average working hours in other countries.[92]

The opinion is irritating for its failure either to mention the precedent it was relying on or to deal with a contradictory ruling. During this period it was almost impossible to predict with any accuracy the result in the Supreme Court in any case involving economic regulation or the grounds for the result. But the significance of the *Bunting* case is that the same type of evidence employed in *Muller* had now been used to justify legislation not restricted to women, and that the power of the state to do for men what it had done for women had been accepted. *Muller* had proved to be a useful foot in the door leading to acceptance of state economic regulation for all citizens, not just especially vulnerable ones. It was no longer thought that like legislation for men was not necessary, and it could now be sustained.

MINIMUM WAGE LEGISLATION, 1912-1937: THE REVIVAL AND FINAL DEATH OF FREEDOM OF CONTRACT

I have discussed the conditions which led to the passage of minimum wage laws by several states between 1912 and 1915. Inevitably, these laws found their way into the courts. Oregon's 1913 law, establishing an Industrial Welfare Commission with the power to set maximum hours and minimum wages for women and minors "adequate to supply the necessary cost of living for such women and to maintain them in good health," was the first to be so challenged; it got to the Supreme Court before any other case was decided. The Commission had established a minimum wage of $8.64 per week for women employees in manufacturing. Investigation had showed that this was just about enough to cover the ordinary living expenses of a single woman, including room, board, clothing (a working dress, a best dress, shoes, hat and coat, sleepwear, underwear, etc.), transportation, medical expenses, a movie a week or its equivalent, and a donation to the church collection plate.[93]

Frank Stettler, a Portland factory owner, and Elmira Simpson, one of his employees, brought suit to enjoin enforcement of this law. Stettler alleged that he could not pay the minimum wage without going out of business and that his workers who earned less than this wage were incompetent to earn more.[94] Simpson insisted that she could maintain herself in health and comfort on less money, and that she would lose her job if the order were enforced.[95]

The Oregon Supreme Court unanimously rejected both suits, in March and April of 1914.[96] The *Stettler* opinion quoted *Muller* at length, but did not clarify the connection between "woman's physical structure and the performance of maternal functions"[97] and the need for a special minimum wage for women. But the Court went on to cite the findings of state investigations and other authorities that the majority of women workers did not receive wages sufficient for their support, and that many became undernourished or found ways of supplementing their income which were of questionable legality or morality.[98] The Court found a reasonable connection between wages and public health and welfare, and even quoted from a dissent in *Lochner*.[99]

The U.S. Supreme Court heard these cases together. Unable to decide on the first hearing, the Court scheduled reargument. As in *Bunting,* Brandeis did not participate; the remaining eight justices divided evenly and thus affirmed the lower court decision without opinion.[100] The absence of any doubt as to which side the ninth justice would have been on probably gave the result a public legitimacy that it might not otherwise have received. State courts went along, usually in unanimous opinions, with notable enthusiasm.[101] These decisions were based upon recognition of women's inferior economic position and a willingness to agree with legislatures that income had a reasonable relation to health, welfare, and morals.

But after World War I, the movement for minimum wage met with discouragement. Although these laws had originally found a ready public acceptance, post-war advocates of minimum wage laws found employers vigorously opposed and the public apathetic. According to Commons:

> . . . In the postwar years the employer opposition to miminum wage had become organized and effective. Merchants and manufacturer's associations of all kinds were becoming more active and powerful. They were engaging intelligent young executives' secretaries and legislative agents who adopted the methods of their opponents and adapted them to their own use. These young men could use statistics and surveys and questionnaires. They could marshal "contented" workers to appear at legislative hearings and protest against a statute which they had been told would cost them their jobs. All this, of course, impressed the legislatures.[102]

It would also impress the courts. The manufacturers had realized what had hit them, and were arming themselves against it. The fact that wages had risen in the years since the war helped buttress their argument.[103] Unfortunately, despite these increases, many women's earnings still were not sufficient for their needs. Investigations of the Women's Bureau and various state agencies in the postwar years showed that throughout the country thousands of women workers in factories, laundries, and other mercantile establishments did not earn a living wage, and that despite postwar increases, real wages had frequently dropped in relation to the cost of living, determined by standards similar to those employed earlier.[104]

But only one new minimum-wage law was passed between the war and the Depression. In 1918, Congress, by an overwhelming majority, enacted a law authorizing the fixing of minimum wages for adult women in the District of Columbia. A year later, Women's Bureau investigators found that the average rate of pay for women hotel, restaurant, and hospital workers was $15.40 per week; the Bureau of Labor Statistics estimated that the minimum cost of living that year was $18.43 per week.[105] In March 1920, the wage board established by the law issued an order setting a minimum wage of $16.50 per week for women working in hotels, lodging houses, apartment houses, or hospitals. (Compare this with Oregon's 1913 minimum wage, and also with the cost of living estimated by the Bureau of Labor Statistics.) The Children's Hospital of the District of Columbia, and a woman elevator operator in a hotel, sued to enjoin enforcement. Because the illness of a judge on the Supreme Court of the District of Columbia necessitated reargument (which got to be a thorny issue itself), the case took over three years to get to the U.S. Supreme Court, accompanied by the one Brandeis brief which failed to convince a court.

The opinion, issued on April 9, 1923,[106] ranks with *Lochner* as an exhibit in the Chamber of Horrors of Substantive Due Process. The law was invalidated on the grounds that it unduly restricted freedom of contract, and that it bore no reasonable relation to health and morals. The case was decided by a vote of five to three (Brandeis not participating because his daughter was a member of the Minimum Wage Commission), and the dissents were as emphatic as those in *Lochner* had been. The public reaction was overwhelmingly critical, indicating that this decision was out of step with opinion on all sides, even in the legal profession. Law reviews had nothing good to say about it.[107] The New York *World* typified the reaction of the press in a cartoon showing Justice Sutherland, the author of the majority opinion, holding out the decision to a figure labelled, "Woman wage earner." The caption read: "This decision, madam, affirms your constitutional right to starve."[108] So much for the freedom that the law curtailed.

For my purposes, the important parts of the opinion are those in which Sutherland rejects the argument that the government may provide special legislation for wage protection for women. His first task was to distinguish this from the hours cases:

> In the *Muller* case the validity of the Oregon statute, forbidding the employment of any female in certain industries more than ten hours during any one day was upheld. The decision proceeded upon the theory that the difference between the sexes may justify a different rule respecting hours of labor in the case of women than in the case of men. It is pointed out that these consist of maternal functions, and also in the fact that historically woman has always been dependent upon man, who has established his control by superior physical strength. The cases of *Riley, Miller* and *Bosley* follow in this respect the *Muller Case.* But the ancient inequality of the sexes, otherwise than the physical, as suggested in the *Muller Case* has continued "with diminishing intensity." In view of the great—not to say revolutionary—changes which have taken place since that utterance, in the contractual, political, and civil status of women, culminating in the Nineteenth Amendment, it is not unreasonable to say that these differences have come almost, if not quite, to the vanishing point. In this aspect of the matter, while the physical differences must be recognized in the appropriate cases, and legislation fixing hours or conditions of work may properly take them into account, we cannot accept the doctrine that women of mature age, *sui juris,* require or may be subjected to restrictions upon their liberty of contract which could not be lawfully imposed in the case of men under similar circumstances.[109]

The effort to distinguish *Muller* is curious. Although Brewer had explicitly denied that the disfranchisement of women was a factor in that decision, the *Adkins* court appears to see the vote as a matter of primary importance, The majority apparently assumes that, since the Nineteenth Amendment, the only differences between the sexes which can justify special legislation are the physical ones—which, admittedly, do not seem to be directly related to living expenses. Except for the reliance on suffrage, however, the reasoning in *Adkins* is entirely compatible with that in *Muller*. Brewer had implied that changes in the social position of women might eventually make some special legislation for women obsolete, but that the physical differences between the sexes would always necessitate some special protection for women. Sutherland has accepted both portions of this argument. He insists that the changes anticipated by Brewer have now occurred: that women no longer suffer contractual, political, and civil disadvantages which formerly might have justified regulations like that at issue here. But he agrees with Brewer that physical differences may still provide a basis for regulations reasonably connected with them (as he shows a year later in *Radice*). Since Sutherland can see no connection between women's physical characteristics and wages, he concludes that minimum wage laws for women are unconstitutional.

As Brewer had done, Sutherland ignores economic differences between the sexes, in their incomes and working opportunities and in the conditions they had to endure—differences whose existence was demonstrated, in both cases, by the evidence in the briefs. In *Muller,* that inattention did not make much difference, since physical distinction provided plausible justification for hour limitation. But no such clear connection obtains between physical distinctions and wage regulation. In the latter area, economic factors are crucial. However great the political and social changes since 1908— and surely the *Adkins* Court exaggerates them—the economic differences between the sexes were nowhere near the vanishing point, Nineteenth Amendment or no Nineteenth Amendment. Nearly 350 pages of evidence of this fact were presented to the Court. As one critic wrote:

> Will the learned justices of the majority be pardoned for over-
> looking the cardinal fact that the minimum wage legislation
> is not and never was predicted on the political, contractual,
> or civil inequalities of women? It is predicated rather upon
> evils to society resulting from the exploitation of women in
> industry who *as a class labor under a tremendous economic
> handicap.* The problem is one of economic fact, not of po-
> litical, contractual, or civil status.[110]

The dissents, too, betray confusion as to what *Muller* had decided and what was being decided now. Chief Justice Taft was uncertain as to what the status of *Muller* now was, in light of the passage from the Sutherland opinion which I quoted. On its face, that passage seems to me to say quite plainly that hours limitations are justified by physical differences even if the political ones have diminished (which is, of course, exactly what Brewer said), but Taft was apprehensive. He argued that the present case was controlled by *Muller,* declaring, "I don't think we are warranted in varying constitutional construction based on physical differences between men and women, because of the Nineteenth Amendment."[111] But Taft does not explain how the wage regulations are "based on physical differences between men and women." Do women need a certain minimum income because they may bear children, or because they are usually weaker than most men? If so, precisely what is the connection between either or both of these characteristics and living expenses? Taft does not give us any useful hint.

Holmes' dissent is even more intriguing. With characteristic bluntness, he wrote: *"Muller v. Oregon,* I take it, is as good law today as it was in 1908. It will take more than the Nineteenth Amendment to convince me that there are no differences between men and women, or that legislation cannot take them into account."[112] But this does not help clarify the issue at all. The *Adkins* decision does not change the status of *Muller.* And the new decision does not suggest that there are no differences between the sexes which law can take into account; indeed, it specifically says just the opposite with respect to physical differences.

Furthermore, Holmes tells us no more than Taft did about the relationship between sexual differences and minimum wages. Neither dissent adequately responds to the majority opinion.

The significant division on the Court seems to be between those who think that now that women have gained political, contractual, and civil rights, *only* physical differences can justify special legislation, and do not justify this type of it (the majority), and those who believe that the physical differences do justify this, and probably, from their language, any kind of differential treatment (the dissenters). This interpretation is reinforced by the *Radice* decision a year later, where the Court unanimously upheld a law on the basis of physical characteristics. These two decisions indicate the extent to which judges' attention was increasingly focused on the physical and permanent differences. They also indicate great confusion on the part of these judges about what the real issue was. For the question is not whether there is a rational relationship between sexual characteristics and a given regulation. The question should be, rather, whether there is a rational relationship between an evil which is substantive and a law which purports to mitigate that evil. For example, certainly there is a rational connection between physical strength and working hours. But the important point is whether there is a causal connection between ill health, accidents and so forth, and the number of hours one works. In night work, the question is whether prohibition of this work can reasonably be said to prevent the evils identified. In minimum wage regulation, the point is whether the dangers of an inadequate income can be mitigated by a fixed wage. But the courts obscure this question. Ironically, the result is that women's freedom of contract is sustained in a situation where in fact it did not exist, and curtailed in a situation where it did exist. This comment is not a defense of minimum-wage laws which apply only to women—I find them vulnerable to the same criticisms I made of women's hours laws—but I include it to emphasize the fact that the result of both *Radice* and *Adkins* was not to help, but to harm, women workers.

The few state appellate courts which heard subsequent minimum-wage cases followed *Adkins,* but their compliance was notably grudging in at least one case.[113] Washington State and California continued to enforce their regulations. The important employers' organizations declared their willingness to comply, which suggests that they had found the limitations less than devastating for their prosperity.[114]

This situation was dramatically altered by the Depression, during which twenty-one states passed new minimum-wage laws, either for all workers or for women and minors, or began enforcing old ones.[115] These laws were, of course, only one manifestation of a radical change in the approach of both federal and state governments to the economy, a change which, after a short, bitter struggle, was accepted by the judiciary. The history of the New Deal, the "nine old men," the Court-packing bill, and the "switch in time" is too well known to need retelling here. An examination of the two Supreme Court cases which involved a women's minimum wage regulation —the latter of which became a landmark in American constitutional history—will suffice to understand the relevance of the "switch in time" to the future of women's labor legislation.

In 1933 New York had enacted its first minimum-wage law, establishing a commission. The statute declared that it was against public policy

for any employer to employ any woman at an oppressive or unreasonable
wage, defined as one "both less than the fair and reasonable value of the
services rendered and less than sufficient to meet the minimum cost of
living necessary for health."[116] It was hoped that the first clause would
prevent defeat under the *Adkins* precedent, which had dwelt at length
on the fact that Congress had made no mention of the value of services
rendered. But the addition did not save the new law, which the Court
invalidated by the usual five to four vote.[117] Writing for the majority,
Justice Butler quoted *Adkins* at length, emphasizing freedom of contract.[11]
Furthermore, the Court insisted, the act was an arbitrary discrimination
against women:

> Much, if not all, that in them is said in justification of the
> regulations that the Act imposes in respect of women's wages
> applies with equal force in support of the same regulation of
> men's wages. While men are left free to fix their wages by
> agreement with employers, it would be fanciful to suppose
> that the regulation of women's wages would be useful to pre-
> vent or lessen the evils listed in the first section of the Act.
> Men in greater numbers than women support themselves and
> dependents and because of need will work for whatever wages
> they can get and that without regard to the value of service
> and even though the pay is less than minima prescribed in
> accordance with this Act. It is plain that under circumstances
> such as those portrayed in the "Factual Background," pre-
> scribing of minimum wages for women alone would unrea-
> sonably restrict them in competition and tend arbitrarily to
> deprive them of employment and a fair chance to find work.[119]

This conclusion directly contradicted the evidence in the briefs[120] and
the appellate court opinion.[121] Even during depressions, men do not take
women's jobs at women's wages.[122]

Chief Justice Hughes, in dissent, attempted to refute the Court's argument by citing the statistics submitted in the state's brief which illustrated
these facts.[123] Another dissenter, Justice Stone, argued a point which
might seem obvious to anyone except an appellate court judge: "In the
years since the Adkins case we have had opportunity to learn that a wage
is not always the resultant of free bargaining between employees and em-

ployers; that it may be one forced upon employees by their economic necessities and upon employers by the most ruthless of their competitors."[124] Both dissents, signed by Brandeis and Cardozo as well, left open the possibility of minimum-wage laws for all employees, not just women and minors.

The *Morehead* decision was to all intents and purposes reversed less than a year later, while the Court-packing fight was raging, in *West Coast Hotel Co. v. Parrish.*[125] For whatever reasons, Justice Roberts had changed his opinion in the interim, and now the vote was five to four for affirmance. The law at issue was that enacted by Washington State in 1913, which, as I mentioned, had been enforced consistently thereafter, regardless of the *Adkins* decision. The majority, speaking through Hughes, sustained the restriction of the scope of the law to women. The opinion relied on the *Muller* argument that the health of women was directly related to "the health and vigor of the race" and that "there is that in her disposition and habits of life which will operate against a full assertion of rights."[126] Hughes also discusses the exploitation of women as he had in dissent a year before.[127] But the opinion went even further. It settled, once and for all, the status of freedom of contract, demoting it from its position as a fundamental constitutional right:

> What is this freedom? The Constitution does not speak of freedom of contract. It speaks of liberty and prohibits the deprivation of liberty without due process of law. In prohibiting that deprivation the Constitution does not recognize an absolute and uncontrollable liberty. Liberty in each of its phases has its history and connotation. But the liberty safeguarded is liberty in a social organization which requires the protection of law against the evils which menace the health, safety, morals and welfare of the people. Liberty under the Constitution is thus necessarily subject to the restraints of due process, and regulation which is reasonable in relation to its subject and is adopted in the interests of the community is due process. . . .
> Freedom of contract is a qualified and not an absolute right. . . . Liberty implies the absence of arbitrary restraint, not immunity from reasonable regulations and prohibitions imposed in the interests of the community.[128]

Freedom of contract was no longer to be treated as a fundamental personal liberty, immune from all but the most urgently needed restriction. To call any liberty a fundamental right had been fairly safe before 1937, since up to that time the prevailing rule of adjudication had been that even fundamental rights could be abridged if the restriction was reasonable (as was made quite clear in the early free-speech cases).[129] The old courts were in error not only in elevating freedom of contract to a status it had never before held, but also in their absurdly narrow conception of what was involved in protecting the public welfare. The courts had begun to broaden their outlook on the latter issue even before 1937; much economic legislation was sustained even under the old doctrine of freedom of contract.

But in the light of post-1937 constitutional developments, the demotion of freedom of contract became extremely significant. The Court was beginning to develop what has been called a two-tier theory of "liberty" within the meaning of the Due Process Clause of the Fourteenth Amendment. The first, lower level of liberty consists basically of the individual's right to do whatever he or she wants. The government's power to infringe this liberty is broad; restraints are presumed to be constitutional. But even these must meet certain standards of "reasonableness." The second, higher level of liberty contains "fundamental" rights, of such a character that they cannot be denied without violating basic principles of justice. Infringements of this liberty are presumed to be unconstitutional. They must meet stronger standards than reasonableness; they can stand only upon proof of a *compelling* state interest in abridging the right.[130] At the same time that the Court relinquished its powers in economic cases, it began to extend its role by recognizing the Bill of Rights guarantees as fundamental rights in this stronger sense. In the 1930s and 1940s, the Court began to assign these rights a "preferred position."[131] One significant result of the *Parrish* case was that freedom of contract did not receive the benefit of the tougher standards.

The impact of all this is that the one constitutional doctrine which—whatever its validity—could have provided some measure of protection for women's rights in employment had now been abandoned. If freedom of contract had been assigned to the higher level of liberty, where the tougher standards apply, infringements of this right would have been presumed unconstitutional, and could have survived scrutiny only upon showing of a pressing need for them. As I hope the next chapter will show, it is unlikely that the laws reviewed by courts in this area after

1937 could have survived such a test. But they never had to. *Parrish* firmly assigned freedom of contract to the lower level of liberty. Economic rights gained virtually no judicial protection after 1937. Freedom of contract could now be curtailed as long as such restriction had some reasonable relation to a legitimate governmental purpose.

The only successful challenge under the U.S. Constitution which could thereafter be made to employment legislation which discriminated on the basis of sex was that such a law had no reasonable relation to a legitimate state purpose. In the next chapter, I try to make a case that no such relation existed in the important post-1937 employment cases. But the courts did not see this as the dispositive question. They saw the question of reasonableness as being whether classification on the basis of sex was itself reasonable, not whether there was a reasonable connection between restrictions upon one sex and a governmental purpose. On the face of it, it might seem that some sex-based classifications are reasonable in this sense, and some are not. But the unbroken line of decisions from *Muller* to *Radice* was interpreted by courts as establishing the principle that permanent rather than situation-bound distinctions between the sexes justified any sex-based employment discrimination. These early decisions had not gone so far, but in the last forty years judges have frequently behaved as though to deny the validity of sex-based discrimination was to deny the existence of any sexual differences.

That judges have ruled in this way may be unfortunate, but it is not surprising. Not only did such decisions mirror the prevailing social views in those years, but the courts were not confronted with any sustained pressure to rule in ways counter to these views, as had been the case in other situations. However understandable the judicial approach to these cases, its results in the last three decades have been, first, to obscure important changes in the situation of women workers which have reduced the need for protection, and, second, to allow the use of the law to restrict, rather than protect, American women.

NOTES

1. 300 U.S. 379 (1937).
2. See Robert McCloskey, "Economic Due Process and the Supreme Court," *Supreme Court Review* (1962), pp. 34-62.
3. See, e.g., Harold U. Faulkner, *The Quest for Social Justice* (New York: Macmillan Co., 1931), pp. 162-65; U.S. Bureau of the Census, *1950 Census of Population* 1 (Washington, D.C.: U.S. Government Printing Office, 1952): 1-3.

4. Stephen B. Wood, *Constitutional Politics in the Progressive Era* (Chicago: University of Chicago Press, 1968), p. 1.

5. John R. Commons, *History of Labor*, 3:474-79.

6. *Born Female* (New York: David McKay Co., 1968), p. 61.

7. See Margaret Mead, *Male and Female* (New York: William Morrow & Co., 1949), pp. 159-60.

8. U.S. Senate Report, *Wage-Earners*, 9:23-27.

9. John R. Commons and John B. Andrews, *Principles of Labor Legislation* (4th rev. ed., New York: Harper & Brothers, 1936), p. 181.

10. C. E. Persons, "Women's Work and Wages in the United States," *Quarterly Journal of Economics* 29 (February 1915): 201-34.

11. See, e.g., U.S. Senate Report, *Wage-Earners*, 5:21.

12. Ibid., p. 17.

13. Ibid., pp. 32-35.

14. People *ex rel.* Morehead v. Tipaldo, 270 N.Y. 233, 258 (1935) (Lehman, J., dissenting).

15. Brief for Plaintiff in Error, pp. 10-76, Stettler v. O'Hara, 243 U.S. 629 (1917).

16. Ibid., pp. 57-58.

17. Appendix to the Briefs Filed on Behalf of Respondent, pp. 108ff., Stettler v. O'Hara, 243 U.S. 629 (1917).

18. *The Unheavenly City* (Boston: Little, Brown & Co., 1970), pp. 95-97.

19. See, e.g., Thomas Reed Powell, "The Judiciality of Minimum-Wage Legislation," *Harvard Law Review* 37 (March 1924): 545-73.

20. Brief for Plaintiff in Error, pp. 108-36, Stettler v. O'Hara, 243 U.S. 629 (1917); Brief for Appellants, pp. 302-03, Adkins v. Children's Hospital, 261 U.S. 525 (1923).

21. Brief for Plaintiffs in Error, pp. 162-79, Stettler v. O'Hara, 243 U.S. 629 (1917).

22. Ibid., pp. 188-92; Brief for Appellants, pp. 362ff., Adkins v. Children's Hospital, 261 U.S. 525 (1923).

23. Withie v. Bloehm, 163 Mich. 419 (1910); Commonwealth v. Riley, 210 Mass. 387 (1912); State v. Somerville, 67 Wash. 638 (1912); *ex parte* Miller, 162 Cal. 687 (1912).

24. *Ex parte* Miller, 162 Cal. 687, 691; Miller v. Wilson, 236 U.S. 373, 382-83; Bosley v. McLaughlin, 236 U.S. 385, 386-87 (1915).

25. See, e.g., Keokee Coal Co. v. Taylor, 234 U.S. 224 (1914); Jeffrey v. Blagg, 235 U.S. 571 (1915).

26. Ritchie v. Wayman, 244 Ill. 509 (1910); People v. Elerding, 254 Ill. 579 (1912); Hawley v. Walker, 232 U.S. 718 (1914).

27. Goldmark, *Fatigue*, Part II, pp. 339-410.

28. Riley v. Massachusetts, 232 U.S. 671 (1914).

29. Miller v. Wilson, 236 U.S. 373 (1915); Bosley v. McLaughlin, 236 U.S. 385 (1915).

30. Wood, *Constitutional Politics*, p. 97.

31. Brief for Complainant, p. 7, Bosley v. McLaughlin, 236 U.S. 385 (1915).

32. Ibid.

33. 244 Ill. 509 (1910).

34. 214 N.Y. 395, 108 N.E. 639 (1915).

35. 244 Ill. 509, 527 (1910).

36. Ibid., pp. 520-21, 530.

37. Summary of Facts of Knowledge Submitted on Behalf of the People, p. 47, People v. Charles Schweinler Press, 214 N.Y. 395, 108 N.E. 639 (1915).

38. Ibid., pp. 10ff.

39. Ibid., pp. 114, 187ff, 251.

40. Ibid., p. 244.

41. Ibid., p. 142.

42. Ibid., p. 187. Cf., supra, 27-28; U.S. Senate Report, *Wage-Earners*, 13: 109.

43. "Facts of Knowledge," p. 252, People v. Charles Schweinler Press, 214 N.Y. 395, 108 N.E. 639 (1915).

44. Ibid., p. 113.

45. Bunting v. Oregon, 243 U.S. 426 (1917).

46. Brief for Defendant in Error, pp. 63-192, 265-359, Bunting v. Oregon, 243 U.S. 426 (1917).

47. Ibid., pp. 414-27.

48. "Facts of Knowledge," pp. 84-85, People v. Charles Schweinler Press, 214 N.Y. 395, 108 N.E. 639 (1915).

49. Brief for Appellants, pp. 8-9, People v. Charles Schweinler Press, 214 N.Y. 395, 108 N.E. 639 (1915).

50. Ibid., p. 14.

51. Ibid., p. 26.

52. Ibid., p. 21.

53. Ibid., p. 31.

54. Griswold v. Connecticut, 381 U.S. 479, 502-06 (1965) (White, J., concurring).

55. Aptheker v. Secretary of State, 378 U.S. 500 (1964). For further illustrations, see Wieman v. Updegraff, 344 U.S. 183 (1953); Schware v. Board of Bar Examiners, 353 U.S. 232 (1957).

56. 108 N.E. 639, 643-44 (1915).

57. Ibid., p. 643.

58. Brief for Appellants, p. 18, People v. Charles Schweinler Press, 214 N.Y. 395, 108 N.E. 639 (1915).

59. Ibid., p. 26; "Facts of Knowledge," p. 195.

60. "Facts of Knowledge," p. 195.

61. Ibid., p. 89.

62. Brief for Defendants, p. 91; Plaintiff's Assignment of Error, pp. 38-39, 110, Radice v. New York, 264 U.S. 292 (1924).

63. Affidavit for Plaintiff on Appeal, p. 65, Radice v. New York, 264 U.S. 292 (1924).

64. 264 U.S. 292 (1924).

65. Affidavit for Plaintiff on Appeal, p. 38, Radice v. New York, 264 U.S. 292 (1924).

66. Ibid., pp. 39, 41.

67. Brief for Plaintiffs, p. 23.

68. Ibid., p. 195, 252; Affidavit for Plaintiff on Appeal, pp. 35, 40-41, 165; Supplementary Brief for Plaintiff, pp. 4-5.

69. Supplementary Brief for Defendants, p. 2.

70. Brief for Defendants, p. 195.

71. Supplementary Brief for Defendants, p. 7.

72. See Baker, *Protective Labor Legislation,* pp. 362-66, 424-28, 432.

73. Ibid., pp. 362-66.

74. 261 U.S. 525 (1923).

75. 264 U.S. 292, 295.

76. Ibid., p. 294.

77. See e.g., Keokee Coal Co. v. Taylor, 234 U.S. 224 (1914); Jeffrey v. Blagg, 235 U.S. 571 (1915); Central Lumber Co. v. South Dakota, 226 U.S. 157 (1912); Royster Guano Co. v. Virginia, 254 U.S. 412 (1920).

78. 264 U.S. 292, 295.

79. Supra, ch. 1.

80. Atkin v. Kansas, 191 U.S. 207.

81. See Holden v. Hardy, 169 U.S. 366 (1898); in re Morgan, 26 Colo. 415 (1899).

82. Commons, *History of Labor,* 3: 548.

83. Ibid., p. 559.

84. 243 U.S. 426 (1917).

85. Baker, *Protective Labor Legislation,* p. 434.

86. Brief for Defendant in Error (filed by George M. Brown, Attorney General of Oregon), pp. 5-50, Bunting v. Oregon, 243 U.S. 426 (1917).

87. Brief for Defendant in Error (filed by Felix Frankfurter and Josephine Goldmark), pp. 499-531.

88. Ibid., pp. 532-71.

89. Goldmark, *Fatigue,* Part II, pp. 252-60, 302-17.

90. U.S. Bureau of the Census, Monograph #19, "Women in Gainful Occupations, 1870 to 1920" (Washington, D.C.: U.S. Government Printing Office, 1929), p. 77.

91. 243 U.S. 426, 435-36 (1917).

92. Ibid., pp. 438-39.

93. See U.S. Senate Report, *Wage-Earners,* vol. 5, passim.

94. Brief for Plaintiffs in Error, p. 8, Stettler v. O'Hara, 243 U.S. 629 (1917).

95. Ibid., pp. 9-10.

96. Stettler v. O'Hara, 69 Ore. 519, 139 P. 743; Simpson v. O'Hara, 70 Ore. 261, 141 P. 158.

97. 208 U.S. 412, 421 (1908).

98. 139 P. 743, 748-49.

99. Ibid., pp. 746, 750.

100. Stettler v. O'Hara, 243 U.S. 629 (1917).

101. See State v. Crowe, 130 Ark. 272 (1917); Williams v. Evans, 139 Minn. 32 (1917); Holcombe v. Creamer, 231 Mass. 99 (1918); Larsen v. Rice, 100 Wash. 642 (1918); Miller v. Minimum Wage Commission, 145 Minn. 262 (1920); Spokane v. Younger, 113 Wash. 359 (1920); Poye v. Texas, 230 S.W. 161 (Tex. Crim. App. 1921).

102. *History of Labor,* 3:529.

103. Ibid.

104. Brief for Appellants, Part II, pp. 887-1022, Adkins v. Children's Hospital, 261 U.S. 525 (1923); Commons, *History of Labor,* 3:518-19, 524-25.

105. U.S. Women's Bureau, Bulletin no. 61, *The Development of Minimum-Wage Laws in the United States 1912 to 1927* (Washington, D.C.: U.S. Government Printing Office, 1928), pp. 130-36, 340-42.

106. Adkins v. Children's Hospital, 261 U.S. 525.

107. See, e.g., comment, "Constitutional Law: Police Power: Minimum Wage for Women," *California L. Rev.* 11 (July 1923): 353-62; Harry Cohen, "Minimum Wage Legislation and the Adkins Case," *N.Y.U. L. Rev.* 2 (March 1925); "The Minimum Wage Decision," *Kentucky L. Rev.* (November 1923): 1-9; Powell, "Judiciality."

108. Thomas I. Parkinson, "Minimum Wage and the Constitution," *American Labor Legislation Rev.* 13 (June 1923): 131-36.

109. 261 U.S. 525, 552-53 (1923).

110. Comment, "Minimum Wage," p. 357. Emphasis in the original.

111. 261 U.S. 525, 567 (1923).

112. Ibid., pp. 569-70.

113. Topeka Laundry Co. v. Court of Industrial Relations, 119 Kans. 12 (1925); see also Murphy v. Sardell, 269 U.S. 530 (1925); Donham v. West-Nelson Mfg. Co., 273 U.S. 657 (1926); Folding Furniture Works v. Industrial Commission, 300 F. 991 (1924).

114. Commons, *History of Labor,* 3:515.

115. See Ora Marshino and Lawrence J. O'Malley, "Wage and Hour Legislation in the Courts," *George Washington L. Rev.* 5 (May 1937): 865-78.

116. Laws of 1933, ch. 584.

117. Morehead v. New York *ex rel.* Tipaldo, 298 U.S. 587 (1936).

118. Ibid., pp. 610-11.

119. Ibid., pp. 616-17.

120. Motion for Leave to File Brief as *Amicus Curiae* (filed by John W. Bricker, Attorney General of Ohio), pp. 26ff, Morehead v. New York *ex rel.* Tipaldo, 298 U.S. 587 (1936).

121. People *ex rel.* Morehead v. Tipaldo, 270 N.Y. 233, 258 (1935) (Lehman, J., dissenting).

122. For an illustration, see Corning Glass Works v. Brennan, 417 U.S. 188, 195-96 (1974), a case arising under the Equal Pay Act of 1963. At issue was a pay differential between women day-shift inspectors and men night-shift inspectors which dated from 1925-1930, when Corning began night-shift operations. Because state laws prohibited night work for women, Corning had to hire men; it was forced to pay them more because the men, even after 1929, refused to work for the wages paid to women.

123. 298 U.S. 587, 626-27 (1936).

124. Ibid., p. 635.

125. 300 U.S. 379 (1937).

126. Ibid., pp. 394-95.

127. Ibid., pp. 398-99.

128. Ibid., p. 391.

129. See, e.g., Gitlow v. New York, 268 U.S. 657, 666-67 (1925); Whitney v. California, 274 U.S. 357 (1927); Near v. Minnesota, 283 U.S. 697 (1931).

130. See Bates v. Little Rock, 361 U.S. 516, 524 (1958); Poe v. Ullman, 367 U.S. 497, 542-44 (1961) (Harlan, J., dissenting); Judith Baer, "Griswold v. Connecticut: The Zone of Privacy and Freedom" (unpublished, University of Chicago, 1970), pp. 47-48.

131. See U.S. v. Carolene Products, 304 U.S. 144, 152, n. 4 (1938); Cantwell v. Connecticut, 310 U.S. 246 (1940); Bridges v. California, 314 U.S. 256, 262 (1941); Murdock v. Pennsylvania, 319 U.S. 105 (1943); Kovacs v. Cooper, 336 U.S. 77 (1949).

4

FALLING BETWEEN
SELF-ERECTED BARRIERS:
WOMEN'S RIGHTS AND
THE CONSTITUTION,
1937-1976

The first striking fact about the performance of American courts between 1937 and 1971 in cases involving the constitutionality of sex discrimination is that they got very little chance to perform at all. This statement may sound inaccurate to those who have observed the flood of decisions on sex discrimination which the courts have produced in the last few years, but most of the decisions have involved not constitutional adjudication but statutory construction.

There are only scattered instances of constitutional cases in state and federal courts, on subjects too varied[1] and with results too disparate[2] to permit the development of any trends in judicial decisions. Of these cases, only three got to the Supreme Court,[3] and the Court refused review in five others.[4] The remaining cases, including both favorable and adverse decisions to feminist claims, were not appealed; and there were very few of them to begin with, partly because there were almost no new laws.

Only a small proportion of the cases—and only one which reached the Supreme Court—pertained directly to employment restrictions. The others concern us directly only to the extent that they use, or fail to use the decisions involving labor as precedent. As three legal scholars specializing in sex discrimination have pointed out,[5] *Muller,* which had to do only with hours legislation, has been cited as controlling precedent in cases "upholding the exclusion of women from juries, differential treatment in licensing various occupations, and the exclusion of women from state-supported colleges,"[6] with the almost mechanical repetition of the phrase "Sex is a valid basis for classification" (for which the reader will search the *Muller* opinion in vain). But here again, there are too few cases to permit description of this out-of-context citation as a trend or habit. There are other cases which uphold sex-based discrimination which do not cite employment cases as precedent.[7]

With one exception, the courts which decided employment cases between 1937 and 1971 upheld the challenged laws. And the one exception —the most recent case, decided at a time when feminism had again become a viable political issue—was the result of judicial overkill. It could have been resolved under Title VII of the Civil Rights Act of 1964, without any mention of the Constitution.[8] And interestingly enough, *every* law regulating women's employment which was upheld by the U.S. Supreme Court has been repealed or substantially modified by the legislature which passed it.

It would be tempting to describe the bulk of these decisions as "horrible examples," except for the fact that they are not examples. They are the only cases. Furthermore, they must be viewed in the context of other decisions involving economic problems. These cases were decided at a time when courts had virtually abandoned the power to review the constitutionality of economic regulation. Judges no longer demanded any showing that a given statute or a classification had a reasonable relation to a legitimate governmental purpose; they upheld laws whenever it was remotely possible to assume that such a relationship might exist.[9] The decisions involving sex discrimination are neither more nor less permissive than the resolutions of other economic cases. It is instructive to compare the results in employment cases with those of cases involving sex discrimination in other areas, where women's claims have frequently been accepted in some jurisdictions even while other courts were rejecting these claims,[10] or with the courts' construction of statutes prohibiting sex discrimination, where they have frequently taken the law more seriously than did the dominant members of the legislature which passed it.[11]

The courts did not establish themselves as champions of women's rights, but it is difficult to sustain an accusation that they have been any more antifeminist than the rest of society. The opinions are not innocent of sexism, but the courts' reluctance to interfere in employment cases had additional, more complex causes. This fact does not preclude criticism of these decisions. But we do not get anywhere if we confine that criticism to exposure of antifeminist prejudice inherent in the decisions, or attribute the results solely to the overwhelmingly male composition of the judiciary and the privileged position that appellate court judges enjoy in our society.[12] These factors do not explain why legislatures, also composed predominantly of men who are exposed to prevailing social attitudes, were prone to relax restrictions which courts had sustained, or thy the same privileged male judges did not maintain a united front against women's claims in other areas.[13]

In a series of cases decided in the past few years, the Supreme Court had departed from the almost unbroken line of precedents to limit significantly governmental power to discriminate on the basis of sex. The first such decision, *Reed v. Reed*,[14] struck down an Idaho law which gave an automatic preference to men over equally qualified women in appointing the administrator of a decendent's estate. A unanimous Court declared that "to give a mandatory preference to members of either sex over members of the other . . . is to make the very kind of arbitrary legislative choice forbidden by the Equal Protection Clause of the Fourteenth Amendment."[15] Since *Reed*, the Court has invalidated differences in dependency benefits for male and female military personnel,[16] mandatory maternity leaves for public employees,[17] automatic exemptions from jury service for women,[18] and the Social Security Act's provision for benefits to widows, but not widowers, with minor children.[19]

Victims of sex discrimination had had enough success by 1973 to cause one scholar to write, "Thus far the Burger Court seems to have taken only Women's Lib under its protective wing."[20] I have argued elsewhere that this conclusion is wrong. The Court has rejected important claims,[21] and displays a sympathy for "compensatory" discrimination which it does not adequately explain or defend.[22] Furthermore, the changes seem to me to be due not so much to an emerging feminist consciousness on the part of the justices as to the Burger Court's original approach to equal protection cases in general.[23] Any skepticism was vindicated by *General Electric v. Gilbert*,[24] in which the Court reversed the Equal Employment Opportunity Commission and all U.S. Courts of Appeals to rule that Title VII permitted the exclusion of disabilities related to pregnancy from employee sickness and accident benefit programs. I shall discuss this decision more fully in Chapter 5. For now, it is enough to say merely that it has substantially weakened the Court's reputation as a friend of women's rights. Whatever the source or the limitations of the new policy, however, it is clear that discriminations based on sex are no longer accorded absolute constitutional validity, and this applies to discriminatory employment legislation.

To a great extent, the constitutional fate of women's labor legislation
was the result of historical accident. One of those accidents was the choice
of a women's hours case as the subject of the first Brandeis brief, and
another was the choice of Brewer rather than a less conservative justice
to write the *Muller* opinion, but these are the simplest ones. Judicial response to this legislation has been largely determined by three sets of developments in constitutional history which had nothing directly to do
with women. The first was the development of the doctrine of freedom
of contract and the almost infinite expansion of the doctrine of class
legislation as tools for the invalidation of economic legislation. These
widely accepted doctrines made the sustaining of legislation pertaining
to women (powerfully urged by that first brief) possible only if differences, preferably permanent differences, between the sexes were
emphasized. The second set of these developments comprised the retreat
from these positions after 1937, after which the courts were loath to
scrutinize any form of economic intervention. The third and most recent
series of changes has been what Gerald Gunther has described as "an
emerging model of modest intervention [which] would have the courts do
more than they have done in the last generation to assure rationality of
means, without unduly impinging on legislative prerogatives regarding
ends."[25] Several of the Court's recent decisions overturned policies so
poorly related to legislative ends that they could not withstand this more
rigorous scrutiny.[26]

Women's employment legislation between 1937 and 1971 thus fell between two sets of judicially erected barriers; judges were unlikely to overturn these laws for two reasons. First, the language of *Muller* and its successors implied that to question the validity of any sex-based discrimination was to suggest that the sexes were identical. Second, the abandonment of the power of review in economic cases extended to those involving sex discrimination. Even if courts had been willing to examine the
relationship between sexual differences and particular kinds of discrimination, they would still have been restrained by their tendency to assume,
rather than question, the legitimacy of labor regulation.

A third contributing factor to this judicial passivity may have been
that courts were simply not presented with enough cases to force them to
take women's claims seriously. The return of women to the home after
World War II, and their unprotesting absorption in the traditional female
role during the next two decades, created a climate of opinion which

neither encouraged nor welcomed feminist complaints. This passive mood was reflected in the lack of political activity, including litigation, in support of women's rights. It was easy to dismiss a few barmaids from Michigan or a wrestler from Oregon as aberrations.

But once all this has been said in explanation of the courts' behavior, these decisions are nevertheless vulnerable to criticism. The opinions are replete with unsupported assumptions, unexamined premises, and generally careless reasoning. And they demonstrate serious flaws in the precedent cases by showing where the reasoning of those earlier opinions could lead.

IS BARTENDING UNLADYLIKE?
PROTECTIVE LEGISLATION AFTER WORLD WAR II

The states did not expand their protective labor legislation to safeguard the women who entered the labor force during the war (as European countries had done during World War I),[27] nor was this legislation widely used as a weapon after the war to force women to yield jobs to returning veterans. Women did leave the labor force in large numbers, but not because changes in the laws forced them to. Their retirement was not always enthusiastic, or even voluntary,[28] but it was not the law that made them quit.

The next case, however, is suspicious. Michigan's law providing that applicants for bartenders' licenses in cities of more than 5,000 people must be males over twenty-one, except for the wives and daughters of male owners of bars, arouses distrust because of the date of its passage —April 30, 1945—and the date the Michigan Liquor Control Commission began enforcing it—May 1, 1947. Between those two dates, the executive board of the International Union of Hotel and Restaurant Employees and Bartenders had adopted a resolution to resume the policy of excluding women from bartending which it had abandoned during the war. The Union vigorously pursued this goal for the next several years.[29] The conclusion that this law was designed to injure women while inconveniencing men as little as possible can be inferred from its text.

Valentine Goesaert, the owner of a bar in Dearborn, Michigan, her daughter Margaret, and two other women employees sued for an injunction on the grounds that the law violated their rights under the Fourteenth Amendment. The briefs and records contain no evidence that women bartenders posed or might pose a threat to health, safety, welfare, or morals of the people of Michigan. No evidence is presented that drunken patrons were creating increased dangers to women bartenders, or that the presence of women bartenders caused any "moral" problems, or that any segment of the female population of Michigan was forced into bartending. Nor was there any evidence that the rest of the Western world had been beset by these problems and that Michigan needed some preventive medicine. There are speculations that the legislature might have supposed that the first problem existed, but they remain speculations. The state stuck to the new law, not the facts. Michigan's thirty-three-page brief cited *Radice* as controlling on the issue of sex discrimination,[30] and *Miller v. Wilson* on the issue of the exception.[31] Most of the brief was devoted to citing cases establishing the broad scope of the legislature's power to classify in general, and the constitutionality of state regulation of the liquor trade.[32] We have come a very long way from the Brandeis brief.

The plaintiffs, however, got affidavits from twenty-three women bartenders, and from both male and female owners, stating that the law would do them irreparable injury, that the women bartenders were in no physical danger, and that, in fact, "women barmaids [sic] are an asset to the business because men refrain from becoming intoxicated and from using profanity in the presence of women."[33] On the law, the plaintiffs insisted that the exemption for wives and daughters of male owners (even those not on the premises who, therefore, could scarcely protect members of their families) was arbitrary and capricious.

The Goesaerts did not get very far. A three-judge district court rejected their suit in an opinion marked by its use of the subjunctive mood:

> It is conceivable that the Legislature was of the opinion that a grave social problem existed because of the presence of female bartenders in places where liquor was served in the larger cities of Michigan. It may have been the Legislature's opinion that this problem would be mitigated to the vanishing point in those places where there was a male licensee ultimately responsible for the condition and the decorum maintained in his establishment. It may have determined that the self interest of male licensees in protecting the immediate members of their families would generally insure a more wholesome atmosphere in such establishments. The Legislature may

also have considered the likelihood that a male licensee could
provide protection for his wife or daughter that would be beyond the capacity of a woman licensee to provide for herself
or her daughter. The power of the Legislature to make special
provision for the protection of women is not denied . . . .

We conclude that the Legislature may also have reasoned
that a graver responsibility attaches to the bartender who has
control of the liquor supply than to the waitress who merely
receives prepared orders of liquor from the bartender for service at a table. It may have concluded that the presence of
female waitresses does not constitute a serious social problem
where a male bartender is in charge of the premises. . . . It
may reasonably be conceived that the Legislature deemed it
necessary to have male control in the establishment but that
it was not necessary to regulate the routine tasks of the waitresses in bringing food and drinks to patrons at individual
tables.[34]

On appeal, the Supreme Court upheld by a vote of six to three. The
dissenters found the discrimination between male and female owners to
be unconstitutional. Justice Frankfurter—who, we should remember, had
been deeply involved in earlier litigation involving women's employment
—found the case as simple of solution as had the court below.

His opinion is less than three pages long. He indicates approval of the
lower court's resolution of the issue of the distinction between bartenders
and waitresses, and does not elaborate on this point. He refers jocosely to
the "historic calling" of "the alewife, sprightly and ribald, [met] in Shake-
speare," and speaks of "barmaids," a term found most often in dirty jokes
and bawdy songs. He generally exhibits the capacity for amusement for
which he was noted. But quotation from the serious portions of his opinion will display the quality of the reasoning which this brilliant jurist
brought to this problem.

Beguiling as the subject is, it need not detain us long. To
ask whether the Equal Protection Clause of the Fourteenth
Amendment barred Michigan from making the classification
the State has made between wives and daughters of owners
of liquor places and wives and daughters of non-owners, is

one of those rare instances where to state a question is in effect to answer it. . . .

The Fourteenth Amendment did not tear history up by
the roots, and the regulation of the liquor traffic is one of
the oldest and most untrammeled of legislative powers. Michigan could, beyond question, forbid all women from working behind a bar. This is so despite the vast changes in the
social and legal position of women. . . . The Constitution
does not require legislatures to reflect sociological insight, or
shifting social standards, any more than it requires them to
keep abreast of the latest scientific standards. . . . Since bartending by women may, in the allowable legislative judgment,
give rise to moral and social problems against which it may
devise protective measures, the legislature need not go to the
full length of prohibition if it believes that as to a defined
group of females otner factors are operating which either
eliminate or reduce the moral and social problems otherwise
calling for prohibition. Michigan evidently believes that the
oversight assured through ownership of a bar by a barmaid's
husband or father minimizes hazards that may confront a
barmaid without such protecting oversight. This Court is certainly not in a position to gainsay such belief by the Michigan
legislature. If it is entertainable, as we think it is, Michigan
has not violated its duty to give equal protection of the laws.
We cannot cross-examine either actually or argumentatively
the mind of Michigan legislators nor question their motives.
Since the line they have drawn is not without a basis in reason, we cannot give ear to the suggestion that the real impulse behind this legislation was an unchivalrous desire of
male bartenders to try to monopolize the calling.[35]

The Court indicates that it considers the issue of sex discrimination
closed, but not, apparently, so much because precedents have determined
that sex is always a permissible basis for classification as because the entire
issue of economic regulation is closed. It does not cite a single authority
for its statement that "Michigan could forbid all women from working
behind a bar," but quickly moves on to the question of the exemptions.
A glance at the cases cited in the majority opinion indicates that the

Court regarded this case as a successor not of the *Muller* line of decisions, but of those involving economic due process and equal protection in a broader sense.[36]

Frankfurter emphasizes a very recent precedent, *Kotch v. Board of River Pilot Examiners.*[37] Here, eighteen months before, the Court had sustained a Louisiana statute requiring an apprenticeship program for river pilots against a charge that the law permitted arbitrary discrimination by giving incumbent pilots unfettered discretion to choose apprentices. The evidence presented in favor of this law was as skimpy as that in *Goesaert,* but Justice Black, writing for the majority, used language reminiscent of the lower court's opinion in the Michigan case: "We can only assume that the Louisiana legislature weighed the obvious possibility of evil against whatever useful function a closely knit pilotage system may serve," and "the benefits to morale and esprit de corps which family and neighborly tradition might contribute . . . might have prompted the legislature."[38] But nowhere does the state attempt to tell the Court how it reached these conclusions.

The tone of *Goesaert v. Cleary* is offensive, to be sure, but its reasoning is no worse than that employed in *Kotch* and similar cases.[39] But the relative length of *Goesaert* to that of these opinions, and the apparent amount of intellectual effort that went into each, indicates that the Court took the claims of river pilots, advertisers, and opticians more seriously than those of female bartenders. This whole line of cases raises serious questions about the appropriate role of the courts in reviewing economic regulation.

Either of two possible changes in rules of constitutional interpretation might permit different results in these cases. First, courts might grant freedom of contract and other economic rights the status of fundamental rights, thus assigning them to the higher level of liberty. Alternatively, they might preserve the secondary status these rights now have, but toughen the test of reasonableness that restraints on these rights must satisfy. The first step would, in my view, be unwise, both because it might undermine much necessary regulation[40] and because it is not defensible as constitutional interpretation. That property rights and freedom of contract were highly regarded by the framers is beyond doubt, but these rights are neither guaranteed by the Constitution nor readily inferable from rights contained therein. The second possible step, however, seems to me to be desirable; it would permit the protection of much liberty without jeopardizing general governmental power.

Certainly, no one wants to return to *Lochner*. The state and federal governments must be allowed wide latitude in regulating labor and business, and courts should be reluctant to substitute their own judgments on these issues for that of officials who are better informed and whose duty it is to cope with economic problems. But, while judges are expected to recognize that the rightness of public policy is not their concern, it seems to me that the quality of the reasoning involved is quite properly their concern. Reasoned, principled judgments are precisely what we rely on the courts for in a system which includes judicial review. Surely it is a part of the courts' job to point out to a state when necessary that its conclusions, in the form of challenged laws, do not follow, as a matter of reason and logic, from the evidence it presents in their favor. The relevant courts could properly have done this in *Schweinler* and *Radice,* as my discussion suggested, and surely any of the courts which heard the case could have performed a similar task in *Goesaert,* considering the character of the evidence presented by the state there.

An argument similar to this has been advanced by Gerald Gunther in his foreword to the *Harvard Law Review*'s evaluation of the Supreme Court's 1971 term.[41] Professor Gunther approves of the "emerging model of modest intervention" which he identifies. I will have more to say later about the Court's appropriate role in reviewing legislative ends, but I find Gunther's suggestion that the Court should be willing to judge the rationality of the connection between announced ends and chosen means entirely compatible and neatly in tune with my own position.

Reluctance to substitute judicial for legislative opinion need not result in the automatic affirmance of all economic policies. Even if the state is abridging no fundamental right, it is restricting freedom and injuring some people, and it ought not to exercise such power lightly. Surely it would not impose an intolerable burden upon governments to ask that their attorneys include in the briefs a discussion of the history of a disputed law. (Suppose a woman bartender had been murdered by a drunken patron in Michigan during the 1940s. If the Supreme Court had been told that, would it not have lent credence to the state's contention? This did not happen, but it would be a useful example.) Such a defense would not require a Brandeis-style brief, but it should permit the use of simple past and present tenses, and the indicative rather than the subjunctive mood.

If legislators are in the habit of enacting laws without the superior information that we assume them to have, without having any clear idea of what they are doing, the courts and the public should, perhaps, begin finding out, and maybe such laws do not deserve the presumption of constitutionality. The laws invalidated in the notorious due process cases— *Lochner, Adkins,* and the like—could have survived efforts to demonstrate their reasonableness if freedom of contract had had only the status it has now. But we cannot readily tell whether the laws tested in *Goesaert, Kotch, Railway Express Agency v. New York,*[42] and *Williamson v. Lee Optical Co.*[43] could, since they never had to.

If the Court had undertaken any independent review of the Michigan law, it would have had to examine three questions: the validity of the denial of employment opportunities on the basis of sex, the reasonableness of the exemption for the wives and daughters of male owners, and the reasonableness of the distinction between bartenders and waitresses. These questions still might not have detained the Court long. It might have resolved them by citing the *Muller* successors, some of which, like *Miller, Bosley,* and *Radice,* involve discriminations among differently situated women.

If the Court had decided to ask whether this particular law was a valid exercise of police power, it would have had to inquire as to whether the state could show that sufficient dangers to safety and morality existed to make the prohibition of female bartenders advisable; whether there was much evidence that even absent male owners of liquor establishments could protect their female relatives from such dangers; whether the maintenance of the integrity of the family as an economic unit justified permitting male, but not female, owners to employ their daughters;[44] and whether it was so reasonable to conclude that the controllers of the liquor supply would be in greater danger from inebriated (and, therefore, by definition unreasonable) patrons than servers of prepared drinks.

The bars of the 1940s were not, after all, the saloons of the Wild West, those scenes of frequent brawls and shootouts. Indeed, some of the evidence in the brief suggests, and it is entirely plausible to conclude, that bars are less violent places in recent years precisely because women patronize and work in them. And most people have long ago discarded the notion that "morality" requires the separation of the sexes in social contexts (a point not argued by the state, anyway). Even if women bartenders were in some danger from drunks, an argument could be made similar to that regarding night work thirty years earlier: the choice of occupation was voluntary (except, quite possibly, for the very women exempted from the prohibition). Some women are stronger than most men, or are trained in self-defense, and are therefore able to protect themselves, and their entering the bartending trade would not force weaker women into it. Virtually no evidence is presented here either about the nature and the gravity of the evil the state is trying to prevent, or the need for the restriction in order to prevent it. Furthermore, the evidence presented by the Goesaerts indicates that the law represents a significant curtailment of individual freedom which existed in fact, not just on paper.

To accept the state's justification for this law requires reasoning so convoluted as to verge on nonsense. It would go something like this: "Women must be protected from assaults by drunks. Therefore, we must forbid them to tend bar. But they may safely serve as waitresses, even though waitresses get closer to patrons, with no intervening structure, because serving liquor is not as dangerous as controlling the supply. But not all women bartenders are equally endangered by drunks. Male owners of bars (but not male employees) will be able to protect their wives and daughters (but not other female employees) from injury, simply by posing an implicit threat to potential troublemakers. Even if the male owner is never on the premises, the tone of the establishment will be affected by the fact of his existence, whether known to the patrons or not." Surely a law which requires that kind of reasoning to justify it should be regarded with some skepticism.

If we "give ear to the suggestion that the real impulse behind this legislation was an unchivalrous desire of male bartenders to try to monopolize the calling,"[45] we can construct another line of reasoning: "In order to allow male bartenders a monopoly, we must deny this occupation to females. Since men have little desire for waiters' jobs—which are less skilled and lower paid—there is no need to keep women from this work. But prohibiting all women from tending bar would work hardship on the owners of liquor establishments who could otherwise employ their wives (whom they are not legally obligated to pay) or daughters. Therefore, we will exempt these women." Nice, neat, and logical. Even if one agrees that questions of motive are beyond judicial reach, judges can ask questions about actual or potential effect.

But if the Court had found the former line of reasoning implausible, it would not have been obliged to argue that the latter explanation actually was that which had convinced the legislators of Michigan. And if it had felt itself obliged to find an alternative justification for the law, and had adopted the one I have advanced, its troubles would not have been over.

In discussing another economic equal protection case, Alexander Bickel has raised an analogous question. A New York City ordinance prohibited the carrying of advertising for hire on the sides of vehicles, but made an exception for owners of trucks who advertised their own wares on their vehicles, and did not reach nonvehicular displays such as those in Times Square. The Railway Express Agency, which has for years sold space on its trucks for advertising, was fined for violating this ordinance, and attacked its discriminations as arbitrary. The Supreme Court upheld the city, insisting that the distinctions were reasonably related to the ordinance's alleged purpose of improving traffic safety: "The local authorities may well have concluded [the subjunctive again] that those who advertise their own wares on their trucks do not present the same traffic problem in view of the nature or extent of the advertising which they use."[46]

Bickel comments:

> . . . if the sole purpose of the New York ordinance was traffic safety, then it is hard to defend the rationality of the classifications. The legislative purpose, however, may have been not merely to regulate traffic and protect the public, but also to discriminate. Two policies may have been served in tandem, one of them being to discriminate—that is, to foster . . . owner operation of trucks, and certain commercial activity around Times Square. These are surely not capricious ends; they involve choices in the ordering of social activity, made along lines of significant differences. Yet to say these ends are not immaterial is to leave open the question of whether they are good. It is not irrational either, in the present state of our society, to take account of the differences between black and white, or Jew and Catholic. We are prepared to lay it down as to the latter that it is bad and impermissible to favor the one over the other. For the rest, where a discrimination has no rational relation to the stated purpose of governmental action, we dispose of it on that ground. But since the purpose may be to discriminate, we must face the question, as a matter of principle, whether that purpose is allowable, for it is in itself not irrational.[47]

The import of these remarks for *Goesaert* is clear. If the Michigan liquor law is examined in the way Bickel wanted to scrutinize the New York traffic ordinance, one important question is this: Is discrimination on the basis of sex, for the purpose not of the protection of women but of the preferential treatment of men, constitutionally permissible? It is not prohibited in the Constitution, any more than is discrimination in favor of owner-operate trucks. Could discriminatory laws stand on showing of a reasonable relation ship to the preferential treatment of men? The first question is of course one of the crucial problems of this study and I shall devote considerable space to trying to resolve it. What must be recognized here—and what the courts have not recognized—is that it is a very different question from that of the permissibility of protective legislation. In laws of the former type, the question becomes not whether the restriction is necessary or advisable in the interests of women, but whether the interests of women are outweighed by those of men; the second, not the first, of the crucial questions I identified in the introduction to this book. By refusing to entertain the possibility that sexual discrimination in employment might restrict women as well as protect them, and acquiescing so meekly in all economic cases, the Court opened the way for public policies which curtail women's opportunities in the interests of men, and permitted the two questions to be confused with each other.

The passage just quoted from Bickel also indicates the limits of the rationality-scrutiny approach described by Gunther in achieving sexual equality under the Constitution. If discrimination on the basis of sex is seen as a legitimate goal—and nothing in the Constitution precludes that possibility, except with respect to voting—then policies rationally related to this goal can survive.

Municipal ordinances similar to the Michigan law were sustained by the supreme courts of Illinois in 1953,[48] New Jersey in 1956,[49] and Pennsylvania in 1963.[50] Michigan's supreme court sustained a revised version of that law, now exempting the daughters of female owners, too, in 1953.[51] Each of these decisions was very short indeed, citing *Goesaert* (but not *Muller* or any other case) as controlling authority and employing a few more "may haves." The Pennsylvania court did suggest that both the protection of women and the preservation of morality might have justified the law, refusing to choose between these principles.[52]

Goesaert was also relied upon in a series of cryptic decisions upholding so-called "B girl" ordinances, which typically prohibited female employees in bars from standing, sitting, or drinking at bars or mingling with customers.[53] None of these decisions shed any light on why standing at a bar to drink was any more dangerous than standing there to pick up ordered drinks, or why morality (which, on the face of it, appears to be the primary consideration behind these regulations) demands the restriction of only one sex. Nor was any justification offered for citing a decision which appeared, to the intermediate court at least, to rely on the conclusion that the law was necessary for the purposes of protection, as valid precedent for sustaining laws which appeared to be based on considerations of morality. But then the "B girl" cases did not discuss the rationale behind these laws at all. The prevailing interpretation of *Goesaert* after 1948 seemed to be that any legislature could restrict women's activity in such establishments for any reason at all, a reading given support by the Frankfurter opinion.

STATE v. HUNTER: *MALE INSECURITY WRESTLES WITH FEMALE COMPETITION*

State v. Hunter, following after *Goesaert v. Cleary,* provides ample reinforcement for that version of Murphy's Law which states that however bad things are, they can get worse, and usually do. The Oregon supreme court, that old defender of protective legislation, did not—unfortunately—flinch from the question of whether discrimination is allowable. That state had a law which prohibited persons "not of the male sex" from participating in, or being licensed to participate in, any wrestling competition or exhibition. A woman named Jerry Hunter did participate in such a competition in Clackamas County, Oregon, on October 25, 1955. She claimed that the law deprived her of equal protection of the laws, and, predictably, she lost (the case, that is; there is no record of how she fared in the match). The court's unanimous opinion is worth quoting at length:

> In addition to the protection of the public health, morals, safety, and welfare, what other considerations might have entered the legislative mind in enacting the statute in question? We believe we are justified in taking judicial notice of the fact that the membership of the legislative assembly which enacted this statute was predominantly masculine. [The membership of the Oregon Supreme Court in 1956 was exclusively masculine.] That fact is . . . important in determining what the legislature might have had in mind with respect to this

particular statute, in addition to its concern for the public weal. It seems to us that its purpose, although somewhat selfish in nature, stands out like a sore thumb. Obviously it is intended that there should be at least one area on the sea of life reserved for man that would be impregnable to the assault of woman. It had watched her emerge from long tresses and demure ways to bobbed hair and almost complete sophistication; from a creature needing and depending upon the protection and chivalry of man to one asserting complete independence. She had already invaded practically every activity formerly considered suitable and appropriate for men only. In the field of sports she had taken up, among other games, baseball, basketball, golf, bowling, hockey, long distance swimming, and racing, in all of which she had become more or less proficient, and in some had excelled. In the business and industrial fields as an employee or as an executive, in the professions, in politics as well as in almost every other line, she had matched her wits and prowess with those of mere man, and, we are forced to concede, in many instances had outdone him. In these circumstances, is it any wonder that the legislative assembly took advantage of the police power of the state in its decision to halt this ever-increasing feminine encroachment upon what for ages had been considered strictly as manly arts and privileges? Was the Act an unjust and unconstitutional discrimination against women? Have her civil or political rights been unconstitutionally denied her? Under the circumstances, we think not.[54]

Muller and *Bunting* are then cited as "authorities that might shed some light on this power."[55]

That is a familiar argument, one that most feminists have heard before. This argument, if taken seriously, can bring out the man-hater in the least rancorous of feminists: the insistence of poor, insecure little boys that they need to build up their shaky egos by curtailing women's freedom. How ironic it is that women's weaknesses are used as grounds for denying them freedom, and men's weaknesses are also used as grounds for denying women freedom. And how contemptuous a view of their own sex is that expressed by men who make this argument.

The position is infuriating enough when confined to its usual habitats. It becomes a far more serious matter when legislators restrict women to shore up the self-esteem of male citizens like themselves, and graver yet when the Constitution of the United States is invoked to sanction this kind of protection.

Whatever the motives which impel men to impose restrictions on women—and, in all fairness to the Oregon legislature, we do not know whether the court has interpreted its action correctly—the significance of the case is that the restriction of women for the benefit of men has been accepted as constitutionally legitimate. A court has gone so far as to say that a group which is virtually unrepresented in public office may be curtailed by one which has a near-monopoly of public office, acting for its own benefit. This court has cited as authority for its conclusion a case which sustained the power of the government to curtail the freedom of powerful groups within society for the benefit of a relatively powerless group. A decision which ratified governmental action for the noblest of purposes is now invoked to justify governmental action for the meanest of purposes.

But should the opinion be taken seriously? Is the judge perhaps writing with his tongue in his cheek? There is no pressing reason to believe that he is. Although he is clearly trying for a light touch—rather laboriously, I must say—his humor does not appear to be any more central to his point than was Frankfurter's in *Goesaert*. However ludicrous this argument may seem, it is frequently made in all seriousness; George Gilder's book, *Sexual Suicide,* [56] is an example. Considering that the Oregon court did, after all, uphold the law, facetious treatment of the issues would indicate dereliction in its duties, as well as a distressing tendency to find the claims of women amusing. But there is little basis for concluding that the opinion is not straightforward, or for softening my criticism on the grounds that the judges really did not mean what they said.

Hunter is, to be sure, an isolated case, but that may be mere accident. If more groups had chosen to enlist the power of state legislatures to keep women out of predominantly male occupations, and more women had challenged these laws in court, might there have been more laws and decisions like this? I think so, for two reasons. First, the courts which decided the early cases had engaged in judicial overkill. By emphasizing the physical and quasi-permanent, rather than the social and situation-bound, differences between the sexes as justifications for differential labor legislation, the judges had not only resolved immediate cases, but had given an indelible stamp of approval to any future legislation, which could be shown to have some plausible relation to these differences. The emphasis on sexual differences was so strong that an equally crucial difference—that between protection and restriction—was overlooked. Secondly, the post-1937 abandonment of judicial review in economic cases had given the legislatures almost unfettered power in regulating employment. The combination of these two factors, both of which I have already discussed, produced the judicial acquiescence in legally sanctioned sex discrimination which one scholar described as "an almost josephic aversion to women."[57] The cumulative weight of all these precedents created a deadlock from which there seemed no way out, short of a constitutional amendment.

But in these same years, the judicial system was forced to grapple with an ever-increasing number of due process and equal protection cases of a very different kind, cases which confronted them again and again with Bickel's question. Thanks mainly, at first, to the efforts of the NAACP, claims of racial discrimination—for which the Fourteenth Amendment had beyond doubt been principally intended—were brought before the courts, which began to recognize, or re-recognize, race as an illegitimate basis for legal classification. Gradually, other individuals and groups, perhaps encouraged by this development, began challenging other kinds of classifications, such as ethnicity, income, and circumstances of birth, as vulnerable under the principles which made racial discrimination illegitimate. In responding to these claims, the courts have slowly developed a new constitutional doctrine, which has begun to provide a basis for attacking sex discrimination.

SUSPECT CLASSIFICATION: SAIL'ER INN AND FRONTIERO

The Fourteenth Amendment provides that "no state shall . . . deny to any person within its jurisdiction the equal protection of the laws." The framers of this amendment agreed that this clause forbade legal discrimination on account of race, color, or former slave status, toward black residents of the country—but they agreed on very little else which the provision might mean. They could not even reach a consensus on its application to the other racial problem which the United States then had: prejudice against Chinese and Japanese immigrants.[58]

The few members of the Thirty-ninth Congress who discussed these questions were sure that the post-Civil War amendments and statutes did *not* prohibit discrimination on the basis of either sex or age.[59] However, these two issues were never explored at length, and, as the editor of these debates has pointed out, the arguments in defense of sex discrimination were not always convincing.[60] These discussions of the issue are, at best, inconclusive.

The issues raised by the Equal Protection Clause were even more confused by the courts, which could not agree on what constituted racial discrimination,[61] or state as opposed to private action,[62] but which displayed great eagerness to declare that the clause prohibited all forms of "arbitrary" discrimination, a term to which, as I have said,[63] they gave wide latitude in striking down efforts to regulate industry. William Crosskey, in a different context, once described the Supreme Court's performance by a paraphrase of the Episcopal Book of Common Prayer which is apposite here: "They have left undone those things which they ought to have done, and they have done the things they ought not to have done."[64]

But the original errors have been rectified. As no one who can read can help knowing, the Supreme Court has not only stopped invalidating economic legislation under the Fourteenth Amendment, but has used it to strike down racial discrimination, not only against blacks but against Orientals[65] and Mexican-Americans.[66] The Court also continued, though infrequently, to invalidate other classifications it considered arbitrary or capricious.[67]

A sort of two-tiered theory of equal protection emerged, analogous to that of due process. Racial classifications have been assigned to the second, higher tier; they can be sustained only "upon showing a subordinating state interest which is compelling."[68] In practice, this has meant that, with one deplorable exception,[69] racial classifications cannot stand at all. Most other classifications belong on a lower tier, and need only to answer the more lenient criteria of reasonableness, intelligibility, and compliance with constitutional guarantees.

But in recent years the courts have added classifications other than racial ones to the higher tier as "inherently suspect." If the intentions of the authors of a constitutional provision were the only guide to its meaning, this interpretation would be hard to defend. But the meanings of the words used in the constitutional text, and the search for "fundamental propositions rooted in history to which widespread acceptance may be attributed,"[70] also form a necessary part of constitutional interpretation, and they can support the concept of suspect classification.

Alienage has achieved such a status, for example. *Takahishi v. Fish and Game Commission*[71] not only affirmed the inclusion of Orientals in the protection against racial discrimination but declared that "the power of a state to apply its laws exclusively to its alien inhabitants as a class is confined within narrow limits."[72] As recently as 1971, *Graham v. Richardson*,[73] striking down Arizona and Pennsylvania laws denying welfare benefits to aliens, stated that "classifications based on alienage, like those based on lineage and race, are inherently suspect and subject to close judicial scrutiny."[74] This conclusion was affirmed in *In re Griffiths*,[75] which invalidated a Connecticut law excluding aliens from admission to the bar. For this study it is perhaps not irrelevant to note that the alien involved was a woman resident married to a United States citizen. But the reasoning of some of these decisions seems rather dubious; one wonders whether, for example, "close judicial scrutiny" would be required for laws denying the franchise to aliens.

Economic status as a basis for classification has been viewed most warily by the Supreme Court. As early as 1946, in *Thiel v. Southern Pacific Co.*,[76] it reversed a verdict in a civil suit because the jury panel had intentionally and systematically excluded people who worked for a daily wage. "Were we to sanction an exclusion of this nature," the opinion declared, "we would encourage whatever desires those responsible for the selection of jury panels may have to discriminate against persons of low economic or social status."[77] Ten years later, an Illinois law which forced defendants in noncapital criminal cases to pay for copies of their own transcripts on appeal was invalidated in *Griffin v. Illinois* on the grounds that "in criminal trials a State can no more discriminate on account of poverty than on account of religion, race, or color."[78] This treatment of economic status has obviously been buttressed by the long series of cases involving the right to counsel for poor defendants.[79]

However, not all members of the present Supreme Court agree on this point. Justice Powell, writing for the majority in *San Antonio Independent School District v. Rodriguez*, insisted that the Court has never held economic status to be a suspect classification,[80] arguing that *Griffin* and similar cases established not the suspect nature of the category but the primacy of procedural rights in criminal trials. But there seems to be considerable disagreement on this point among Powell's colleagues.[81] His reading of *Griffin* is defensible, but I think he has misinterpreted the prevailing doctrine here.

Several Supreme Court decisions can be interpreted as adding other classifications to the list. In a concurring opinion in a 1971 case, Justice Douglas reviews a few of them.[82] The 1942 decision which invalidated Oklahoma's criminal sterilization law because of its "arbitrary" exemption for embezzlers[83] suggests that social class and caste (terms which Douglas appears to consider synonymous) are suspect. He interprets *Sherbert v. Verner,*[84] which upheld a Seventh Day Adventist's right to refuse Saturday work, as giving a similar status to religious discrimination. That religion is a suspect classification can hardly be doubted, but the Establishment and the Free Exercise Clauses of the First Amendment, as well as the provision in Article VI, Section 3, that religious tests for public office are forbidden, are at least as important as any one case in achieving this result. Two 1968 cases which Douglas does not mention (rather surprisingly, since he himself wrote for the Court) can be read as establishing the marital status of one's parents at birth as a suspect classification. In *Levy v. Louisiana*[85] and *Glona v. American Guarantee and Liability Insurance Co.,*[86] invalidating laws restricting the right to sue for wrongful death of a parent to "legitimate" children, the majority seems to be on the verge of making such a stipulation, but does not do so explicitly.

To summarize, race, ethnicity, alienage, and religion have been declared suspect classifications, and therefore subject to careful judicial scrutiny. Economic status, social class, and caste are probably, and circumstances of birth possibly, included with these. This does not mean that any other distinction between human beings has been considered an acceptable basis for any and all kinds of discrimination which law could impose. No distinction (even sex) has achieved universal, irrevocable validity. In each instance, the reasonableness of the connection between the distinction and the particular kind of discrimination must be shown, not assumed. The difference between suspect and non-suspect classifications is not that the former never justify discrimination and the latter always do, but that the former are presumed invalid (though not irrefutably), whereas no presumption, positive or negative, attaches to the latter.

What do suspect bases for discrimination have in common? We may learn more about the nature of suspect classification by examining and contrasting distinctions which we consider legitimate bases for discrimination. Perhaps the most obvious one is age. Although the law cannot deprive children of certain fundamental rights,[87] it may prevent them from doing things adults do (e.g., voting, working, signing contracts), and oblige them to do things adults do not have to do (e.g., go to school). The law may also restrict the freedom of people over a certain age (e.g., oblige them to pass drivers' tests more frequently than others), or grant them special privileges (e.g., Medicare, additional tax exemptions). We may argue whether a specific discrimination is just or unjust—a controversy seems to be brewing over compulsory school attendance, for instance[88]—but no one seriously questions the legitimacy of any and every distinction based on age.

We agree that age is a valid basis for some classifications partly because we observe a relationship between age and capacity. Children usually do not have good business sense or the ability to make sophisticated moral judgments, so we do not let them engage in business or make them criminally responsible. But some children do have good business sense, and the restriction still applies to them. (At least, as far as we can tell, most children do not have these qualities. I would hate to make the common error of underestimating the intelligence of children.) Despite the fact that not all members of the class share the observed disabilities, we accept the classification because most of them do, and because making individual determinations in each case would be difficult, if not impossible.

Another basis for special treatment which we consider reasonable is disability. We deny drivers' licenses to people with severe visual or motor impairment, for instance. We also have compensatory programs such as rehabilitation services for the mentally and physically handicapped, and additional tax exemptions for the blind. But this kind of distinction can be misleading, because it is not really a class distinction. First, to say that the handicapped compose a class is to create a category so unwieldy as to be unmanageable; there are too many varieties of disability. Second —whatever society assumes—the law does not conclude on the basis of observable disability that a person is subject to, or qualifies for, special treatment. Instead, the determination of capacity is made in each individual case. The license examiner does not assume that a person in a wheelchair, or one with a telescopic lens attached to his or her spectacles, cannot qualify for a driver's license; motor ability and vision are tested before that determination is made. In the same way, disability must be proved before a person becomes eligible for rehabilitation services or tax exemptions.

Why does the state assume a burden here which it need not accept in cases of age? Understandably, some of the reasons are financial; no government wants to provide expensive services unless they are necessary. But these considerations alone do not explain the hesitancy. The crucial difference between age and disability is that the former characteristic is temporary, and the latter, usually, is permanent. (If not, a person can be "retested" and the restrictions lifted, or the benefits removed.) Children grow up, and we reach the other end of life only after many years, if at all. Restrictions based on age are tolerable partly because they are temporary, but restrictions based on disability must be endured for a lifetime. It is no light matter to impose them, and they are imposed only to prevent harm to the individual and to others. But these non-classifications are also non-suspect.

What characteristics do suspect classifications share which distinguish them from age and disability? One of these classifications—religion—really does not belong conceptually with the others; it achieves its status through a prevenient political decision that it is not the government's business. The other classifications share several characteristics, though not all of them have all of these traits.

First, they are categories into which the individual is usually locked, by factors beyond his or her control. Second, they are permanent or persistent (with the exception of alienage, whose inclusion I find unpersuasive, as I have stated). An individual cannot change his or her race or ethnic background. Changing social class or economic status is possible, but extremely difficult. To impose discriminations on the basis of characteristics an individual does not control permanently relegates her to a position which she cannot change. Such treatments impose heavy burdens, so heavy that they should not be imposed without overpowering evidence that they are needed.

A discussion of this concept from one of the relevant decisions well describes the character of suspect classifications. *Sail'er Inn, Inc. v. Kirby*[89] is a landmark case in the area of women's rights, for, in considering yet another law excluding women from bartending, the California Supreme Court addressed itself to the question of whether sex, too, was a suspect classification, and answered it in the affirmative. In a case decided two years later, four members of the U.S. Supreme Court agreed, quoting almost verbatim from *Sail'er Inn*.[90] The unanimous opinion of the California court declared:

> Sex, like race and lineage, is an immutable trait, a status into which the class members are locked by the accident of birth.

What differentiates sex from nonsuspect statuses, such as intelligence or physical disability, and aligns it with the recognized suspect classifications is that the characteristic frequently bears no relation to ability to perform or contribute to society. The result is that the whole class is relegated to an inferior legal status without regard to the capabilities or characteristics of its members. Where the relation between characteristic and evil to be prevented is so tenuous, courts must look closely at classifications based on that characteristic lest outdated social stereotypes result in invidious laws or practices.[91]

The two factors which most of the suspect classifications have in common, then, are, first, that they are categories into which people are inadvertently and permanently locked (unlike age, but like disability) and, secondly, that there is little or no relation between the classification and individual competence (like age, but unlike disability). Whether this relationship is indeed lacking in some of these statuses is, of course, open to debate. No one needs to be reminded of recent efforts to establish the existence of a causal relationship between heredity and intelligence. Less well known is the casual acceptance by another scholar as recently as 1968 of "the assumption that a correlation exists between wealth and talent."[92] However, the validity of these conclusions is extremely dubious, and even if they were someday proved correct by new evidence, the statement of the *Sail'er Inn* court that the relationship is frequently lacking would still hold. With respect to the relationship between sex and most legally imposed discriminations, the generalization as stated is obviously true, but that does not resolve the issue.

Clearly, sex fulfills the first set of conditions. The tough questions arise when we try to decide whether it fulfills the second. *Muller v. Oregon* concluded that a relationship between sex and capacity existed in enough cases to justify the restriction on working hours.

But the reasoning in *Muller* and its successors was as faulty as the laws were overinclusive. The real justification for special labor legislation lay not in women's physical, but their socioeconomic, weaknesses. The history of minimum-wage legislation illustrates this point. These factors justified only some, not all, restrictions on women; it is difficult to see how they justified denial of bar admission in 1869, and, as we have seen, they provided very weak justification for the prohibition of night work in 1915 and 1924.

Hours and wage legislation was not adopted because women needed more rest or money than men did, but because, in fact, women worked longer hours than men, and did not earn enough money. (No serious effort was ever made to raise their incomes to the level of men's.) These situations did not justify the broad and discriminatory laws which were actually passed, and, in the case of hours limitations, sustained. The desired results could have been reached by laws which did not mention sex, much as it is possible to prohibit rape or grant maternity leaves without mentioning sex. The strongest possible defense of the *Muller* line of cases is that, given women's economic vulnerability and the box the courts had painted themselves into by the beginning of the twentieth century, the results benefitted working women more than any other likely result would have. But that is not a very strong defense.

As I have suggested, the emphasis on physical differences, combined with the changes in standards of constitutional interpretations over the years, virtually froze these laws into a legitimate place, even as their effects changed from protective to restrictive. Defending Justice Brewer and his colleagues by pointing out that they did not have the advantage of 1976's hindsight into the temporary character of 1908's conditions will not work. A rereading of the opinion will reveal that Brewer anticipated social change, but nevertheless chose to base his conclusion on physical (and assumed psychological) differences. The only changes he did not anticipate were medical advances.

As early as 1915, the *Muller* doctrine was used to uphold a law which was supported by evidence of dubious relevance and conclusions of questionable validity about the relationship between sexual differences and the particular restriction. By the time the Supreme Court sustained this law nine years later, the arguments in its favor were even less convincing. And with *Goesaert* and *Hunter,* the relationship between the classification, individual characteristics, and legitimate governmental purposes had become so tenuous as to be nonexistent. The *Sail'er Inn* opinion speaks to these points:

> . . . Laws which disable women from full participation in the political, business and economic areas are often characterized as "protective" or beneficial. These same laws applied to racial

or ethnic minorities would be recognized as invidious or impermissible. The pedestal upon which women have been placed had all too often, upon closer inspection, been revealed as a cage.[93]

Which set of judges is right? Is sex a permissible classification for all discriminatory purposes, or should it be suspect for any purpose? Or is the truth somewhere in between these two positions?

Litigation under federal antidiscrimination laws in the 1960s and 1970s has confronted judges again and again with the issue of sex-based classification, whether direct or indirect. The constraints imposed by clear legislative mandates for sexual equality have forced these judges to approach these problems in new ways, and the resulting interpretations have provided insights which are valuable in attempting to answer the questions I posed. I have devoted the next chapter to an analysis of this group of cases.

NOTES

1. E.g., Goesaert v. Cleary, 74 F Supp. 745 (E.D. Mich. 1947), Guill v. Hoboken, 127 N.J. 574 (1956), prohibiting women bartenders; State v. Hunter, 208 Ore. 252, 300 P. 2d 455 (1956), prohibiting women wrestlers; Heaton v. Bristol, 317 S.W. 2d 86 (Tex. Civ. App. 1957) and Allred v. Heaton, 336 S.W. 2d 251 (Tex. Civ. App. 1960), sex segregation in state-supported colleges; Hoyt v. State, 119 So. 2d 691 (Sup. Ct. Fla. 1960) and State v. Hall, 187 So. 2d 861 (Sup. Ct. Miss. 1966), jury service; Clem v. Brown, 207 N.E. 398 (Ct. of Common Pleas of Ohio, Paulding Co., 1965), Krohn v. Richardson-Merrill, Inc., 406 S.W. 2d 166 (Sup. Ct. Tenn. 1966), Karczewski v. Baltimore and Ohio R.R., 274 F. Supp. 169 (N.D. Ill. 1967), and Miskunas v. Union Carbide Corp., 399 F. 2d 847 (7th Circ. 1968), consortium; U.S. ex rel. Robinson v. York, 281 F. Supp. 8 (E.D. Conn. 1968) and Commonwealth v. Daniel, 430 Pa. 642 (1968), prison sentences.

2. Cf., e.g., Goesaert v. Cleary, 74 F. Supp. 745, and Guill v. Hoboken, 127 N.J. 574, and Sail'er Inn, Inc. v. Kirby, 5 Cal. 3rd 1, 485 P. 2d 529 (1971); Krohn v. Richardson-Merrill, 406, S.W. 2nd 166, and Miskunas v. Union Carbide, and Clem v. Brown and Karczewski v. B & O; Heaton v. Bristol and Allred v. Heaton, and Kirstein v. University of Virginia, 309 F. Supp. 184 (E.D. Va., 1970).

3. Goesaert v. Cleary, 335 U.S. 464 (1948); Hoyt v. Florida, 368 U.S. 57 (1961); U.S. v. Yazell, 382 U.S. 341 (1966).

4. Heaton v. Bristol, *cert. den.* 359 U.S. 230 (1957); Allred v. Heaton, *cert. den.* 364 U.S. 517 (1960); Krohn v. Richardson-Merrill, *cert. den.* 386 U.S. 970 (1967); State v. Hall, appeal dismissed 385 U.S. 98 (1967); Miskunas v. Union Carbide Corp., *cert. den.* 393 U.S. 1066 (1968).

5. Kanowitz, *Women and the Law*, p. 154; Pauli Murray and Mary Eastwood,

"Jane Crow and the Law: Sex Discrimination and Title VII," *George Washington L. Rev.* 34 (December 1965):232-56.

6. Murray and Eastwood, "Jane Crow," p. 237, citing Commonwealth v. Welosky, 276 Mass. 398, *cert. den.* 284 U.S. 684 (1932), jury exclusion; People v. Case, 157 Mich. 98 (1908), and State v. Hunter, 208 Ore. 252, 300 P. 2d 455 (1956), licensing; Heaton v. Bristol 317 S.W. 2d 86 (1957) and Allred v. Heaton, 336 S.W. 2d 251 (1960), state-supported colleges.

7. See, e.g., Hoyt v. Florida, 368 U.S. 57 (1961); U.S. v. Yazell, 382 U.S. 341 (1966).

8. Sail'er Inn, Inc. v. Kirby, 5 Cal. 3rd 1, 485 P. 2d 529 (1971).

9. See, e.g., Robert McCloskey, "Economic Due Process and the Supreme Court"; Wallace Mendelson, "From Warren to Burger: The Rise and Decline of Substantive Equal Protection," *American Political Science Review* 66 (December 1972):1226-33.

10. See n. 2, supra; U.S. *ex rel.* Robinson v. York, 281 F. Supp. 8 (1968), and Commonwealth v. Daniel, 430 Pa. 632 (1968); cf., People *ex rel.* Rago v. Lipsky, 327 Ill. App. 63 (1945) and State *ex rel.* Krupa v. Green, 114 Ohio Appl. 497 (1961), right of woman to retain original surname after marriage.

11. See Ch. 5 infra.

12. See John D. Johnston, Jr., and Charles Knapp, "Sex Discrimination by Law: A Study in Judicial Perspective," *N.Y.U. L. Rev.* 46 (October 1971):675-747.

13. See notes 1 and 10 supra.

14. 404 U.S. 71 (1971).

15. *Ibid.,* pp. 76-77.

16. Frontiero v. Richardson, 411 U.S. 677 (1973).

17. Cleveland Board of Education v. La Fleur, 414 U.S. 632 (1974).

18. Taylor v. Louisiana, 419 U.S. 522 (1975).

19. Weinberger v. Wiesenfeld, 420 U.S. 636 (1975).

20. Philip B. Kurland, "The New Supreme Court," *John Marshall Journal* 7 (Fall 1973):10-11.

21. See, e.g., Forbush v. Wallace, 405 U.S. 970 (1972), refusing to review an Alabama law requiring married women to get driver's licenses in their husband's names; Geduldig v. Aiello, 417 U.S. 484 (1974), upholding the exclusion of pregnancy-related conditions from California's disability insurance program.

22. Kahn v. Shevin, 416 U.S. 351 (1974); Schlesinger v. Ballard, 419 U.S. 498 (1975).

23. See Judith A. Baer, "Sexual Equality and the Burger Court," prepared for delivery at the annual meeting of the American Political Science Association, San Francisco, Calif., September 2-5, 1975.

24. 45 U.S. Law Week 4031 (1976).

25. "In Search of Evolving Doctrine on a Changing Court: A Model for a Newer Equal Protection," *Harvard Law Review* 86 (November 1972):23.

26. For an argument along these lines, see Baer, "Sexual Equality," pp. 6-7, 9-10, 12-13.

27. Summary of the Fact of Knowledge Presented on Behalf of the People, pp. 409-22, People v. Charles Schweinler Press, 214 N.Y. 395, 108 N.E. 639 (1915).

28. Bird, *Born Female*, p. 33.

29. Note, "The Union Role—Good Faith Protection of Women or Self-Interested Protection of Men?" in Barbara Babcock et al., eds., *Sex Discrimination and the Law: Cases and Remedies* (Boston: Little, Brown and Co., 1975), pp. 277-78.

30. Brief for Appellees, pp. 7, 14, Goesaert v. Cleary, 335 U.S. 464 (1948).

31. Ibid., p. 27.

32. Ibid., pp. 23-28; 15-22.

33. Brief for Appellants, p. 23, Goesaert v. Cleary.

34. Goesaert v. Cleary, 74 F. Supp. 745, 749 (1947).

35. 335 U.S. 464, 465-68.

36. Roschen v. Ward, 279 U.S. 337 (1929); Tigner v. Texas, 310 U.S. 141 (1940); Carter v. Virginia, 321 U.S. 131 (1944).

37. 330 U.S. 552 (1947).

38. Ibid., p. 563.

39. See Railway Express Agency v. New York, 336 U.S. 106 (1949); Barsky v. Board of Regents, 347 U.S. 442 (1954); Williamson v. Lee Optical of Oklahoma, 348 U.S. 483 (1955).

40. McCloskey, "Economic Due Process."

41. "Newer Equal Protection," p. 23.

42. 336 U.S. 106 (1949).

43. 348 U.S. 483 (1955).

44. This argument is not made, but it is a possible one.

45. 335 U.S. 464, 468.

46. 336 U.S. 106, 110.

47. *The Least Dangerous Branch* (New York: Bobbs-Merrill Co., 1962), p. 225.

48. Henson v. Chicago, 415 Ill. 564.

49. Guill v. Hoboken 127 N.J. 574.

50. *In re* Kovalchuck, 202 Pa. Super. 389, 195 A. 2d 828.

51. Nephew v. Liquor Control Commission, 336 Mich. 120.

52. 195 A. 2d 828, 829.

53. Miami v. Kayfetz, 92 So. 2d 798 (Sup. Ct. of Fla., 1956); People v. King, 115 Cal. App. 2d Supp. 875 (1957); Milwaukee v. Piscuine, 18 Wis. 2d 599 (1963).

54. 300 P. 2d, 455, 457-58.

55. Ibid.

56. (New York: Quadrangle Books, 1973).

57. Robert J. Harris, *The Quest for Equality* (Baton Rouge.: Louisiana State University Press, 1960), p. 73.

58. Alfred Avins, ed., *The Reconstruction Amendments' Debates* (Richmond: Virginia Commission on Constitutional Government, 1967), pp. 223-25, 229, 460-63.

59. Ibid., pp. 157-60, 221, 231, 251, 299-300, 309-10, 354-55, 361-62.

60. Ibid., p. xv.

61. Plessy v. Ferguson, 163 U.S. 537 (1896).

62. Civil Rights Cases, 109 U.S. 3 (1883).

63. Supra, ch. 2.

64. *Politics and the Constitution* (Chicago: University of Chicago Press, 1953), p. 1161.

65. See, e.g., Oyama v. California, 332 U.S. 631 (1948); Takahashi v. Fish and Game Commission, 334 U.S. 410 (1948).

66. Hernandez v. Texas, 347 U.S. 475 (1954).

67. See, e.g., Skinner v. Oklahoma, 316 U.S. 535 (1942); Morey v. Doud, 354 U.S. 481 (1957).

68. Bates v. Little Rock, 361 U.S. 516, 524 (1958).

69. Hirobayashi v. United States, 320 U.S. 81 (1943); Korematsu v. United States, 323 U.S. 214 (1944), the first two Japanese Exclusion Cases.

70. Sweezy v. New Hampshire, 354 U.S. 234, 255, 266-67 (1957) (Frankfurter, J., concurring).

71. 334 U.S. 410 (1948).

72. Ibid., p. 420.

73. 403 U.S. 365 (1971).

74. Ibid., p. 372.

75. 413 U.S. 717 (1973).

76. 328 U.S. 217.

77. Ibid., pp. 223-24.

78. 351 U.S. 12, 17.

79. Gideon v. Wainwright, 372 U.S. 335 (1963); Escobedo v. Illinois, 378 U.S. 478 (1964); Miranda v. Arizona, 384 U.S. 436 (1966).

80. 411 U.S. 1 (1973).

81. Ibid., p. 59 (Stewart, J., concurring); p. 62 (Brennan, J., dissenting); pp. 70-137 (Marshall, J., dissenting); Boddie v. Connecticut, 401 U.S. 371 (1971).

82. Boddie v. Connecticut, 401 U.S. 371, 383-89 (1971).

83. Skinner v. Oklahoma, 316 U.S. 535 (1942).

84. 374 U.S. 398 (1963).

85. 391 U.S. 68.

86. 391 U.S. 73.

87. *In re* Gault, 387 U.S. 1 (1967).

88. See, e.g., Wisconsin v. Yoder, 406 U.S. 205 (1972).

89. 5 Cal. 3rd 1, 485 P. 2d 529 (1971).

90. Frontiero v. Richardson, 411 U.S. 677 (1973).

91. 485 P. 2d 529, 540-41.

92. Paul Eidelberg, *The Philosophy of the American Constitution* (New York: Free Press, 1968), pp. 155-56.

93. 485 P. 2d 529, 541.

5

THE PEDESTAL AND
THE CAGE: THE COURTS
AND EMPLOYMENT
DISCRIMINATION,
1964-1976

Women's rights was not a major concern of lawmakers in the 1960s. But in that decade Congress passed two laws which greatly benefit working women. The first was the Equal Pay Act of 1963, which was accompanied by a substantial legislative history and subjected to serious debate.[1] The second was Title VII of the Civil Rights Act of 1964. The inclusion of sex in a bill which originally banned employment discrimination because of race, color, religion, or national origin has frequently been described as a "joke." This description is inaccurate. It is true that Representive Howard Smith of Virginia, the author of the amendment, hoped to "[sink] the bill under gales of laughter"[2] and that a few legislators discussed the issue in a tone similar to that of Frankfurter in *Goesaert*, but the amendment survived because several women members of Congress refused to join the liberals in opposing it.[3] However, the provision is almost barren of legislative history, and what evidence there is does not suggest that it represented a firm collective commitment to sexual equality.

Whatever the intent of Congress, both laws, by empowering federal agencies to hear complaints and to interpret the statutes, provided weapons against sex discrimination, and, by giving complainants the right to sue, assured that the issues would reach the federal courts. Although the laws have by no means proven to be panaceas, in the hands of the agencies—the Wage and Hour Division of the Department of Labor for the Equal Pay Act and the new Equal Employment Opportunity Commission (EEOC) for Title VII—and the courts, they have been used to combat sex

discrimination and to extend employment opportunities for women with
some degree of success. This result was not a foregone conclusion, for
both laws contain serious weaknesses as weapons against discrimination.
The Equal Pay Act provides that no employer covered by it "shall discriminate . . . between employees on the basis of sex by paying wages to
employees . . . at a rate less than the rate at which he pays wages to employees of the opposite sex . . . for equal work on jobs the performance
of which requires equal skill, effort, and responsibility and which are performed under similar working conditions."[4] I have already pointed out
that men and women usually perform different jobs and that men usually
earn more for what they do than women for what they do. The Wage and
Hour Administration's Guidelines make it clear that the Act does not
permit inquiry into whether dissimilar jobs require equal skill, effort, and
responsibility:

> It is clear that Congress did not intend to apply the equal pay
> standard to jobs substantially differing in terms and conditions.
> Thus the question of whether a female bookkeeper should be
> paid as much as a male file clerk required to perform a substan-
> tially different job is outside the purview of the equal pay pro-
> visions. It is also clear that the equal pay standard is not to
> be applied where only men are employed in the establish-
> ment in one job and women are employed in a dissimilar
> job.[5]

Nevertheless, women were found to be working for less money than
men in the same jobs often enough that, between 1964 and 1973, the Labor Department found that workers were owed about 65.6 million dollars
under the Act.[6] The law has been effective because sex discrimination is
frequently so blatant.

Title VII's defects lie both in its substance and in its enforcement procedures. The Act contains an exception—discrimination is permitted when
sex, religion, or national origin (but never race) is a "bona fide occupational
qualification reasonably necessary to the normal operation of that particular business or enterprise"[7]—which virtually invites its nullification. But
as this chapter will show, both the EEOC and the courts have interpreted
this exception narrowly. Procedurally, "the act stated the admirable goal
of eliminating employment discrimination while providing absolutely no

viable means of doing so."[8] Until the Equal Employment Opportunity Act of 1972 empowered the EEOC to bring charges, only individuals (and the Attorney General, who rarely did so) could initiate complaints and bring suit. Antidiscrimination laws which depend on the victim for enforcement are inherently weak; most victims hesitate to initiate complaints, whether through ignorance of their legal rights, fear of reprisal, lack of funds to pay lawyers, pessimism, or whatever motivation.[9] But it only takes one victim to start an action, and there have been enough complaints to establish valuable precedents.

In the mid-1970s, sex discrimination in employment remains the rule, not the exception. There is no cause for complacency. Legislation has not cured the disease. But it has alleviated the symptoms.

The federal courts have played a significant part in the careers of these laws. Presented with mandates for sexual equality, the judges, with a few exceptions, have evinced neither great friendliness nor animosity toward this legislative purpose. Their performance in this area reinforces the argument I made in Chapter 4: that male chauvinism has not been the judges' primary motivation. If it had been, one would expect grudging interpretations of the provisions and lavish interpretations of the exceptions. Neither law has in fact been interpreted in this way. The courts have shown a willingness to follow Congress' lead—deference to the legislature, which so long harmed working women, now operated in their favor—and a lawyerlike demand for proof that exceptions apply to particular cases. On the other hand, the courts have not been eager to read more into the laws than Congress or the agencies put there. If judges are not demonstrably more sexist than the rest of society, neither are they more feminist. Where they have most grievously fallen short, I think, is in their occasional failure to perceive subtle, indirect sex discrimination. *General Electric v. Gilbert*[10] is the most glaring recent example of this.

This litigation directly touches protective labor legislation. I have remarked that protection of this type is inevitably also restriction. The question raised by Title VII is this: Do laws which prevent women from working under certain conditions conform to the federal law? Through extensive litigation, this question has been decisively answered in the negative. Viable protective labor legislation no longer exists in the United States. The Equal Pay Act confronts these laws less directly, but litigation under it has uncovered instances where wage discrimination originally resulted from state laws.[11]

In this chapter, I devote much attention to the fate of protective legislation, and the judges' growing recognition that, as the California Supreme Court declared, a pedestal may be a cage.[12] I also examine other major Title VII and Equal Pay Act cases to assess the current status of equal employment, and to gain some insights into the moral questions raised by these cases.

THE EQUAL PAY ACT: WHEN IS EQUAL NOT EQUAL? WHEN IS SIMILAR NOT SIMILAR? WHEN IS SEX OTHER THAN SEX?

The 1963 amendment to the Fair Labor Standards Act of 1938 reads:

> No employer having employees subject to any provisions of
> this section shall discriminate within any establishment in
> which such employees are employed, between employees
> on the basis of sex by paying wages to employees in such es-
> tablishment at a rate less than the rate at which he pays
> wages to employees of the opposite sex in such establish-
> ment for equal work on jobs the performance of which re-
> quires equal skill, effort, and responsibility, and which are
> performed under similar working conditions, except where
> such payment is made pursuant to (i) a seniority system;
> (ii) a merit system; (iii) a system which measures earnings
> by quantity or quality of production; or (iv) a differential
> based on any other factor other than sex: Provided, that an
> employer who is paying a wage rate differential in violation
> of this subsection shall not, in order to comply with the pro-
> visions of this subsection, reduce the wage rate of any em-
> ployee.[13]

Labor organizations, too, are forbidden to "cause or attempt to cause" employees to violate this subsection.[14] The administration and enforcement procedures of the parent act apply to the amendment: the Secretary of Labor may sue under it[15] (a power the EEOC did not have for Title VII for its first eight years); willful violations may bring criminal penalties;[16] and it is subject to the interpretive rulings of the Wage and Hour Administration.[17]

All courts which have interpreted the amendment have agreed that the Secretary has the initial burden of proof both that workers of one sex are paid more than workers of the opposite sex and that the work they perform is equal. Once this is shown, the burden of proof shifts to the employer, who must show that one of the exceptions applies.[18] Since 1966, after the first of these decisions, the Wage and Hour Administration has accepted this interpretation.[19] Most litigation under the equal pay provisions has raised one or more of the following questions: whether the skill, effort, and responsibility required by the jobs are equal; whether the conditions under which the work is performed are similar; or whether the differential is based on a factor other than sex. I take up each series of cases in that order.

SKILL, EFFORT, AND RESPONSIBILITY

In earlier chapters, I indicated that our society has usually assigned men and women to different tasks, that the tasks men perform are more highly valued than those women perform, and that men are rewarded accordingly. The Equal Pay Act, as I have said, does not touch this situation. What these cases reveal is that even when men and women have the same tasks, the men get paid more, and that any difference in tasks, however tiny, will result in a higher wage for men. The law is aimed at this situation, and has been interpreted to bar this kind of discrimination.

In the typical case, men and women perform the same tasks, with some additional task assigned to men. An early case was *Wirtz v. Dennison Mfg. Co.*, decided in 1967. Women machine operators ran machines and checked machine tag processing, while male operators ran machines, made repairs, and got their own materials and took them to the machines. The men earned from fifteen to fifty cents an hour more than the women. The judge ruled that the skill and effort required to repair machines and move material (which took about ten percent of the men's time) were significantly greater than what was required merely to operate them: "the men . . . did have to possess a significant degree of mechanical skill in order to change their machines from job to job."[20] This conclusion sounds defensible in the circumstances, but the decision is troubling because, as Leo Kanowitz points out, it

"gives very little attention to the circumstances under which these jobs were assigned to men and women in the first place.

> . . . How many American women now work at jobs requiring
> little skill or responsibility, not because they are incapable of
> acquiring the skill or assuming the responsibility of higher
> paying jobs, but because, in the past, they have been denied
> the opportunity to do so by the discriminatory practice of
> employers, labor organizations, and employment agencies?"[21]

This may be an instance where Title VII and the Equal Pay Act comple-
ment each other, but the Equal Pay Act alone does not speak to it.

Dennison did not set a pattern for this litigation. Two months earlier,
in *Wirtz v. Rainbo Baking Co.,*[22] a Federal District Court in Kentucky
heard a case involving bakery workers. The facts revealed a phenomenon
which is all too typical of these cases: a change in job title, but not in
pay, after the law went into effect. Until 1966, Rainbo, in an agreement
with the bakery workers' union, had classified women employees in its
distribution department as "Female Help" and men as "Wrapping Machine Helpers." The latter received an additional twenty-five cents per
hour. Then "Female Help" became "Bun Packers" with no change in
pay. All five workers in the department, two women and three men,
boxed and bagged rolls and buns. The men also occasionally rolled bin
trucks or lifted heavy containers; one man replaced the truck loader
(who was paid the same wage as the wrapping machine operators) one
day a week. Although this employee spent twenty percent of his time
in heavy work compared to ten percent in *Dennison,* the court ruled in
favor of the Department of Labor:

> The preponderance of the evidence shows that there are
> no significant differences in these jobs, or in the skill, effort
> and responsibility required to perform them, or in the work-
> ing conditions under which they are performed. . . . [The
> heavy work is] only incidental and so incidental that it would
> not justify making a distinction here. . . . The evidence shows
> that the twenty-five cents per hour difference in pay is based
> solely on sex. . . .
> Application of the equal pay standard is not dependent
> on job classification, but depends rather on actual job re-
> quirements and job performance. Equal does not mean iden-
> tical. Jobs are seldom identical in every respect; small differ-
> ences in job requirements can easily be made but make no

real difference where the work is substantially the same. The incidental and occasional performance of a task which women might be physically inadequate to perform is not sufficient to render the jobs unequal or to justify a difference in pay. The jobs as a whole should be viewed over the entire work cycle. The fact that one of the men replaces the truck loader one day a week is not a justification for paying him the entire week at a wage rate higher than that paid the women.[23]

Three years later, two circuits followed this lead, and this interpretation has prevailed. *Shultz v. Wheaton Glass Co.*[24] ruled that the work done by male and female selector-packers did not justify a ten-percent pay differential, although the men were assigned additional tasks and occasionally had to work more than ten hours a day, which state law prohibited to women. All the additional tasks, most involving heavy work, were usually assigned to "snap-up boys," who were paid two cents an hour more than the female selector-packers. The company testified that the male selector-packers spent approximately eighteen percent of their time doing the work of snap-up boys, but there was no finding of fact on this. In ruling for the government, the Third Circuit Court of Appeals insisted that even a finding that the additional tasks did occupy a large portion of the men's time would not have justified the differential: "For there would be no rational explanation why men who at times perform work paying two cents an hour more than their female counterparts should for that reason receive twenty-one and a half cents per hour more than females for the work they do in common."[25] Thus, the Secretary met his burden of proof when he showed that a differential existed, that men and women performed identical primary tasks, and that the additional work performed by the men was itself paid at a rate only slightly higher than that of the females.[26] The court went on to discuss some of the problems that had been ignored in *Dennison:*

Just as it has not been made clear by any finding that all male selector-packers perform or are available for the work of snap-up boys, so there is an absence of any finding on the ability of any female selector-packers to perform the work of snap-up boys. The fact that some female selector-packers,

unlike some male selector-packers, may have been unwilling
or unable to do the work of snap-up boys might justify a
wage differential between them. But it would still leave open
the question why the company did not include under its
flexibility requirement the female selector-packers who are
both able and willing to do the work of snap-up boys. . . .

    These disparities in rates of pay . . . take on an even more
discriminatory aspect when viewed in the light of their history. For as the district court indicated, the classification
of female selector-packers at the lowest rate of pay of these
three categories was made at a time of labor shortage when
the company was forced to hire women and the union insisted on conditions which would minimize their future competition against the men with whom they would now be working. The motive therefore clearly appears to have been to
keep women in a subordinate role . . . and to emphasize this
subordination by both the ten percent differential between
male and female selector-packers and the two cents differential betewen snap-up boys and female selector-packers.[27]

    The import of *Wheaton Glass* was "its holding that jobs meriting equal
pay need not be *identical,* but only *substantially equal.*"[28] This standard
has been followed by all appellate courts which have heard similar cases.[29]
The Eighth Circuit independently reached this result two months after
Wheaton Glass in *Shultz v. American Can Co.—Dixie Products,*[30] rejecting not only the contention that male machine operators who spent between two and seven percent of their time handling and loading paper
deserved twenty cents an hour more than female operators, but also the
notion that day shift and night shift were dissimilar working conditions
and the claim that the differential was based on a training program which
did not in fact exist.

    After *Wheaton Glass,* not only is the standard "substantially equal,"
but it is clear that additional tasks which require only part of a worker's
time will not justify a wage differential over the entire time span. The
case of *Hodgson v. Daisy Manufacturing Co.*[31] carried the notion of substantially equal work even further. The district judge refused to accept
the argument that a pay differential between male and female press operators was justified because males performed heavy work not required of

females, not because these tasks were minimal or incidental, but because the women had to perform all high-speed operations, with a great attendant risk of getting their hands mangled in the machinery. The court ruled that the fear and mental exertion involved in these tasks (for which the women received no extra pay) were equivalent to the greater physical exertion required of the men.[32]

This ruling arguably goes further than Congress intended, if the Guidelines I quoted earlier are correct. For the first time, in *Daisy* the focus has turned from whether the "male" job actually requires greater skill, effort, and responsibility to whether the "female" job might also make additional demands on workers. This court, unlike the *Wheaton Glass* and *American Can* courts, has independently examined the "female" job to discover what it requires. I do not find any departure from congressional intent here; it can be argued that "equal pay" requires that if workers of one sex are compensated for special demands made on them, workers of the opposite sex must be similarly compensated for such demands.[33]

Taken as a whole, the cases on "equal work" are encouraging. The courts display not only that deference to legislative goals which they like to claim for themselves, but a willingness to go beyond such formal evidence as official job descriptions to examine the actual working situation. But some of the cases do suggest that similar sets of facts may be subject to varying interpretations. Therefore, the outcome of any given case is unpredictable.

SIMILAR WORKING CONDITIONS: AS DIFFERENT AS NIGHT AND DAY?

The typical case on working conditions involves men and women workers who do the same jobs, the women on day shifts and the men on evening or night shifts. The legislative history suggests that Congress meant to incorporate into the Act the language of the formal, complex job evaluation plans used by most of American industry; these plans quantified four factors—skill, effort, responsibility, and working conditions—in determining compensation.[34] "The fact of the matter is that the concept of 'working conditions' as used in the specialized language of job evaluation systems simply does not encompass shift differentials."[35] However, there are indications that Congress did mean to include shift differentials under the general exception of "any factor other than sex."[36] But, as an exception, this is an instance where burden of proof falls on the employer, not the

Department of Labor. The Guidelines state that any rate which distinguishes between all male and all female employees will be strictly scrutinized, and that the employer must establish the absence of sex as a factor, whether direct or indirect, in the scheme.[37] In cases where only or almost only men work at night and only or almost only women during the day, the differentials have been held to violate the Act. So this provision, too, has worked to the advantage of women workers.

The only equal pay case yet to reach the Supreme Court involved conflicting decisions from two circuits on shift differentials in the Corning, New York, and Wellsboro, Pennsylvania, plants of Corning Glass Works.[38] At both plants, males performed night shift inspection, and were paid more than female day shift inspectors. When the night shift had been introduced, between 1925 and 1930, both New York and Pennsylvania law prohibited women from working at night. The men hired as night shift inspectors demanded, and received, higher wages than the women day workers were then receiving. The Pennsylvania and New York statutes were amended in 1947 and 1953, respectively, to allow women to work at night, but Corning's hiring policy did not change until 1966, when it began to allow women to bid for night jobs as vacancies occurred. In 1969 (the year both states repealed their laws entirely), a new system was instituted by which all subsequently hired inspectors would receive the same wage, a rate higher than the previous night shift rate, regardless of either shift or sex. Previously hired inspectors, however, would get a higher rate on the night shift, thus perpetuating the basic pay difference (since women hired before 1969 had been assigned to the day shift and could not get onto the night shift unless a vacancy occurred). The Department of Labor brought claims for back pay and injunctive relief.

In the Courts of Appeals, dispute centered not around the question of working conditions but around the "factor other than sex" provision. The Second Circuit Court, in New York, declared, "The plain fact is that the differentials here at issue arose because men would not work at the low rates paid the women day-time inspectors to perform what the men called 'female work.' This is the very condition at which the Equal Pay Act was aimed."[39] In other words, since sex (perhaps "gender" is a clearer word in this context) was the cause of the original wage difference, the policy came within the prohibitions of the Act. The Third Circuit, ruling on the Wellsboro case, did not concern itself with the history of Corning's policy, but only with the legislative history of the Act. It cited the report of the House Subcommittee on Labor, which listed shift differentials as a legitimate factor other than sex.[40] This implied, the judges thought, that shift differentials were excluded from the Act regardless of their origin.

The Supreme Court followed the lead of several lower courts[41] in ruling for the government. It concluded that neither Congress nor American industry viewed day shifts and night shifts as creating dissimilar working conditions.[42] Reaffirming that the burden of proof thus shifted to Corning, Justice Marshall, writing for the majority, turned to the policies of that company. He pointed out that the differential began at a time when no other night workers at Corning got higher pay than corresponding day workers; that the differential existed only among inspectors, the only employees divided into all-male and all-female shifts; and that the differential arose only because men would not work at the low wage paid women inspectors, and thus from its inception was based on sex. "That the Company took advantage of such a situation might be understandable as a matter of economics," Marshall wrote, "but its differential nevertheless became illegal once Congress enacted into law the principle of equal pay for equal work."[43] And the fact that the night shift did not command higher pay than the day shift on all jobs suggested that the working conditions were not generally viewed as being different.

Corning Glass Works v. Brennan and related decisions do not forbid all wage differentials based on the time of day worked. They do, however, insist that sex must not continue to be a factor in the organization of workers into day and night shifts. The case law on similar working conditions has developed in ways parallel to that on equal skill, effort, and responsibility. Here again, the courts are not satisfied with pat references to job descriptions or legislative history but follow the Labor Department's lead in going beyond these to look at what is actually happening in the plant and why it has happened that way. And even when it happened that way partly because of protective labor legislation (as was true in *Wheaton Glass* as well as in *Corning*), the pay differential is invalidated. In a muted confrontation between protective labor legislation and antidiscrimination law, the latter wins. Thus, wage discrimination which appears to be sex-neutral has been shown to be sex-linked, and the letter and spirit of the Act have been followed rather than thwarted.

FACTORS OTHER THAN SEX

The shift differential cases I have discussed under the heading of "working conditions" also involve the "factor other than sex" provision, as the foregoing discussion has indicated. The rulings suggest that a factor other than sex must be truly that, not an apparently neutral criterion which in fact reflects sex discrimination. This principle has been followed with varying degrees of consistency. One situation which has recurred in equal pay litigation is the "training program," in which employees enrolled in such a program earn more than other employees doing similar work. In a bank, for example, the employee who cashes one's check may be either a female "teller" permanently assigned to this job or a male "management trainee" rotating through the department on a temporary basis, earning perhaps an additional one hundred dollars a month. The Wage and Hour Administration's first set of Guidelines, issued in 1966, recognized the legality of a differential based on a "bona fide training program," but warned that programs which appeared to be available only to workers of one sex would be scrutinized closely to determine whether they were in fact bona fide.[44]

No training program has yet survived scrutiny. In *Shultz v. First Victoria National Bank*[45] in 1969, the court found not only that the training program was limited to men but that it amounted to "little more than an understanding that the male employees—or 'trainees'—could, if they performed well over some indefinite period, become officers."[46] No differences were found between the work assignments of female tellers and male management trainees. The American Can Company lost a case because no evidence could be found that the program it claimed actually existed;[47] two years later, an Iowa bank lost not only because its male trainees rotated through the bank's various departments as randomly as did tellers, but also because the men did not even know that they were "trainees" enrolled in such a program.[48] In some cases, the courts found that the programs were indeed bona fide, but decided in favor of the government because, somehow, no woman had ever been hired as a trainee,[49] or the employer had never considered women suitable for the program.[50] These cases have presented few difficulties; they, too, reveal the lengths to which employers will go to discriminate against women.

A disturbing trend has appeared in the "factor other than sex" cases. The Robert Hall clothing store in Wilmington, Delaware, paid its salesmen both higher salaries and higher periodic increases than its saleswomen. The store defended its policy on the grounds that the men's department showed a larger dollar volume in gross sales and a larger gross profit than the women's, because the men's merchandise was of higher price and better quality. Only men worked in men's clothes and only women in women's clothes, a practice not complained of in the litigation (and not yet ruled on in a Title VII case). Both the Federal District Court and the Court of Appeals ruled that economic benefit to the employer did justify a differential for full-time sales personnel, and the appellate court accepted it for part-time workers as well.[51] The latter court found that a "factor other than sex" included factors related to any legitimate business purpose: "The saleswomen are paid less because the commodities which they sell cannot bear the same selling costs that the commodities sold in the men's department can bear. Without a more definite indication from Congress, it would not seem wise to impose the economic burden of compensation on employers. It could serve to weaken their competitive position."[52] Robert Hall need show only that one department was consistently more profitable than the other, the court ruled, and need not correlate individual pay to individual performance: "It would be too great an economic and accounting hardship to impose upon Robert Hall the requirement that it correlate the wages of each individual with his or her performance"[53] in the absence of any clear indication that this was Congress' intention.

The *Robert Hall* decision is vulnerable to at least three criticisms. First, the brief for the Secretary of Labor, which both courts had before them, showed that over three months several women had a greater dollar sales volume per hour than most of the men, even though, since they were selling less costly merchandise, they had to work harder and faster to do this.[54] The inequity of the sex-based average for these women is clear. Second, the court's solicitude for business seems out of place in a law which restricts business for the benefit of employees. Finally, the conclusion that a factor other than sex is present here is curious. The distinction between men's clothes and women's clothes, from which the pay difference arises, is by definition a factor based on sex. The decision is a questionable one indeed.

Despite the criticisms I have made of some of these decisions, the equal pay cases have unquestionably done working women more good than harm. The courts' performance is generally praiseworthy, but there are enough exceptions to demand caution in making judgments and predictions. But at least the strongest limitations of the Equal Pay Act as a guarantee of sex equality have not been engrafted onto it by the federal judiciary.

THE DEATH OF PROTECTIVE LEGISLATION: TITLE VII OF THE CIVIL RIGHTS ACT OF 1964

As I have shown, the legislative history of Title VII offers small encouragement to feminists. The early performance of the agency created to enforce it was equally an invitation to pessimism. Herman Edelsberg, the first executive director of the EEOC, publicly stated in 1966 that the sex provision was a "fluke" that had been "conceived out of wedlock." These remarks drew strong criticism from Representative Martha Griffiths on the House floor, and it soon became clear that not all EEOC employees shared Edelsberg's views.[55] Agency attitudes have been less of a barrier to change than have the agency's organic weakness and a staff too small to cope with its case load. Both the EEOC's Guidelines and its performance suggest that even if Congress and some bureaucrats thought the law was a fluke, the agency does not. Neither have the federal courts. Although, as I have indicated, the text of the Act all but issues a license to nullify it, the courts have usually interpreted the antidiscrimination provisions broadly and the exceptions narrowly. As in the equal pay litigation, there are exceptions to this rule—and one exception, in the wrong place (the Supreme Court) at the wrong time, is so crucial that it gravely weakens the law. But on Title VII litigation, too, the verdict is positive, though with reservations.

In deciding these cases, the judges have been confronted with some of the questions dealt with in the earlier decisions: the validity of sexual stereotypes, the appropriate role of women in family life, and the ideal relationship between sexual differences and working conditions. For the most part, the answers reached in these decisions are opposed to those embodied in decisions like *Muller.* Under the guidance of new federal law, the judges have been led to reexamine old conclusions. It is probably no accident that the courts began to reconsider the constitutionality of sex discrimination after a few years of dealing with Title VII and equal pay cases.[56]

Title VII prohibits employers covered by the Act—since 1972, all but the federal government, Indian tribes, government corporations, private membership clubs, agencies of the District of Columbia, or those who employ fewer than fifteen full-time workers—from failing to hire, discharging, limiting, classifying, or otherwise discriminating against any individual on the basis of sex, unless the sex of an employee is a bona fide occupational qualification reasonably necessary for that enterprise. Labor organizations are prohibited from discriminating on the basis of sex and from influencing employers to so discriminate.[57] Any person who believes that she or he has suffered such discrimination may file a Charge of Discrimination with the EEOC. These may be either individual or class actions. The EEOC may itself bring charges, and they may be brought by third parties on behalf of others. If a similar agency exists in the state where the alleged violation took place, the Charge is deferred for sixty days to that agency, but state action or inaction does not preclude federal investigation. After this time has elapsed, the EEOC must attempt to reach a conciliation agreement between the charging party and the employer, union, or employment agency.[58] In most cases, this effort has failed.[59] Either the charging party or (since 1972) the EEOC then has the right to sue the respondent in federal court. If the court finds for the plaintiff, it may order "such affirmative action as may be appropriate," including hiring, reinstatement, or back pay.[60]

EVIDENCE OF DISCRIMINATION

Litigation under Title VII has centered around two questions: first, whether discrimination has actually been based on a particular forbidden characteristic, and secondly, in all cases except those involving racial discrimination, whether the characteristic is a "bona fide occupational qualification" (or, BFOQ). On the first question, Title VII does not demand, any more than does the Equal Pay Act, that discrimination be intentional. It is no defense (except against *criminal* penalties under the Equal Pay Act) for an employer to allege, or even to prove, that he did not take whatever action he took in order to discriminate on the basis of sex. The courts rarely inquire into motivation; these are, after all, civil, not criminal, actions.

If proof of intent is not required to prove discrimination, what is? The principal cases here involve not sex discrimination but race discrimination, which is perhaps fortunate, as racial equality was the primary goal of the Civil Rights Act and the long debate over the law, as well as the civil rights struggle itself, had sensitized citizens, including judges, to the complexity of race discrimination. These decisions have been held to be binding precedents in all other cases of discrimination. In 1970, *Parham v. Southwestern Bell Telephone Co.*[61] held that statistics which revealed that between 1.82 and 4.5 percent of a company's employees were black, most of these in menial jobs, and that the population of the state was nearly twenty-two percent black, established a violation of Title VII: "In cases concerning discrimination, statistics often tell much and courts listen."[52] *United States v. Hayes International Corporation,*[63] another racial case (and one of the few where the Attorney General instigated the court suit), cited *Parham* as binding, but appeared to soften it somewhat, holding that a gross discrepancy between the percentage of blacks in a city's population and the percentage of blacks in office and technical jobs in a company within that city was prima facie evidence (and thus not, as in *Parham,* proof) of discrimination. But the company was unable to defend its hiring policies in any way which proved that race was in no way a factor. *Parham* and *Hayes International* have been relied on, without elaboration, in sex discrimination cases, on the issue of prima facie evidence, not proof, without any judge seeing a possible discrepancy between the two cases.[64]

The Supreme Court spoke on this issue in 1973, in *McDonnell Douglas Corporation v. Green.*[65] Here, the Court set out guidelines for "one-on-one" cases, where the issue is not whether a pattern of discrimination exists but whether an individual has suffered discrimination. Declaring that under Title VII the complainant must carry the initial burden of establishing a prima facie case of discrimination, the Court ruled that this might be done by showing (1) that the individual belongs to a racial minority; (2) that he applied and was qualified for a job for which the employer was seeking applicants; (3) that, despite his qualifications, he was rejected; and (4) that after his rejection, the position remained open and the employer continued to seek applicants.[66] The Court then remanded the case for a decision on the merits. These were cited without comment as controlling standards for sex discrimination cases a year later in *Jurinko v. Edwin L. Wiegand Co.,*[67] without anyone reflecting that women are not a "sexual minority."

The first of the four *McDonnell Douglas* standards thus presents a real problem. Did the Court mean to suggest that only minorities, not disadvantaged majorities, or only minorities and/or disadvantaged groups, not majorities or dominant groups, are protected from discrimination? The law does not say this, and, indeed, explicitly disavows any intention of requiring preferential discrimination in favor of any group.[68] But the major impact of the decision, like that of *Parham* and *Hayes International,* has been to shift the focus of inquiry from the motives of the employer to the effects of his decisions. Evidence of discrimination is, of course, not proof and the employer may still prove that his decisions were not based on race or sex. But the complainant need not prove that they were. And on a prima facie case has been made, the burden of proof is the employer's, not the complainant's. So far, no employer has been able to meet this burden. The three decisions I have examined put plaintiffs in a favorable position.

INDIRECT DISCRIMINATION

Any choice involves discrimination. To hire one applicant and reject another is inevitably to discriminate. Title VII forbids the use of five characteristics in making these choices: race, color, religion, sex, and national origin may not be considered in making hiring decisions. But the text of the act leaves open two questions. First, may a person be rejected because of a coalescence of a forbidden factor and a neutral factor? For instance, may jobs be denied, not to all women, but to all married women; is that discrimination based on sex, or on the neutral factor of marital status? Second, is a policy which on its face is neutral with respect to the forbidden characteristics, but which has discriminatory effects when applied, permissible under the law? The first type of indirect sex discrimination—"sex plus" discrimination, as it has been called—has been decisively rejected both by the EEOC[69] and the federal courts. Facially neutral policies with discriminatory effects have had an erratic fate in the courts, as this chapter will show. There is a third kind of policy which I classify by itself because I do not know how else to classify it: regulations pertaining to pregnancy. Obviously, they are not neutral on their face with respect to sex; even the Supreme Court, in its recent decision, does not quite take that absurd position. But because they do not specify one sex, neither are they "sex-plus" regulations. The problem here is conceptual, whereas in the above example it is physiological. However, these regulations do seem to belong conceptually with this group of cases, perhaps because of the way courts have treated them.

"Sex Plus" Discrimination. The "sex plus" cases are important here because they directly raise the issue of women's role in family life. These cases typically involve either discrimination against married women or against women with young children. The Supreme Court's first decision on the sex provisions of Title VII, *Phillips v. Martin-Marietta Corp.,*[70] involved the latter situation. Ida Phillips had applied for a job with Martin-

Marietta, which had informed her that it did not accept applications from women with preschool-age children. The company did employ men with children of that age. The EEOC ruled for Phillips, but was unable to reach a conciliation agreement. Phillips' suit failed in the lower courts, the Court of Appeals ruling that

> a per se violation of the Act can only be discrimination based solely on one of the categories, i.e., in the case of sex, women vis-à-vis men. When another criterion of employment is added to one of the classifications listed in the Act, there is no longer apparent discrimination based solely on race, color, religion, sex, or national origin. It becomes the function of the courts to study the conditioning of the elements outlined in the statute . . . and to determine if any individual or group is being denied work due to his race, color, religion, sex or national origin. . . . [The law] does not prohibit discrimination on any classification except those named within the Act itself. Therefore, once the employer has proved that he does not discriminate against the protected groups, he is free thereafter to operate his business as he determines, hiring and dismissing other groups for any reason he desires. . . .
>
> [The EEOC has] left us only with the alternative of a congressional intent to exclude absolutely any consideration of the differences between the normal relationship of working fathers and working mothers to their pre-school age children, and to require that an employer treat the two exactly alike in the administration of its general hiring policies. If this is the only permissible view of Congressional intention available to us, as distinct from concluding that the seeming discrimination here involved was not founded upon "sex" as Congress intended that term to be understood, we have no hesitation in choosing the latter. The common experience of Congressmen is surely not so far removed from that of mankind in general as to warrant our attributing to them such an irrational purpose in the formulation of this statute.[71]

This brings us right back to *Muller, Schweinler,* and *Radice.* Once again, notions of the normal relationship between women and their families are relied upon to restrict women's employment opportunities. The only difference here between Martin-Marietta in the 1960s and the State of Oregon in the 1900s is that the former restricts only some women, while the latter restricted all of them. The Court of Appeals sees this factor as crucial: a policy discriminating against all women would be impermissible, but a rule which discriminates only against certain women, distinguished by some characteristic, may stand. Even a law which expressly forbids sex discrimination is here interpreted to allow discrimination based on sex-role stereotypes.

This decision appears in an even worse light if one believes that the assignment of child care almost exclusively to women is itself an injustice. From that viewpoint, it means that one injustice may be used to justify another. And there are practical as well as ideological objections to the decision. As a dissenting judge pointed out, "If 'sex plus' stands, the Act is dead."[72] Nothing, he continued, would prevent employers from adding such requirements as minimum shoulder width, weight, and lifting ability.

"Sex plus" did not stand. The Supreme Court reversed this decision in 1971, in a *per curiam* opinion. But despite the result, the decision is disappointing and disturbing. The Court wrote:

> Section 703(a) of the Civil Rights Act of 1964 requires that persons of like qualifications be given employment opportunities irrespective of their sex. The Court of Appeals therefore erred in reading this section as permitting one hiring policy for women and another for men—each having preschool-age children. The existence of such conflicting family obligations, if demonstrably more relevant to job performance for a woman than for a man, could arguably be a basis for a distinction under . . . the Act. But that is a matter of evidence tending to show that the condition in question is a "bona fide occupational qualification reasonably necessary to the normal operation of that particular business or enterprise." The record before us, however, is not adequate for resolution of these important issues.[73]

The Court should have stopped after the first two sentences. The problem and its resolution are neatly expressed there. But the rest of the opinion is superfluous and ominous. In the first place, the BFOQ issue was not properly before the court; that portion of the opinion is mere dicta (and has been followed in no subsequent case). In the second place, as

Justice Marshall wrote in a separate opinion, "I fear that . . . the Court has fallen into the trap of assuming that the Act permits ancient canards about the proper role of women to be a basis for discrimination."[74] Suppose Martin-Marietta could prove that many, or most, or nearly all mothers of preschool-age children had primary responsibility for their care, and that job performance was harmed by this? Would it be right for the company to deny a job to an individual on the basis of such a generalization?[75] *Phillips* hands an unnecessary invitation to employers who wish to continue to discriminate. So far, no one has taken the Court up on this.

One fruitful source of "sex plus" cases, as of Title VII cases in general,[76] has been the airlines. It was their long-standing practice to require that stewardesses be single when hired and remain single under penalty of discharge. This rule was first challenged in 1967, in *Cooper v. Delta Airlines, Inc.*,[77] where a district judge ruled that the policy was legal because the discrimination was based on marital status, not sex, though Delta's male employees were not required to remain single. Since no men were hired by Delta as flight attendants at that time, the judge may have seen the case only as one of discrimination between single and married women, although viewed differently it might seem to be one of double-edged discrimination.

A similar case, *Lansdale v. United Air Lines,* was also decided in favor of the rule, but after the Supreme Court's decision in *Phillips,* the Court of Appeals vacated this decision.[78] The first case which reached an appellate court was *Sprogis v. United Air Lines,*[79] decided five months after *Phillips.* The Seventh Circuit, too, invalidated "sex plus" discrimination, but also ruled on the BFOQ issue.

The airline maintained that it adopted its no-marriage rule after it had received complaints from husbands about their wives' schedules. United also relied on the testimony of psychiatrists and marriage counselors that marriage tended to change women's attitudes toward their jobs, and alleged that married stewardesses were more likely than single ones to get pregnant and thus endanger themselves and embarrass the airline.[80] The EEOC had apparently sided with United, which claimed that it had a letter to that effect from the agency's general counsel. However, this letter was never introduced in evidence.[81] But the court ruled otherwise.

> Even assuming that Title VII might justify hiring only females for that position,[82] that conclusion would not automatically legitimate the no-marriage rule imposed exclusively

upon stewardesses. A valid discrimination in favor of women generally in filling that occupational position need not warrant the imposition of an additional qualification which operates discriminately against those employees by comparison to United's male employees. United's no-marriage rule must stand upon its own feet.[83]

Having thus implicitly disposed of *Cooper,* the court continued:

United has failed to offer any salient rationale in support of its marital status policy. The only reason specifically addressed to that rule is that United was led to impose the requirement after it received complaints from husbands about their wives' working schedules and the irregularity of their working hours. This is clearly insufficient. Section 703(e)(i) specifically requires a connection between the condition of employment and satisfactory performance of the employees' occupational duties. The complaints of spouses do not suffice as an indicator of employee competence. . . . United has presented no direct, rational, or reasonably limited connection between marital status, job performance, and its no-marriage rule for stewardesses.[84]

Thus, conventional notions about wives may no more suffice as grounds for discrimination than may conventional notions about mothers. But in both these cases, the reader of the decisions is struck by how very close a call it was. Each discriminatory practice was upheld by the court of first instance, and challenged successfully only on the appellate level. The lower courts were not very sensitive to sex discrimination until the higher courts directed them to be.

Facially neutral policies. The problem posed by a standard which is neutral on its face is this: suppose a member of a disadvantaged group is denied employment because he or she falls short of the standard, but this deficiency is to some degree traceable to membership in the group? The landmark case in this area is *Griggs v. Duke Power Co.,*[85] decided by the Supreme Court two months after *Phillips,* and, like that case, decided unanimously. *Griggs* was a case of alleged racial discrimination. At Duke's generating plant in North Carolina, the employees were organized into five departments: Labor, Coal Handling, Operations, Maintenance, and Labo-

ratory and Test. Until 1965, blacks were hired only in the Labor department, where the highest-paying jobs paid less than the lowest jobs in the
other four departments. Duke began requiring a high school diploma for
initial assignment to any department except Labor in 1955; ten years
later, it stopped restricting blacks to Labor but kept the diploma requirement. On July 2, 1965, the date Title VII went into effect, Duke began
requiring a minimum score on two professionally prepared aptitude tests
for employment in all departments except Labor (the required scores
approximated the national median for high school graduates, and thus
was an even more restrictive standard.)

These facts permit the inference that Duke intended to circumvent
the law. If so, the company had reason to anticipate success. During the
congressional debates on the Civil Rights Act, the Illinois Fair Employment Practices Commission had issued a decision which suggested that
no standardized test on which whites performed better than blacks could
legally be used as an employment criterion in that state. This ruling alarmed
several members of Congress. Senator John Tower of Texas introduced
an amendment the substance of which was incorporated into the law: ". . .
nor shall it be an unlawful employment practice for an employer to give
and to act upon the results of any professionally developed ability test
provided that such test, its administration or action upon the results is
not designed, intended or used to discriminate because of race, color, religion, sex, or national origin."[86]

Griggs filed a complaint, alleging that the result of the requirements
was to deny employment to blacks. Both the Federal District Court and
the Court of Appeals referred to the legislative history in ruling against
Griggs.[87] Neither court considered the possibility that the timing of
Duke's new regulations might have had some relationship to the company's
design or intent.

The Supreme Court did not raise that point either, but it did rule that
a violation had been found. Chief Justice Burger referred to evidence that
showed that whites performed better than blacks on the tests, and made
the familiar suggestion that both the tests and the diploma requirement
might be suspect because of the inferior educational opportunities which
blacks had received. He continued:

> Congress has now provided that tests or criteria for employ-
> ment or promotion may not provide equality of opportunity
> merely in the sense of the fabled offer of milk to the stork

and the fox. On the contrary, Congress has now required
that the posture and condition of the job-seeker be taken
into account. It has—to resort again to the fable—provided
that the vessel in which the milk is proffered be one all seek-
ers can use. The Act proscribes not only overt discrimination
but also practices that are fair in form, but discriminatory in
operation. This touchstone is business necessity. If an employment practice which operates to exclude Negroes cannot
be shown to be related to job performance, the practice is
prohibited.[88]

On the record, he concluded, "neither the high school completion requirement nor the general intelligence test is shown to bear a demonstrable
relationship to successful performance of the jobs for which it was used."[89]

But did Congress require or invite this conclusion? The Act does permit any test not "designed, intended, or used"[90] to discriminate in illegal
ways. But designed by whom: the author of the test, or the employer? We
have learned that standardized tests are biased in various ways; there is no
way of determining at this late date whether this was or was not intentional. "Used" is an even more confusing verb; its connection to motive is less
direct, whoever the actor is. It may refer to effect as well as to motive. But
the Court's failure to address this question is a disturbing gap in its opinion.

The import of *Griggs* is this: any standard used to evaluate workers, by
which one race does better than another, must be job-relevant to conform
to Title VII. *Griggs* and *McDonnell Douglas,* taken together, imply that if
any member of a racial minority applies for a job, is rejected because of a
facially neutral standard which is not shown to be job-relevant, and the
employer continues to seek applicants, a prima facie case of racial discrimination exists. And the burden of proof is on the employer to show the
relevance of the criterion. Later in 1971 a Court of Appeals interpreted
the test of "job relevance" as being "whether there exists an overriding
legitimate business purpose such that the procedure is necessary to the
safe and efficient operation of the business,"[91] a standard which the
EEOC has adopted in all cases of discrimination.[92]

These rules are also applied in sex discrimination cases. *Meadows v.
Ford Motor Company*[93] ruled that a requirement that all production line
employees must weigh at least 150 pounds was discriminatory because
only twenty percent of all women between eighteen and twenty-four in

the United States weigh this much, while seventy percent of the men of that age do; that Ford had made exceptions for male applicants who weighed between 135 and 150 pounds; and that Ford had neither made physical examinations on underweight female applicants nor had made studies or tests to determine the relative strength of people over and under the weight limit.[94] Similarly, in *Pond v. Braniff Airways*,[95] an employee was denied a transfer to the position of customer service agent, to which she had an absolute seniority right under union contract, because she did not meet the 5'8" minimum height requirement. A man who was not a Braniff employee got the job. She won, not because of statistics on the relative heights of men and women, but because she had been given no opportunity to demonstrate her ability to handle the job (which occasionally included lifting luggage), and Braniff had tested neither her nor the successful applicant to determine their comparative ability.[96] In neither case did the court say that the test used was not relevant to job performance; they found simply that relevance was not shown. In a fashion typical of lawyers, the judges are insisting on careful proof, here as in the "sex plus" cases. This lawyer-like attitude has frequently served to benefit the women plaintiffs, but it can, of course, work the other way around. In 1975, a Court of Appeals refused to invalidate an antinepotism rule as having a disproportionate negative effect on women because the plaintiff had not shown that such an effect existed.[97]

These cases are encouraging, but they are not conclusive; none of them represents a full confrontation between an employer armed with statistics and arguments for job-relevance and an applicant with data to refute these contentions. Perhaps such a case will not soon arise; even in occupations in which performance does seem related to physical strength, such as police work, on analysis the job turns out not to demand that quality as much as one might assume.[98] And as I shall indicate, another Title VII case has set a very strict standard of proof for the employer.

Pregnancy. I have expressed my reluctance to classify policies relating to pregnancy as either "sex plus" or "facially neutral" discrimination. The Supreme Court had no similar problem in semantics, refusing to recognize any discrimination at all. Until *Gilbert,* the Court had dealt only with the constitutionality of such regulations, not their legality under Title VII. In spite of its increasingly suspicious attitude toward sex discrimination, it had found sex discrimination in neither of the two cases decided.

Cleveland Board of Education v. LaFleur[99] declared a very long mandatory maternity leave unconstitutional, but on due process, not equal protection, grounds; it had found no rational relationship between the long
leaves and any legitimate governmental purpose. *Geduldig v. Aiello*[100]
sustained California's disability insurance program, which then excluded
from its coverage (but has since been amended to include) all disabilities arising from normal pregnancies, against a similar claim by arguing
that the exclusion did bear a rational relationship to the state's goal of
limiting the cost of the program. Neither case raised any Title VII question. But the EEOC Guidelines stated that all disabilities related to pregnancy and childbirth should be treated like any other temporary disabilities for all purposes,[101] and all Courts of Appeals which had addressed
the question had agreed.[102]

The Supreme Court did not.[103] At issue was General Electric's em-
ployer-financed disability plan, which paid weekly non-occupational
sickness and accident benefits for all disabilities except those arising
from pregnancy. In sustaining it, the Court relied on *Geduldig* as the controlling precedent, although that case had involved the Constitution and
this one a federal law. Justice Rehnquist, writing for the majority, twice
quoted this passage from *Geduldig:* There is no risk from which men are
protected and women are not. Likewise, there is no risk from which wom-
en are protected and men are not."[104] Therefore, no sex discrimination
existed.

The apparent basis for this conclusion is twofold. First, "the 'package'
going to relevant identifiable groups—General Electric's male and female
employees—covers exactly the same categories of risk, and is facially nondiscriminatory,"[105] after which Rehnquist repeats the language I just
quoted from *Geduldig*. The categories of risk covered for both men and
women are these: all disabilities, except those arising from pregnancy. This
above sentence appears to mean that the policy is nondiscriminatory because neither men nor women can get benefits for pregnancy-related conditions. If this is what the Court means, it is patently absurd. Since this
portion of Rehnquist's argument consumes almost half of his opinion,
the reader can understand why critics of this decision have emphasized
this apparent absurdity.

But Rehnquist presents an additional argument for his conclusion, which
only a very careful reading of the opinion can discern. He cites the district
court's findings of fact, which showed that the cost of the plan in 1970 and

1971 "per female employees was at least as high, if not substantially higher, than the cost per male employee,"[106] $62.08 per insured male employee and $112.91 per insured female employee in 1971.[107] Four pages later, just before the passage I quoted above, he again quotes *Geduldig;* there is no evidence, he argues, that the plan's financial benefits "worked to discriminate against any definable group or class in terms of the *aggregate* risk protection derived by that group or class from the program."[108] The plan "did not operate, *in fact,* to discriminate against women"[109]; "pregnancy related disabilities constitute an *additional* risk, unique to women, and the failure to compensate them for this risk does not destroy the presumed parity of the benefits, accruing to men and women alike, which results from the facially evenhanded *inclusion* of risks."[110] The kindest possible interpretation of the majority's argument—an interpretation which one has to go digging to find—is that there is no sex discrimination because the cost of the plan per employee is no less for the women than for the men.

But even this will not wash. I have criticized the *Geduldig* holding elsewhere;[111] to reiterate briefly, a plan such as G. E.'s indeed exposes women to a risk from which men are protected: the risk of incurring a disability for which they will not be compensated. This point is not rebutted by showing that proportionally no less money is paid to women employees than than to men under the plan. Even if women in fact collect as much money as men do, no woman collects any of this money if her disability results from pregnancy or childbirth. The plan may not discriminate in effect against all women (neither, after all, did United's no-marriage rule), but it discriminates against some women, and against no men.

But how can the exclusion be "facially even-handed"? Is this another version of the "no pregnancy benefits for men" absurdity? Rehnquist suggests that it is not, but this argument creates more problems with the opinion. He attempts to defend the neutrality and rationality of the exclusion by stating that pregnancy is "significantly different from the typical covered disease or disability" because it is "often a voluntary and desired condition."[112] But not always—not only is contraception far from failure-proof and abortion not always feasible, but women do get raped, and under family law husbands are still entitled to demand their wives' sexual services. (Whether or not that rule would now survive in court, it could not easily be made sex-neutral.)

Justice Brennan, in dissent, makes an even stronger objection to this reasoning. He points out that G.E.'s inclusion of risks is not facially evenhanded; voluntariness is not consistently applied as a criterion for exclusion. The plan covers voluntarily incurred conditions such as sports injuries and elective plastic surgery.[113] So the one sex-neutral justification for the policy offered in the opinion is struck down. I know of no scheme which does use voluntariness in such a manner; it would be rather difficult, I think, to do so. We know that many disabilities, such as ulcers, liver diseases, and lung cancer, may result wholly or in part from personal habits; where do we draw the line between "voluntary" and "involuntary"?

Rehnquist goes on to make an ominous observation. "We do not therefore infer that the exclusion of pregnancy disability benefits from petitioner's plan is a simple pretext for discriminating against women."[114] But *Griggs* and *McDonnell Douglas* indicate that effect, not intent, is the controlling factor in Title VII cases. Whether Rehnquist means to repudiate these decisions is unclear—a few sentences later he cites both in support of his conclusion that "a prima facie violation of Title VII can be established *in some circumstances*"[115] upon showing discriminatory effect— but the qualification so alarmed two justices in the majority that they explicitly disavowed any repudiation of *Griggs*.[116]

Gilbert is a disaster. The opinion is so badly reasoned and organized that the reader has to search for a marginally acceptable argument, which even then is rebuttable at every step. The ruling is not fully reconciled with two important precedents. It has all the defects of the very dubious case on which it relies. with the additional fault of being blind to sex discrimination even when faced with a law which expressly forbids it. Like *Robert Hall,* it fails to see that sex is the very basis for the classification. "By definition, such a rule discriminates on account of sex, for it is the capacity to become pregnant which primarily differentiates the male from the female."[117] *Gilbert* suggests that only blatant, deliberate sex discrimination may be rejected by the Court; the victories of recent years may have been possible only because such discrimination is so widespread. As the discrimination becomes more subtle—and, in the light of the attempt at evasion which equal pay and Title VII cases have revealed, there is every reason to expect that it will—the gains may stop.

BONA FIDE OCCUPATIONAL QUALIFICATION

Even is sex discrimination is proved, an employer has the defense of showing that sex is a BFOQ. It is this provision which presented the greatest potential danger to the Act. A look at the Guidelines reveals the kinds of interpretation the EEOC found it necessary to warn against. Sex is not a BFOQ when the employer relies on assumptions of comparative employment behavior of men and women, stereotyped characterizations of the sexes, or preferences of customers, coworkers, employees, or clients.[118] That these were no chimeras is demonstrated, for example, by *Diaz v. Pan American World Airways,* in which the airline argued that being a woman was a BFOQ for the position of flight attendant on the basis of psychologists' testimony that anxious passengers would be more reassured by "feminine" attendants. The district court accepted this argument, but the Court of Appeals did not.[119] Male flight attendants are not at all rare today on domestic flights.

The Commission has had to consider whether state protective laws create a BFOQ under the Act. The law does refer to this question, but only to state a tautology: "Nothing in this title shall be deemed to exempt or relieve any person from any liability, duty, penalty, or punishment provided by any present or future law of any State or political subdivision of a State, other than any such law which purports to require or permit the doing of any act which would be an unlawful employment practice under the title."[120] The EEOC never reached an independent resolution of this problem. Its first guideline, issued in December 1965, indicated its belief that the Act was not intended to disrupt state protective laws, and that these laws were a basis for application of the BFOQ exception.[121] Less than a year later, a revised guideline was issued: the EEOC declared it would make no determinations where conflicts existed between Title VII and state protective legislation, "except in cases where the clear effect of the law in current circumstances is not to protect women but to subject them to discrimination," but would notify any complainant of her right to sue.[122] Thus, the EEOC referred the question to the federal courts. The next year a Georgia district court ruled that that state's thirty-pound weight limit (see *Weeks,* to follow) made maleness a BFOQ for the job of telephone switchman.[123]

A 1968 guideline can best be described as firm vacillation. While the Commission reaffirmed its belief that Congress did not intend to disturb these laws, it also stated its own belief that some such laws "have ceased to be relevant to our technology or to the expanding role of women in our society." It announced that it would consider these laws as a basis for the BFOQ exception, but would not accept a law whose effect was clearly discriminatory rather than protective. For example, restrictions on lifting weights would be legal so long as the limit was not unreasonably low.[124] No minimum figure was suggested.

Meanwhile, a case which the EEOC had refused to resolve was moving into the courts.[125] Leah Rosenfeld, employed by the Southern Pacific Railroad, had applied for a transfer to the position of agent-telegrapher. She was denied employment solely on grounds of her sex and a California law which prohibited women from working more than ten hours a day or lifting more than fifty pounds. A male employee with less seniority got the job. Rosenfeld filed a Charge of Discrimination; the EEOC, following its 1966 Guideline, decided to make no determination and advised her of her right to sue. She did, the State of California joining Southern Pacific as a party to the case.[126]

In a terse opinion, listing findings of facts and conclusions of law but making no arguments to support these findings and conclusions, the district court ruled that Rosenfeld must be given a chance to demonstrate her qualifications for the job. The judge concluded that the state laws did not create a BFOQ; that the 1965 and 1966 EEOC Guidelines were not controlling; and that the laws were void under Title VII.[127] But only a month later, in *Gudbrandson v. Genuine Parts Co.*,[128] a federal judge in Minnesota held that that state's forty-pound weight limit ". . . is a bona fide occupational qualification reasonably necessary to the normal operation of its particular business within the meaning of the Act, even though some women may be able to perform the work without hazard, since the process of selecting those few who may be able to do so involves a high risk of danger and inefficiency."[129]

It was the *Rosenfeld* ruling, not that in *Gudbrandson*, which prevailed. The following year, 1969, was a landmark year for protective legislation, at least in the sense that 1937 was a landmark year for freedom of contract. Two decisions, one at the circuit level and one in district court, struck down state laws. Two more decisions invalidated employer policies not dictated by state law.

Weeks v. Southern Bell,[130] decided in March, was the first Title VII sex discrimination case to reach an appellate court. It had been brought on appeal from the Georgia decision I mentioned earlier. Lorena Weeks, refused consideration for a switchman's job, pursued her case. The Fifth Circuit Court of Appeals went a step beyond *Rosenfeld*. It ruled not only that the limit violated Title VII, but that the employer had the burden of proof that sex was a BFOQ, and enunciated the rule that has remained the standard in deciding Title VII cases:

> We conclude that the principle of nondiscrimination re-
> quires that we hold that in order to rely on the bona fide oc-
> cupational qualification exception an employer has the bur-
> den of proving that he had reasonable cause to believe, that
> is, a factual basis for believing, that all or substantially all wom-
> en would be unable to perform safely and efficiently the duties
> of the job involved.
>   Southern Bell has clearly not met that burden here.
> They introduced no evidence concerning the lifting
> abilities of women. Rather, they would have us
> "assume" on the basis of a "stereotyped characteriza-
> tion" that few or no women can safely lift thirty
> pounds, while all men are treated as if they can.
> While one might accept, *arguendo,* that men are strong-
> er on the average than women, it is not clear that any
> conclusions about relative lifting ability would follow.
> This is because it can be argued tenably that technique
> is as important as strength in determining lifting
> ability. Technique is hardly a function of sex. What
> does seem clear is that using the class stereotypes denies
> desirable positions to a great many women perfectly
> capable of performing the duties involved.
>   Southern Bell's remaining contentions do not seem to be
> advanced with great seriousness. . . . It does seem that switch-
> men are occasionally subject to late-hour call-outs. Of course,
> the record also reveals that other women employees are sub-
> ject to call after midnight in emergencies. Moreover, Title
> VII rejects just this type of romantic paternalism as unduly
> Victorian and instead vests the individual woman with the
> power to decide whether or not to take on unromantic tasks.
> Men have always had the right to determine whether the in-
> cremental increase in remuneration for strenuous, dangerous,
> obnoxious, boring or unromantic tasks is worth the candle.
> The promise of Title VII is that women are now to be on an
> equal footing. We cannot conclude that by including the bona

fide occupational qualification exception Congress intended
to renege on that promise.[131]

The connection between protection and restriction, between the pedestal and the cage, is well expressed here. The standard of proof may initially trouble the reader. Even if substantially all women could not do a
job, would that justify rejecting a woman who could, any more than proving that family responsibilities were as a rule more relevant to job performance for mothers than for fathers of young children would justify rejecting an individual for whom this was not true? In practice, however, the
burden imposed by *Weeks* has never been met; proving that all or substantially all women cannot do something, or even offering some evidence to
this effect, appears to be almost impossible. (Certainly, none of the Brandeis briefs met that standard.) *Weeks,* of course, did not and could not
rule that all state protective laws were superseded by Title VII. But it
did present a strong argument for such a step.

In May, the Oregon district court followed this ruling in finding that
state's weight limits in violation of Title VII.[132] The decisions in *Cheat-
wood v. Southern Bell,*[133] from Alabama's district court, and *Bowe v.
Colgate-Palmolive Co.,*[134] from the Seventh Circuit Court of Appeals,
each invalidating a private company's weight limit, followed in July and
September respectively. None of these decisions saw any reason to give
state laws any more deference than private regulations; they all fell.

In August, the EEOC accepted the courts' findings. In a new Guideline, it announced: "The Commission has found that [state protective]
laws do not take into account the capacities, preferences, and abilities
of individual females and, therefore, discriminate on the basis of sex. The
Commission has concluded that such laws and regulations conflict with
and are superseded by Title VII of the Civil Rights Act of 1964."[135] This
regulation still stands.

After this, the decisions kept coming. California's weight limitations
were again invalidated in 1970, in a decision which clarified the relationship between state laws and Title VII:

> Section 703 (e) creates a very narrow exception to the
> Act; it refers to a particular business or enterprise rather
> than to broad categories of employment such as industrial
> or technological occupations. Secondly, it refers to employ-
> ing any individual on the basis of sex and does not permit
> discrimination on the basis of groups. . . . The California

statute in question is much broader than Section 703 (e)
would permit. It applies not to a "particular business" but
to any occupation. It applies not to any individual, but to
a class which comprises over half the population of the state.[136]

Since 1969, every sex-specific state labor law challenged under Title
VII has ultimately been invalidated.[137] At first these decisions stopped
short of ordering back pay, on the grounds that employers had not retro-
actively violated Title VII by complying with state laws (which assumed,
of course, that the laws were being enforced and that it was indeed they
which dictated employers' policies); however, by 1972 courts had become more willing to hold employers liable for past actions, insisting
that reliance on state laws after the 1969 Guideline did violate the federal law and called for compensation.[138]

Women's labor legislation withstood attack under the Constitution,
but it could not withstand federal laws prohibiting sex discrimination.
In the light of Title VII, courts did perceive that protection was discrimination; law after law which purported to protect women was found in fact to
discriminate against them. Protection was revealed as restriction, and found
incompatible with sexual equality. *Weeks* is in direct opposition to *Muller;*
laws designed for women's protection are rejected as paternalistic denials
of freedom of choice. The Title VII cases are, however, in accord with the
"suspect classification" cases, *Sail'er Inn* and *Frontiero,* examined in Chapter 4.

Who is right? In Chapter 1, I identified three assumptions common to
arguments for protection. Only the first of these—that permanent rather
than temporary conditions justify these laws—has been prominent in court
decisions. They have been relatively free of arguments of the second and
third type: ideas about women's "primary function" and about the relationship of women's interests to family interests. The usual platitudes
about women's nature and role have gotten into opinions,[139] but not into
those on labor legislation. Implicit assumptions of this kind pervade the
Brandeis briefs and hover behind the scene in *Phillips* and *Sprogis,* but they
remain implicit; they are de-emphasized in the opinions after *Muller* and
are brushed aside in the Title VII cases. After 1937, even the briefs in constitutional cases do not deal with the issue of family responsibilities (understandably, since it would take some doing to prove these responsibilities relevant to the laws at issue in *Goesaert* and *Hunter*). The question
of the relationship of women's needs to family needs is no longer seen as

crucial, but the relationship between women's and men's interests in employment opportunities is to the fore after 1937 in both constitutional and statutory cases.

The facts observable in 1908, however, were not permanent aspects of women's situation. Women's relative inferiority in physical strength and her reproductive function are not as potentially disabling as they once were. The three factors determining the protective or restrictive effect of any law—the gravity of the evil, the extent to which protection is needed, and the extent to which freedom would be increased by the absence of the law—now make this legislation more restrictive than protective. Women are not now forced to take physically taxing jobs in hazardous conditions. Without legislation, a multiplicity of choices are open to them that did not exist seventy years ago. *Weeks* and its successors are absolutely right in their conclusions. If the justifications for special legislation lie in permanent conditions, one or both of the two other assumptions must be true; the only likely arguments for special treatment which remain are those which hinge on family responsibilities.

Arguments like the one made by Annie MacLean, quoted at the end of Chapter 1, reflect assumptions which have not changed very much. Statements like these suggest that it necessarily follows from the fact that women bear children that this is their *primary* function, along with the related tasks of child care and homemaking. The arguments in several Brandeis briefs that the hours that women serve their employers must be reduced so that they can better serve their families, and employers' allegations in *Phillips* and *Sprogis* that some women cannot adequately serve their employers because they must serve their families, reflect this assumption, which still holds. And not only is this *women's* job, but it is their *primary* job, to which all else must be subordinated.

These assumptions seem to me to raise profound moral questions. For instance, does it follow from the fact that most women are inferior to most men in gross muscular strength that women's participation in some activities should be restricted or prohibited? Even if we concede a plausible logical connection between childbearing and homemaking, does the fact that only women can bear children entail the assignment of domestic tasks to women? Is such assignment fair or just? Whose interests does it serve? How do the answers to the last two questions affect the legitimacy of restrictions imposed upon women because of these functions? Should woman be placed in a class by herself because of these factors, even though not all women lack muscular strength, or bear children, and no woman bears children all the time? Or is such classification inherently suspect? Does compelling justification ever exist for it?

Resolving these questions depends partly on an exploration of the reliable biological and psychological evidence we have about the sexes, and partly upon the adequacy of this evidence as a basis for drawing conclusions about the justifiability of imposing restirctions. The studies of such differences must at least be considered, but it cannot be assumed, as it often has been, that the discovery of significant personality differences or similarities between the sexes would legitimize or condemn any existing policy. It will be necessary to establish criteria for deciding what kinds of data would justify what kinds of discrimination before going to the data. This is the task to which the next chapter will be devoted.

NOTES

1. See Kanowitz, *Women and the Law,* pp. 132-33; Bird, *Born Female,* ch. 1.
2. Bird, *Born Female,* p. 4.
3. Ibid., pp. 6-8.
4. 29 U.S.C. Sec. 206(d)(1).
5. 29 C.F.R. Sec. 800.120.
6. Babcock et al., *Sex Discrimination and the Law,* p. 440.
7. 42 U.S.C. Sec. 2000e 703(e).
8. Jo Freeman, *The Politics of Women's Liberation* (New York: David McKay Co., 1975), p. 178.
9. Ibid., pp. 177-80.
10. 45 U.S. Law Week 4031, 97 S.Ct. 401 (1976).
11. See e.g., Wirtz v. Rainbo Baking Co., 303 F. Supp. 1049 (E.D.Ky.1967); Schultz v. Wheaton Glass Co., 421 F.2d 259 (3rd Cir. 1970); Corning Glass Works v. Brennan, 417 U.S. 188 (1974).
12. Sail'er Inn, Inc., v. Kirby, 485 P.2d 529, 540 (1971).
13. 29 U.S.C. Sec. 206(d)(1).
14. Ibid., Sec. 206(d)(2).
15. Ibid., Sec. 216(c).
16. Ibid., Sec. 216; 29 C.F.R. Sec. 800.166.
17. 29 U.S.C. Sec. 201.
18. See e.g., Wirtz v. Basic, Inc., 256 F.Supp. 786, 790 (D.Nev. 1966); Corning Glass Works v. Brennan, 417 U.S. 188, 196 (1974).
19. 29 C.F.R. Sec. 800.141(b).
20. 265 F. Supp. 787, 789 (D. Mass. 1967). Cf. Kilpatrick v. Sweet, 262 F. Supp. 561 (M.D. Fla. 1966).
21. *Women and the Law,* p. 139.

22. 303 F. Supp. 1049 (E.D. Ky. 1967).

23. Ibid., pp. 1051-52.

24. 421 F. 2d 259 (3rd Cir. 1970), *cert. denied* 398 U.S. 905 (1970).

25. Ibid., p. 263.

26. Ibid., pp. 262-63.

27. Ibid., p. 264.

28. Note, "The Impact of the Wheaton Glass Decision," in Babcock, *Sex Discrimination*, p. 446.

29. Hodgson v. Brookhaven General Hospital, 436 F. 2d 719, 725 (5th Cir. 1970); Hodgson v. Corning Glass Works, 474 F. 2d 226, 234 (2nd Cir. 1973); Hodgson v. Fairmont Supply Co., 454 F. 2d 490, 496 (4th Cir. 1972); Hodgson v. Miller Brewing Co., 457 F. 2d 221, 224, n. 7 (7th Cir. 1972); Hodgson v. Square D Company, 459 F. 2d 805 (6th Cir. 1972); Hodgson v. Daisy Manufacturing Co., 317 F. Supp. 538, 551-52 (W.D. Ark. 1970), affirmed per curiam, 445 F. 2d 823 (8th Cir. 1971).

30. 424 F. 2d 356.

31. 317 F. Supp. 538 (W.D. Ark. 1970).

32. Ibid., p. 544.

33. One inconclusive series of cases on equal work has involved hospital nurses' aides and orderlies. The typical situation is one where the orderlies, who are male, and aides, who are female, have similar primary duties of patient care, cleaning, and record keeping, but have different secondary duties, including heavy lifting, catheterizing male patients, and maintaining security for the orderlies. The Department of Labor has consistently found the work equal, but the court decisions have varied. Hodgson v. Brookhaven General Hospital, 9 F.E.P. Cases 644 (N.D.Tex. 1971), affirmed 470 F. 2d 729 (5th Cir. 1972), ruled that where both aides and orderlies had duties peculiar to their jobs and where the amount of time spent by orderlies on extra duties varied considerably, the evidence did not justify an overall pay differential in favor of the orderlies. F.E.P. Cases 644, 645. But in another Texas case, a different judge found security duties "the gravamen and crux of the real and primary work of the orderly," thus ruling in favor of the hospital and insisting that a case-by-case standard be applied. Hodgson v. Good Shepherd Hospital, 327 F. Supp. 143, 148 (E.D.Tex. 1971). Brennan v. Prince William Hospital, 503 F. 2d 282 (4th Cir. 1974), *cert. denied* 420 U.S. 972, held the jobs equal; Hodgson v. Golden Isles Convalescent Home, 468 F. 2d 1256 (5th Cir. 1972), and Hodgson v. William and Mary Nursing Hotel, 20 W&H Cases 10 (M.D.Fla. 1972), ruled for the hospital. These decisions are frustrating to the Department, which often pursues the strategy of negotiating settlements with several employers after a favorable court decision on a type of occupation. Babcock, *Sex Discrimination,* p. 453. Another problem with these cases is that *Wheaton Glass* would seem to require that, even if the jobs were different, extra pay be given the orderlies only for the time actually spent on extra duties, not for the entire shift worked. One frustrating feature of these decisions is that, although it is plausible that situations might differ in different hospitals, it is impossible for the reader to determine whether there is indeed a difference in objective fact or only a difference in judicial emphasis.

34. Corning Glass Works v. Brennan, 417 U.S. 188, 200 (1974); Hearings Be-

fore the Subcommittee on Labor of the Senate Committee on Labor and Public Welfare, 88th Congress, 1st Session (1963), p. 98; Hearings Before the Special Subcommittee on Labor of the House Committee on Education and Labor, 88th Congress, 1st Session (1963), p. 234.

35. Corning Glass Works v. Brennan, 417 U.S. 188, 202-03 (1974).

36. 109 Cong. Rec. 9210 (1963); Brennan v. Corning Glass Works, 480 F. 2d 1254 (3rd Cir. 1973).

37. 29 C.F.R. Sec. 800.142.

38. Hodgson v. Corning Glass Works, 474 F. 2d 226 (2nd Cir. 1973), for the Secretary; Brennan v. Corning Glass Works, 480 F. 2d 1254 (3rd Cir. 1973), for Corning.

39. 474 F. 2d 226, 233.

40. 480 F. 2d 1254, 1259-60, citing 109 Cong. Rec. 9210 (1963).

41. See, e.g., Wirtz v. Basic, Inc., 256 F. Supp. 786 (D. Nev. 1966); Hodgson v. Miller Brewing Co., 457 F. 2d 221 (7th Cir. 1972), affirming Murphy v. Miller Brewing Co., 307 F. Supp. 829 (D.Wisc. 1969).

42. 109 Cong. Rec. 9210 (1963).

43. 417 U.S. 188, 205.

44. 29 C.F.R. Sec. 800.148.

45. 420 F. 2d 648 (5th Cir. 1969).

46. Ibid., p. 655, n. 14.

47. Schultz v. American Can Co.—Dixie Products, 424 F. 2d 356 (8th Cir. 1970).

48. Hodgson v. Security National Bank of Sioux City, 460 F. 2d 57 (8th Cir. 1972).

49. Hodgson v. Fairmont Supply Co., 454 F. 2d 490 (4th Cir. 1972).

50. Hodgson v. Behrens Drug Co., 475 F. 2d 1041 (5th Cir. 1973), *cert. denied sub nom.* Behrens Drug Co. v. Brennan, 414 U.S. 822 (1973).

51. Hodgson v. Robert Hall Clothes, Inc., 326 F. Supp. 1264 (D.Del. 1971), affirmed in part and reversed in part, 473 F. 2d 589 (3rd Cir. 1973), *cert. denied sub nom.* Brennan v. Robert Hall Clothes, Inc., 414 U.S. 866 (1973).

52. 473 F. 2d 589, 595.

53. Ibid., p. 597.

54. Note, "The Impact of Averaging by Sex," in Babcock, *Sex Discrimination,* p. 489.

55. Freeman, *Politics of Women's Liberation,* p. 54.

56. See., e.g., Reed v. Reed, 404 U.S. 71 (1971); Sail'er Inn, Inc. v. Kirby, 485 P. 2d 529 (1971).

57. 42 U.S.C. Sec. 2000(e) 703.

58. Ibid., 705(a); 706(a)(b).

59. Comment, "Sex Discrimination in Hiring Practices of Private Employers: Recent Legal Developments," *Tulane Law Review* 48 (December 1973): 125, 134.

60. 42 U.S.C. Sec. 2000e 706 (e) (f) (g).

61. 433 F. 2d 421 (8th Cir.).

62. Ibid., p. 426.

63. 456 F. 2d 112 (5th Cir. 1972).

64. See. e.g., Nance v. Union Carbide Corp., 397 F. Supp. 436 (W.D.N.C. 1975);

Kaplan v. International Alliance of Theatrical and Stage Employees and Motion Picture Machine Operators, 525 F. 2d 1354 (9th Cir. 1975).

65. 411 U.S. 792.

66. Ibid., p. 802.

67. 497 F. 2d 403 (3rd Cir. 1974).

68. 42 U.S.C. Sec. 2000e 703 (j).

69. 42 C.F.R. Sec. 1604.4.

70. 400 U.S. 542 (1971).

71. 411 F. 2d 1, 4 (5th Cir. 1969).

72. Phillips v. Martin-Marietta Corp., 416 F. 2d 1257. 1260 (Brown, C.J., dissenting from denial of rehearing).

73. 400 U.S. 542, 544.

74. Ibid., p. 545.

75. This discussion recalls a personal experience with sexism in academia. As a graduate student at the University of Chicago, the author helped found the Women's Caucus of its Political Science Department in 1969. One of the Caucus' first acts was to write a statement about sex discrimination in the Department, which was distributed to all faculty and students. The statement has since been widely reprinted, see, e.g., Morgan, ed., *Sisterhood Is Powerful*, p. 101. It began with a series of comments which had been made by members of the then all-male departmental faculty. The last two comments were: "Of course you'll stop work when you have children. You'll have to," and "You have no business looking for work with a child that age." Nearly everyone to whom the author quoted these remarks asked, "How old was the child?"

76. See Denis Binder, "Sex Discrimination in the Airline Industry: Title VII Flying High," *California Law Review* 59 (September 1971): 1091-1112.

77. 274 F. Supp. 781 (E.D. La.).

78. 2 F.E.P. Cases 461 (S.D. Fla. 1969), 437 F. 2d 454 (5th Cir. 1971).

79. 444 F. 2d 1194 (7th Cir. 1971).

80. Affidavit of United Air Lines, pp. 64-65, quoted at 444 F. 2d 1194, 1207, n. 23 (Stevens, J., dissenting). This dissent (which argued that United was entitled to a hearing on the merits although it seemed "most doubtful" that the airline could win), is interesting less for its content than for its authorship: Stevens was appointed to the U.S. Supreme Court by President Ford. Feminists opposed the nomination, to no avail. In fairness to Stevens, it should be added that he dissented in *Gilbert.*

81. 444 F. 2d 1194, 1200.

82. A policy which had just been ruled illegal by the Fifth Circuit. Diaz v. Pan American World Airways, 442 F. 2d 385 (1971).

83. 444 F. 2d 1194, 1199.

84. Ibid.

85. 401 U.S. 424 (1971).

86. 42 U.S.C. Sec. 2000e 703 (h). See Griggs v. Duke Power Co., 420 F. 2d 1225 (4th Cir. 1970); "Developments in the Law: Employment Discrimination and Title VII of the Civil Rights Act of 1964," *Harvard Law Review* 84 (March 1971): 1109, 1113-55.

87. Griggs v. Duke Power Co., 292 F. Supp. 243, 249-50 (M.D. N.C. 1968); Griggs v. Duke Power Co., 420 F. 2d. 1225, 1234.

88. 401 U.S. 424, 431.

89. Ibid.

90. 42 U.S.C. Sec. 2000e 703 (h).

91. C & R Robinson v. Lorillard, 444 F. 2d 791, 794 (4th Cir. 1971).

92. See "Height Standards in Police Employment and the Question of Sex Discrimination," *Southern California Law Review* 47 (February 1974): 585, 604.

93. 5 F.E.P. Cases 665 (W.D. Ky. 1973).

94. Ibid.

95. 500 F. 2d 161 (5th Cir. 1974).

96. Ibid., p. 166. For a discussion of a job for which height requirements are arguably relevant but on analysis become indefensible, see "Height Requirements," supra n. 92.

97. Harper v. Trans World Airlines, 525 F. 2d 409 (8th Cir.).

98. "Height Requirements," pp. 607-12.

99. 414 U.S. 632 (1974).

100. 417 U.S. 484 (1974).

101. 29 C.F.R. Sec. 1604-10.

102. Communication Workers of America v. A.T.&T., 513 F. 2d 1024 (2nd Cir. 1975); Wetzel v. Liberty Mutual Insurance Co., 511 F. 2d 199 (3rd Cir. 1975); Gilbert v. General Electric Co., 519 F. 2d 661 (4th Cir. 1975); Tyler v. Vickery, 517 F. 2d 1089 (5th Cir. 1975); Satty v. Nashville Gas Co., 522 F. 2d 850 (5th Cir. 1975). The Court has granted certiorari in the Satty case.

103. General Electric Co. v. Gilbert, 45 U.S. Law Week 4031, 97 S. Ct. 401 (1976).

104. 97 S. Ct. 401, 408, 409, quoting 417 U.S. 484, 496-97.

105. 97 S. Ct. 401, 409.

106. Ibid., p. 406.

107. Ibid., p. 405, n. 9.

108. Ibid., p. 409, quoting 417 U.S. 484, 496. Emphasis supplied.

109. Ibid. Emphasis supplied.

110. Ibid., p. 410. Emphasis in the original.

111. Baer, "Sexual Equality and the Burger Court," pp. 10-11.

112. 97 S. Ct. 401, 408.

113. Ibid., p. 416.

114. Ibid., p. 408.

115. Ibid. Emphasis supplied.

116. Ibid., p. 413 (Stewart, J., concurring; Blackmun, J., concurring in part).

117. Ibid., p. 421 (Stevens, J., dissenting).

118. 29 C.F.R. Sec. 1604.2.

119. 311 F. Supp. 559 (S.D. Fla. 1970); 442 F. 2d 385 (5th Cir. 1971), *cert. denied* 404 U.S. 950.

120. 42 U.S.C. Sec. 2000e 708.

121. 29 C.F.R. Sec. 1604.1 (3) (b) (1965).

122. 30 F. R. 14927 (1966).

123. Weeks v. Southern Bell, 277 F. Supp. 117 (S.D. Ga. 1967).
124. 33 F.R. 3349.
125. Rosenfeld v. Southern Pacific Co., 293 F. Supp. 1219 (C.D. Cal. 1968).
126. Ibid., p. 1223.
127. Ibid., pp. 1224-26.
128. 297 F. Supp. 134 (D. Minn. 1968).
129. Ibid.
130. 408 F. 2d 228 (5th Cir. 1969).
131. Ibid., pp. 235-36.
132. Richards v. Griffith Rubber Mills, 300 F. Supp. 338 (D. Ore. 1969).
133. 303 F. Supp. 754 (M.D. Ala. 1969).
134. 416 F. 2d 711 (7th Cir. 1969).
135. 29 C.F.R. Sec. 1604.2 (b) (1).
136. Local 246, Utility Workers Union v. Southern California Edison Co., 320 F. Supp. 1262, 1265 (C.D. Cal. 1970).
137. See, e.g., Caterpillar Tractor Co. v. Grabiec, 317 F. Supp. 1304 (S.D. Ill. 1970) (hours law); Vogel v. Trans World Airlines, 346. F. Supp. 805 (W.D. Mo. 1971) (hours law); Rinehart v. Westinghouse Electric Corp., 3 F.E.P. Cases 851 (N.D. Ohio 1971), and Manning v. General Motors Corp., 3 F.E.P. Cases 968, affirmed 466 F. 2d 812 (N.D. Ohio 1971) (hours, weight limits, and seating requirements); Kober v. Westinghouse Electric Corp., 325 F. Supp. 467 (W.D. Pa. 1971) (hours law); Rosenfeld v. Southern Pacific Co., 444 F. 2d 1219 (9th Cir. 1971), affirming 293 F. Supp. 1219; General Electric Co. v. Young, 3 F.E.P. Cases 561 (W. D. Ky. 1971) (hours law); Garneau v. Raytheon Co., 323 F. Supp. 391 (D. Mass. 1971) (hours law); LeBlanc v. Southern Bell, 333 F. Supp. 602 (E.D. La. 1971) (hours law); Schaeffer v. San Diego Yellow Cabs, 462 F. 2d 1002 (9th Cir. 1972) (hours law); Evans v. Sheraton Park Hotel, 5 F.E.P. Cases 393 (D.D.C. 1972) (hours law); Krause v. Sacramento Inn, 479 F. 2d 988 (9th Cir. 1973) (job prohibition against women bartenders); Homemakers, Inc., v. Division of Industrial Welfare, 509 F. 2d 20 (9th Cir. 1974) (hours law, overtime regulations). Note how often several cases had to be brought in the same circuit before the issue was considered resolved.
138. E.g., Schaeffer v. San Diego Yellow Cabs, 462 F. 2d 1002, 1007; Evans v. Sheraton Park Hotel, 5 F.E.P. Cases 393; Krause v. Sacramento Inn, 479 F. 2d 988.
139. E.g., Hoyt v. Florida, 368 U.S. 57 (1961); Bradwell v. State, 16 Wall. (83 U.S.) 130 (1872).

6

JUSTICE, FAIRNESS,
AND SEX EQUALITY:
APPROACHING THE ISSUES

I have suggested more than once that we cannot assume that the existence of sexual differences justified discriminatory treatment. This statement is contrary not only to American constitutional law but also to much of the conventional wisdom about the sexes, which appears to rest on exactly the assumption I have questioned. We are all familiar with phrases like "vive la difference," remarks like "Madam, I can't conceive" of the differences between the sexes, and suggestions that efforts to improve the position of women are efforts to ignore or obliterate sexual differences, offered in defense of the status quo. Such comments frequently stand alone, unaccompanied by any effort to explain the connections between "la difference" and public policy. And these statements seem to accord with a human habit of using differences between people, not similarities among them, as a basis for assigning status.

SOME WAYS OF NOT THINKING ABOUT SEX EQUALITY:[1]
PITFALLS TO AVOID

Unfortunately for feminists, statements like these have certain inherent appeal. A traditionalist who can suggest that reformers deny the existence of sexual differences has reduced their credibility to the level of those who argue that the world is flat. Furthermore, there is at least a plausible logical connection between the observable sexual differences and the roles assigned to each sex: between childbearing and homemaking, and physical strength and dominance. Another reason statements of the kind I have quoted can be convincing has to do not with physical differences but with overall personality differences which can be equally apparent. It does not take a psychologist to observe differences between the ways most women think, feel, and act and the ways most men think, feel and act, and similarities among the members of each group. We all have frequent occasions to observe this phenomenon, and frequently make predictions about the behavior of others on this basis.

The fact that we observe such differences is not very surprising. Although we cannot trace all such differences to physical differences, males and females lead lives, because of these differences, which are in some respects very dissimilar. There are experiences which all females, and no males, have, and vice versa. However sharply we might disagree with some of the psychoanalytic theories based on these differences,[2] and however much differential socialization has reinforced the effects of physical differences, surely it is plausible that the relative prominence and accessibility of the sexual organs, or the presence or absence of cyclical patterns of hormonal production and the degree of their intensity,[3] influence the development of the personality. If we agree that personality is malleable, and experience influences its development, we should not be surpirsed if males and females develop some differences.

But, after all, we can also observe overall personality differences between Northerners and Southerners, Jews and Gentiles, Irish and Italians, and can make generalizations about ethnic or regional personalities which are true for large segments of the relevant populations. Terms such as "Southern belle," "Jewish princess," and "Irish cop," describe readily identifiable characters (although they can become stereotypes that obscure individuality). And we do not conclude from such differences that discrimination based on race, religion, or national origin is allowable. The law, in particular, treats many people who are very different from one another as if they were alike. Equality is not confused with identicality. But in the area of sex discrimination, traditionalists often talk as though "equal'. did mean "identical."

The psychologist might well object at this point that sexual differences are far more important than ethnic or regional ones. The ways in which males and females differ are likely to influence their sexual development, unsurprisingly. This is true however badly much of the literature in the field has misunderstood these differences.[4] If the sexual drive is viewed, as it has been by many writers in this field from Freud to the present, as the basic force in personality development—"the axis around which the organization of the personality takes place"[5]—it seems to follow that such differences are very basic indeed, and would produce a host of other significant differences. But psychologists do not unanimously assign sex so pre-eminent a position in personality development.[6] Even if they did, we would not be bound to accept a conclusion which frequently has been no more than an assumption. And however significant these differences are, they must still be proved relevant for public policy. Personality theories which rest on abstract assumptions, however plausible, should not be the sole basis for limiting individual opportunities.

There is a second, and related, assumption frequently made in thinking about sex equality which represents a trap the scholar must carefully avoid. The adult male is taken as the norm; the question often becomes not whether the sexes differ from each other but whether the women differ from men. Simone de Beauvoir has provided what is probably the most brilliant analysis of this common error:

> A man would never get the notion of writing a book on the peculiar situation of the human male. But if I wish to define myself, I must first of all say, "I am a woman"; on this truth must be based all further discussion. A man never begins by presenting himself as an individual of a certain sex; it goes without saying that he is a man. The terms *masculine* and *feminine* are used symmetrically only as a matter of form, as in legal papers. In actuality the relation of the two sexes is not quite like that of two electrical poles, for man represents both the positive and the neutral, as indicated by the common use of *man* to designate human being in general; whereas woman represents only the negative, defined by limiting criteria, without reciprocity. . . . It amounts to this: just as for the ancients there was an absolute vertical with reference to which the oblique was defined, so there is an absolute human type, the masculine. Woman has ovaries, a uterus; these peculiarities imprison her in her own subjectivity, circumscribe her within the limits of her own nature. It is often said that she thinks with her glands. Man superbly ignores the fact that his anatomy also includes glands, such as the testicles, and that they secrete hormones. He thinks of his body as a direct and normal connection with the world, which he believes he apprehends objectively, whereas he regards the body of woman as a hindrance,

a prison, weighted down by everything peculiar to it . . . .
Thus humanity is male and man defines woman not in herself but as relative to him; she is not regarded as an autono-
mous being. . . . He is the Subject, he is the Absolute—she
is the Other.[7]

A rereading of the *Muller* opinion will illustrate the phenomenon de
Beauvoir is discussing. We are all so accustomed to thinking in the manner she has described that we see no peculiarity in talking about the "special" needs of over half of the population. It has been a man's world for
so long that we tend to accept unquestioningly the male claim to be the
"self" or the "subject." But the assumption is nevertheless a trap, because,
by begging a crucial question, it biases the argument in favor of the traditionalists. If maleness is accepted as the norm, proponents of sex equality
are forced to argue that, despite the sexual differences which do exist,
women are, overall, more like than unlike men. Perhaps they could win
that argument; if boys and girls were socialized in the same ways, maybe
they would develop similar personalities. But until there are radical changes in our social norms, there will be more evidence which appears, however misleadingly, to refute this assumption than evidence in its favor.

If the assumption is challenged, the question does not have to be argued on these grounds. There is no intrinsic reason why male characteristics should be accepted as the norm for human personality and behavior with deviance from these characteristics accepted as a basis for discrimination. It would be possible to view masculine and feminine as true
polarities with different, but equally normal, characteristics. The superiority of maleness—and the legitimacy of the male claim to be the "absolute human type"—would have to be proved, not assumed. And the
proof would have to involve a showing that men are superior to women
with respect to some quality or qualities.

A third common pitfall is the one into which most of the early court
decisions fell: the assumption that the acceptance of one kind of discrimination based on a particular characteristic justifies any and all discrimination based on that characteristic. The validity of the classification
has to be established separately for each kind of discrimination proposed;
the purpose would have to be examined and evaluated in each instance.
We could not say that "sex is a valid basis for classification" across the
board. Accepting sex-based discrimination in a case involving working

hours neither forces nor permits us to accept it in cases involving night work, jury service, or college admissions, or even in another hours case where the circumstances are different. If we assign sex to the status of a suspect classification, that would still enable us to recognize compelling state need for sex discrimination. For example, if a state department of health had only a limited amount of rubella vaccine, this standard would justify its administration to girls rather than boys, and that would not jeopardize any claims to equality.

After all, we do not accept across-the-board discrimination even in non-suspect categories of age and disability, as poor analogies to sex as these are. Our acceptance of age-based discrimination in contractual rights does not imply acceptance of limits on procedural safeguards in criminal trials, nor does the principle which permits the denial of drivers' licenses to people with visual or motor handicaps so severe that they cannot pass the examination allow us to deny them the vote. The question is not whether any attribute is a valid basis for discrimination, but which kinds of discrimination the attribute might or might not justify. Resolution of this question would demand not only an evaluation of the relevance of the particular attribute to the discrimination proposed, but a determination of the degree of deprivation or benefit provided by the discrimination. The kind of reasoning I described earlier in this chapter will not suffice. Not only do obvious sexual differences not justify differential treatment by themselves, but the justification of one kind of sex-based discrimination does not legitimate any other kind.

A fourth error to avoid is an assumption we have identified as common to arguments for protective labor legislation: the identification of the interests of women with those of their families. The grossest form of this position is exemplified by my quotation in Chapter 1 from Phyllis McGinley: the assumption that women have no legitimate interests separate from those of their families or society. "We are the sacrificers . . . the self-immolators." Women are seen as a permanent crypto-slave class, whose interests are presumed identical with others or just do not rank equally with them.

In a recent book, John Kenneth Galbraith describes women in a capitalist system as a "crypto-servant class,"[8] but I think the stonger term is defensible. Its use in this context is not unique. In an address to the Anti-Slavery Convention in Cincinnati in 1835, Horace Greeley said, "I understand by slavery, that condition in which one human being exists mainly as a convenience of other human beings—in which the time, the exertions, the faculties of a part of the Human Family are made to subserve, not their own development, physical, intellectual, and moral, but the comfort, advantage or caprice of others."[9] Greeley's awareness of the import of his words is suggested by a comment further on in the speech: ". . . how can I devote myself to a crusade against distant servitude, when I deem its essence pervading my immediate community and neighborhood? Nay, when I have not yet succeeded in banishing it from my own household? . . . Be as tenacious that your own wives, children, hired men and women, tenants, etc., enjoy the blessings of rational Liberty as the slaves of South Carolina."[10]

The assumption that women exist mainly for the convenience of others has recurred throughout my examination of protective legislation, even in statements which appear to be motivated by sincere concern for women. These reformers strove to make women healthier and happier crypto-slaves, but their efforts were not directed at changing, and did not change, the status of these women.

It is no answer to this contention to object that in all families each member's interests are frequently subordinated to those of others, and sacrifices and compromises are made on all sides. This is perfectly true; however, much of the available popular literature on family life suggests that the mother's interests are *never* to be given independent consideration. That state of affairs might be perfectly acceptable to some women (or, for that matter, to some men in different contexts). A person might voluntarily choose to place her or his own interests last, and to subordinate them to those of others. Such a choice is defensible, and perhaps, in some circumstances, commendable. But there is a vast difference between the *voluntary* choice of self-sacrifice as a way of life and the *assignment* of a large group of people to such a role by law and custom.

Society's acceptance of women's crypto-slave status is indicated by the popular reaction to Phyllis McGinley's book, which I quoted from. This description of women as self-immolators was published in 1964, and sold well enough to get its author on the cover of *Time* magazine. No one objected to this passage or, as I recall, even mentioned it—and the book was widely discussed in the popular press. Now, it is recognizable to a feminist such as Elizabeth Janeway, who in 1971 was clearly appalled by it,[11] as a statement of an extraordinary social fact.

The press of the 1950s and 1960s bombarded us all with articles which made implicit what McGinley had made explicit. There were, for instance, all those articles on how to keep one's husband alive—a task for which he was assumed to have no responsibility. Some of these ideas surfaced again as late as the spring of 1973, in a thoroughly objectionable article by nutritionist Jean Mayer.[12] Still more revealing was all the discussion about whether or not mothers should work outside the home. Writers usually concluded that outside employment was all right so long as the children (and sometimes the husband) were not harmed or inconvenienced in any way—which, in practice, meant virtually never. It was seldom, if ever, suggested that the potential harm to the children might be weighed against the potential gain to the mother.[13]

This kind of reasoning has not been confined to popular journalism. Respected scholars have also accepted this assumption. One striking example is provided by the studies of infants and children which the British physician John Bowlby has been conducting since the late 1940s, sometimes under the auspices of the World Health Organization. These studies conclude that "what is believed to be essential for mental health is that the infant and young child should experience a warm, intimate, and continuous relationship with his mother."[14] Whatever the validity of Bowlby's conclusions—which is not at issue here—the significant aspect of this study (and its popular and academic reception)[15] for my purposes is his assumption, accepted by his readers, that the actions of the mother are properly determined by the needs of the child. Bowlby assumed that a mother will rarely leave her child; the possibility that she might want outside employment does not even receive his serious attention. For example, he writes, "Naturally a mother will keep the time she is away from her child as short as possible, though in some cases the length of time lies outside her control."[16] Little or no consideration is given to the possibility that the mother might have separate needs which should be taken into account. (This statement is not as callous as it sounds; after all, nobody, even an infant, gets all of her or his needs satisfied, and as every expert since Freud has recognized, growing up is a process fraught with frustrations.)[17]

Compare Bowlby's remarks with those of the political scientist Robert Lane, written in 1959:

> Would it be wise to reinforce the feminist movement, emphasizing politics on the women's page along with the garden club and bridge club news, and making ward politics something like volunteer work for the Red Cross or the hos-

pital auxiliary? No doubt something along this line could be
done but it is too seldom remembered in the American society that working girls and career women, and women who
insistently serve the community in volunteer capacities, and
women with extra-curricular interests of an absorbing kind
are often borrowing their time and attention and capacity
for relaxed play and love from their children to whom it
rightfully belongs.[18]

    This quotation is part of a one-paragraph discussion of the female role;
the assumption made in the last sentence about where women's capacities
should be concentrated is nowhere amplified or examined.
    The statements I am analyzing here should not be confused with argu-
ments that women's own nature and character make their interests in-
separable from those of others. The assertions of McGinley, MacLean,
Bowlby, and Lane are mere unsupported assumptions; the reasoning they
contain is far inferior in quality to the psychological theories I shall examine in the next chapter or to statements like that made by Alexis deTocque
ville:

    [Americans] think that nature, which created such dif-
ferences between the physical and moral constitution of men
and women, clearly intended to give their diverse faculties a
diverse employment; and they consider that progress consists not in making dissimilar creatures do roughly the same
things but in giving both the chance to do their job as well
as possible. The Americans have applied to the sexes the
great principle of political economy which now dominates
industry. They have carefully separated the functions of man
and of woman so that the great work of society may be
performed.[19]

    The Americans' assignment of women to "the quiet sphere of domes-
tic duties,"[20] and Tocqueville's approval of it, are based not on an assumed
fusion or subordination of interests but on an independent determination
of women's interests which in turn is based upon a view of sexual differences in personality and abilities. This view itself is not free of unexamined
assumptions; nature's apparent intentions are merely asserted, not proved.
But despite its faults, Tocqueville's argument is superior to those which I

have been discussing because it is free of the logical fallacy of *ignoratio elenchi:* it does not suppose a point proved or disproved by an irrelevant argument. Arguments about children or families are of dubious relevance to the question of the position of women, unless one shows the link between the needs of children or families and those of women. Tocqueville reasons from a view of the nature of women to a conclusion about their appropriate role. His conclusion might permit the identification of women's interests with family interests, but he does not simply assume that. Both Tocqueville and Lane assign women to the same place in life, but for very different reasons.

De Tocqueville's reasoning is similar to that of Justice Bradley in the first sex discrimination case ever heard by the United States Supreme Court:

> The civil law, as well as nature herself, has always recognized a wide difference in the respective spheres and destinies of man and woman. Man is, or should be, woman's protector and defender. The natural and proper timidity and delicacy which belongs to the female sex evidently unfits it for many of the occupations of civil life. The constitution of the family organization, which is founded in the divine ordinance as well as in the nature of things, indicates the domestic sphere as that which properly belongs to the domain and functions of womanhood. The harmony, not to say identity, of interests and views which belongs, or should belong, to the family institution [N.B.] is repugnant to the idea of a woman adopting a distinct and independent career from that of her husband. . . .
>
> It is true that many women are unmarried and not affected by any of the duties, complications, and incapacities arising out of the married state, but these are exceptions to the general rule. The paramount destiny and mission of woman are to fulfill the noble and benign offices of wife and mother. This is the law of the Creator. And the rules of civil society must be adapted to the general constitution of things, and cannot be based upon exceptional cases.[21]

In the next chapter, I will spend much time scrutinizing views like these; the point which needs to be made here is simply that they are very different arguments than those which assume a connection between women's interests and family interests. If Lane and Bowlby, for example, were pressed to defend their statements, they might express views of female human nature similar to those of Tocqueville or Bradley, and link these views with their statements about children. But the fact that they do not do so indicates how easy it is to slip into the habit of discussing women's position in terms of the needs of others.

And the problem is even more pervasive than these statements imply. It is not confined to the ranking of the wife and mother within the family. Wherever women function, their interests, *qua* women, are implicitly underranked. The opinion in *State v. Hunter* had no difficulty in ignoring women's interests while defending men's right to legislate in their own. Jessie Bernard has discussed this phenomenon extensively in a recent book, *Women and the Public Interest.*[22] She analyzes the "all pervading function of stroking"[23] which women are expected to perform on demand. Whatever they may be doing, they are expected to drop it to build up the egos of men or to assist anyone who may require it.[24] Later in the book Bernard concludes that public policies designed to benefit women "are the least of all priorities."[25]

EQUALITY AND JUSTICE: SOME BASIC CONSIDERATIONS

The automatic assignment of inferior status to the interests of any group does not conform to principles of justice widely accepted in our society; indeed, it is the very essence of injustice. This is true whichever of the two "working definitions" of justice prevalent in this culture one wants to accept—justice as equality or the ideal conception of justice as giving everyone his or her due—or however one tries to combine and reconcile them. We can see this more clearly by examining some of the remarks which Aristotle, not an egalitarian philosopher, makes in the early section of the *Politics.* Aristotle's acceptance of natural slavery and the subjection of women depended on his conviction that it served the interests of the subjects as well as those of the masters:

> Whatever may be said of inanimate things, it is certainly
> possible, as we have said, to observe in animate beings . . .
> the presence of a ruling authority, both of the sort exercised
> by a master over slaves and of the sort exercised by a states-
> man over fellow citizens. The soul rules the body with the

sort of authority of a statesman or a monarch. In this sphere
[i.e., in the sphere of man's inner life] it is clearly natural
and beneficial to the body that it should be ruled by the
soul, and again it is natural and beneficial to the affective
part of the soul that it should be ruled by the mind and the
rational part; whereas the equality of the two elements, or
their reverse relation, is always detrimental. What holds good
in man's inner life also holds good outside it; and the same
principle is as true of the relation of man to animals as is
true of the relation of his soul to his body. Tame animals
have a better nature than wild, and it is better for all such
animals that they should be ruled by man because they
then get the benefit of preservation. Again, the relation of
male to female is naturally that of the superior to the inferior—of the ruling to the ruled. This general principle
must similarly hold good of all human beings generally
[and therefore the relation of masters and slaves].

   We may thus conclude that all men who differ from others
as much as the body differs from the soul, or an animal from
a man (and this is the case with all whose function is bodily
service, and who produce their best when they supply such
service)—all such are by nature slaves, and it is better *for
them,* on the very same principle as in the other cases just
mentioned, to be ruled by a master. A man is thus by nature
a slave if he is capable of being (and this is the reason why
he also actually becomes) the property of another, and if
he participates in reason to the extent of apprehending it
in another though destitute in it himself.[26]

   I have quoted Aristotle at such length not to endorse his doctrines, but
merely to show that even he set up stringent criteria for the assignment of
people to inferior status. Women and slaves should have such status because it benefits them, not because it suits men or masters. Aristotle makes
a separate, though not necessarily correct, judgment of the interests of the
subject groups. He suggests that if any people are to be assigned inferior
rank, such assignment is justified—paradoxical as it sounds—only if the
people are first assumed to rank equally, and they are considered on an
equal basis before it is determined that they will benefit from such rank.

Following my previous statement, I would insist that *each* assignment of status or right be justified *separately* in this way.

But at this point a crucial problem arises: how are we to decide whether such status assignment is beneficial? Is the belief of members of a group that such assignment is to their advantage sufficient to justify it, or must some objective criteria be found? Or must the assignment satisfy both conditions? Aristotle suggests that the slave will understand that it is better for him to be ruled by those who are wiser than he, but to interpret this passage as stating that inferior status must be acceptable to the subject group would be, to say the least, problematical. However, I think I have given enough examples of the difficulties that arise when one group tries to interpret the interests of another group to justify the conclusion that, at the very least, the status assignment must be acceptable to the group itself. (Of course, this formulation leads directly to another problem: what happens if the assignment is accepted by some members of the group and rejected by others? I plan to deal with this important question in some detail later, but will put it aside for now.)

Unfortunately, people can and do misinterpret their own interests, as much feminist literature suggests. It is probable that throughout history most women have accepted their assigned status, but we would not wish to conclude from this that the assignment has been just. Some objective evaluation of whether or not the assignment is beneficial to the group involved is necessary. The assignment would have to be advantageous to the group as well as acceptable to it.

EQUALITY, IDENTITY, AND EQUIVALENCE: A NECESSARY DIGRESSION

Before trying to apply political philosophy to the question of sex discrimination, one must answer an objection which could immediately be raised. I have been discussing assignment to *inferior* status. But this adjective raises again the problem I touched on earlier: the tension between two widely accepted ideas of justice, which can also be expressed as a conflict between notions of equality. Those who oppose changes in the status of women emphatically reject the idea that assigning women to a domestic role (and basing public policy on this assignment) does constitute inferior treatment. Contemporary traditionalists are not comfortable, as Aristotle was, with the notion that women are inferior to men. Rather, they accept the principle of sex equality and argue that this equality is

recognized when both men and women are treated in the ways which
benefit them most, which, for the traditionalist, means different treatment. They argue that women are biologically and psychologically best
suited for a domestic role; the emphasis is usually on female, not male,
personality.

The assumption about the meaning of equality which underlies this
position is unexceptionable. Beyond doubt, we cannot define "equal"
as "identical." The fact that women are channelled into one set of roles,
while men are channelled into another, and that most public policy is
based on that role assignment does not prove that women receive unequal (i.e., inferior) treatment. "Equal" can also mean "equivalent."
Traditionalists have argued that women do have equality with men because each sex is channelled into the roles best suited for it and receives
equivalent rewards. One could develop a sort of "different but equal"
theory here, according to which a domestic role is just as rewarding
for those suited to it as a worker's role is for those suited to it, in the
same way, I suppose, that medicine is "equal" to law as a career.

This notion of equality-as-equivalence would not necessarily lead to
a defense of the status quo. One could take a position between tradition-
alism and feminism, arguing that women do receive inferior treatment because the roles for which they are suited do not have equivalent status or
carry equivalent rewards with male roles. Proponents of such a position
might point to the low prestige of the housewife role; the lack of payment for services, sick leave, vacation, or other benefits; the absence of
supportive services for the housewife, etc. Even if one accepts this role
assignment as justified, a solid argument could be made that women still
do not have equal status with men.

"Different but equal" is not as absurd a concept as "separate but equal"
has been shown to be. It would be hard to prove that "different roles are
inherently unequal," since this would involve denying that people in different occupations can benefit equally. However, I must enter a caveat
here. I realize that the examples of occupational status which I have used
are upper-middle-class ones. Most workers are not doctors or lawyers; far
more hold blue-collar, clerical, or unskilled jobs. These jobs do not enjoy
equal status in the public mind with professional careers (nor, of course,
does homemaking).

But aside from the question of status, jobs such as construction work,
typing, and emptying bedpans may not be as intrinsically rewarding for
people suited to them as professional careers are for those whose talents

lie in those directions. There are two components of the value of a task: the societal need for its performance, and the satisfaction it provides for the person who performs it. These components may not be entirely independent of one another, but they are separable to some degree. Satisfaction may be determined partly by the societal need for the task, but it is also partly dependent upon the effort, skill, and intelligence required to perform the task. And this is nowhere clearer than in the area of human reproduction. The creation of human beings in essential to the continuation of society, and human beings themselves are complex and intricate creatures. But, essential and extraordinary as they are, human beings are very easy to make. It does not require the genius of a Beethoven or a Michelangelo to produce babies. Almost anyone past puberty can participate. This is as true for women as it is for men. The talent required of the producers is grossly disproportionate to the value of the product. Therefore, reproduction itself (distinguished, of course, from childrearing) may not be as inherently fulfilling as popular discussions of sex roles frequently suggest. Arguments which emphasize the creative character of childbearing in the typical glowing terms seem to dwell on the nature of the product, to the exclusion of another component: the nature of the effort involved.[27]

There may be some absolutely necessary tasks which can bring no fulfillment for anybody, and, therefore, some people may have to spend part or all of their lives doing work which gives them no satisfaction. The "different but equal" theory, applied to such jobs, would be as absurd as "separate but equal." *All* different roles presumably are not inherently unequal, but *some* roles may be in relation to others. And therein lies a social problem with which we have not coped very well. For the "different but equal" theory to hold in this area, it would have to be shown that (1) homemaking, certainly a necessity, is or can be a satisfying one, and (2) that women are better suited for it than for any other.

Whatever the intrinsic rewards of housework as an occupation—a subject on which there is wide and vehement difference of opinion—the context in which homemaking takes place, and the compulsory nature of the status assignment, degrade both the job and the person. The housewife in a nuclear family is a peculiarly isolated being, especially when her children are young. For most of the day, she is virtually deprived of any but the most superficial relationships with other adults. She spends her time attending to inanimate objects—the washing machine, the vacuum cleaner, the stove, etc.—and interacting with children on an intellectual level determined by their capacity. Philip Slater has described the housewife as "a nobody" to whom "nothing ever happens, really." He writes:

> The emotional and intellectual poverty of the house-
> wife's role is nicely expressed in the almost universal com-
> plaint: "I get to talking baby talk with no one around all
> day but the children." There are societies in which the do-
> mestic role works, but in these societies the housewife is
> not isolated. She is either part of a large extended family
> household in which domestic activities are a communal ef-
> fort, or participates in a tightly knit village community, or
> both. The idea of imprisoning each woman alone in a small,
> self-contained, and architecturally isolating dwelling is a
> modern invention, dependent upon an advanced technology.
> In Moslem societies, for example, the wife may be a prison-
> er but she is at least not in solitary confinement. In our so-
> ciety the housewife may move about freely, but since she
> has nowhere to go and is not part of anything anyway, her
> prison needs no walls.
>   This is in striking contrast to her pre-marital life, if she is
> a college graduate. In college she is typically embedded in
> an active group life with constant emotional and intellectual
> stimulation. College life is in this sense an urban life. Mar-
> riage typically eliminates much of this way of life for her,
> and children deliver the *coup de grace.* Her only significant
> relationship tends to be her husband, who, however, is ab-
> sent for most of the day. Most of her social and emotional
> needs must be satisfied by her children, who are hardly ade-
> quate to this task.[28]

That this phenomenon is not limited to women college graduates is illustrated in an article by sociologist Patricia Cayo Sexton. Describing her mother's experience as a mechanized seamstress in an automobile plant, Sexton reports that the job, though hardly interesting in itself, gave her mother a network of collegial relationships with fellow workers. On the job, she had people she could talk to; she had no intention of giving it up before she had to.[29] Her feelings strike a responsive chord. For most of us, collegial relationships can be one of the joys (even at the same time that they are one of the pains) of life. We relish, for instance, the "in" jokes which develop among workers in the same office, graduate students in the same department, researchers in the same foundations. A life which lacks these relationships must be impoverished indeed.

We are not without evidence, then, that the domestic role falls short in intrinsic rewards. But there is a case to be made on the other side. A more forceful case can be made for the position that such status assignment constitutes inferior treatment simply by pointing out that it restricts women's opportunities to a very narrow field, while depriving men of only one opportunity. Although few men can in fact choose any job other than homemaking, the point is, first, that men have a wider range of choice, and, second, while relatively few men may have a chance at society's most rewarding careers, they have a virtual monopoly on them. The traditional role assignment appears, on analysis, to be intrinsically inferior, not just different, no matter what one's conception of equality.

POSSIBLE BASES FOR SEX DISCRIMINATION

What differences between men and women might provide the basis for differential status? Aristotle suggested one possibility. Suppose we follow him, and most of classical philosophy, in viewing the capacity for reason as the preeminently human ability, that which makes us unique among animals. Suppose it were true, and could be proved, that men are superior to women in this capacity. Would that give men a legitimate claim to superior status?

Resolving such a question would be fraught with difficulties. First—as much as I agree with the idea—not everyone in our society agrees that reason should rule over emotion. Secondly, we would immediately be faced with the problem of whether men's superiority in reason was founded in inherent personality differences between the sexes or in differential socialization of the sexes, and then with the problem of determining the relevance of the source of the difference. We have ample evidence that girls are taught to play dumb with boys,[30] that they are discouraged from displaying or using their intelligence,[31] that they are socialized into mental passivity,[32] and that they are taught to prefer "warm intuitive knowledge" to "cold unproductive thinking"[33] (as if the two were mutually exclusive)—as, indeed, we have evidence that general differential socialization based on sex begins at birth and continues thereafter.[34] Therefore, no one should wonder if women become less rational than men. It seems a little unfair to penalize people for being what they have been taught to be.

Finally, we would have to remember that no one, even Plato or Aristotle, ever argued that the super-rational thinking machine was the ideal human being. Plato, in particular, emphasized the desirability of having all three parts of the soul—the reasoning, the spirited, and the desiring—in *balance*.[35] Although there is no reason to believe that the psyche organizes itself in this tripartite, oppositional fashion—the ancients, or Freud, to the contrary notwithstanding—certainly the observation that the psyche contains a variety of capacities is sound, and the conclusion that reason should rule, but not tyrannize, in the psyche is, to say the least, defensible. If it is balance which is most desirable, then superior rationality in itself would not qualify men for superior status. One could even suggest that women have the edge here if, indeed, they are more emotive and expressive than men are.

A quality in which men could more easily and less ambiguously be judged superior to women is in physical strength. I have suggested that there is at least a plausible connection between physical strength and dominance. However, as I pointed out much earlier, it is not true that all men are stronger than all women. There is substantial overlap, and this raises a significant question: whether it is fair to assign all members of a class to a particular status because of characteristics shared only by some of them. But even if that problem is left aside, the idea that justice is the will of the stronger was rejected long ago. It is somewhat surprising to find it reappearing in contemporary discussions of this particular problem. But reappear it does, along with the related argument that males are more aggressive than females and therefore will, and should, always dominate.[36]

On analysis, this reveals itself to be a rather extraordinary argument. Usually, references are made to "nature" or the "law of nature" by which the stronger rules the weaker. It is assumed by these thinkers that what is "natural" is humankind in its least disciplined, most selfish state: they seem to share Hobbes' view of "man" in the "state of nature." They do not consider, as Aristotle did, that the natural might be that which is most highly refined and developed. Furthermore, although they share the concept of nature prevalent in modern Western political theory, they refuse to draw from this the conclusion which those thinkers drew: that some form of government is necessary among human beings precisely because the rule of nature is intolerable. However discreditable the social contract theory of the origin of government may be as historical interpretation, the conclusion that one of the functions of government is to substitute a system of established law for the rule of brute force is fully justifiable. This is not an idea to which only serious students of political theory have access; it presents itself to those who undertake even the superficial study of American institutions required of schoolchildren in this country.

But this knowledge is cast aside when people begin thinking about sex equality. In this area, people want to accept the apparent dictates of nature rather than find a preferable alternative for them. Those who would absolutely reject the idea that nature, in this sense, should rule supreme in society mysteriously accept the idea that nature must rule in determining the relative positions of the sexes in society. (These arguments recall a related phenomenon: frequent references to the will or law of God to justify the status quo among people who are not generally comfortable with such terminology.) Once the extraordinary inconsistency is exposed, physical strength seems to provide a very poor basis for status assignment.

The question of strength leads logically to the question of aggression. Many experts have argued that males will always dominate in society because they are inherently more aggressive. Two recent versions of this thesis have been advanced by Lionel Tiger in *Men in Groups*[37] and Stephen Goldberg in *The Inevitability of Patriarchy*.[38] Drawing from anthropology, zoology, and literature, Tiger argues that "males are prone to bond, male bonds are prone to aggress, therefore aggression is a predictable feature of human groups of males."[39] Although he is not sure whether aggression produces bonding or vice versa, he is convinced that both phenomena are by nature more characteristic of males than of females and that "males more than females incline to tough mastery of the environment and a creative rather than reactive interference with physical and social realities."[40] Therefore, he suspects, males will always dominate. Goldberg insists that all societies throughout history have been patriarchal (an interpretation which, he recognizes, is not universally accepted, but which is at least plausible), and reasons from this interpretation that innate psychological factors, common to all men and to all women, like differences in aggression, must have been the cause of this phenomenon. He also suggests that aggression may be caused mainly by hormones such as testosterone, which men's bodies produce at a higher level than do women's. Therefore, he concludes, male dominance is inevitable.[41]

Tiger is vulnerable to criticism because he concludes from the ubiquity of male bonding and aggression that they are natural, not learned, phenomena, and therefore probably inflexible, though he himself recognizes the universality of cultural and physical factors which have produced such differentiation in pre-technological societies. Goldberg's thesis is not the only possible explanation for the near-universality of patriarchy up to the present, as I shall suggest in the next few pages. If my theory rather than his is correct, it does not follow that male dominance is inevitable. Furthermore, his reliance on hormones is suspect. If hormone production is the principal determinant of aggression, there should be virtually no exceptions to the general rule that men are more aggressive than women. But we know that there are many exceptions, which endocrinological explanations cannot handle.

These two arguments are nevertheless interesting as well-reasoned examples of theses which emphasize aggression in defending male dominance. It is a useful exercise to concede them their unproved point that men are more aggressive than women. Insofar as they argue that men *will* always rule because women, being less aggressive, will always submit, one does not have to look very far for individual counterexamples, at least. Insofar as they mean that men *should* always rule, they are subject to exactly the same criticisms as those who advance physical strength as a basis for dominance. It may be essential for civil society that its more aggressive members be *prevented* from dominating others. Equality is probably the best protection.

THE BIOLOGICAL BASIS FOR SEX DISCRIMINATION: REPRODUCTION AND SEXUAL INEQUALITY

Any of these factors—intellect, strength, or aggression—might provide, and indeed has provided, justifications for sex discrimination. But none of them has inspired the commonest traditional argument. The usual starting point for discussion is, of course, differences in reproductive function. Arguments tend to start with the fact that women, and not men, can bear children. Out of all human characteristics, those which the sexes share and those in which they differ, this one is seen as most crucial in determining the place of men and women in society.

It is not difficult to see how things might have gotten that way. As G. P. Murdock has written:

> It is unnecessary to invoke innate psychological differen-
> ces to account for the division of labor by sex; the indisput-
> able differences in reproductive functions suffice to lay out
> the broad lines of cleavage. New tasks as they arise are as-
> signed to one sphere of activities or the other in accordance
> with convenience and precedent. Habituation to different
> occupations in adulthood and early sex typing in childhood
> may well explain the observable differences in sex tempera-
> ment instead of *vice versa*.[42]

Vulnerability to pregnancy, childbirth, and lactation, and relative inferiority in physical strength, apparently combine to dictate a certain sexual division of labor in primitive, marginally viable societies. It is less clear
how society gets from this division of labor to male dominance (and it
may not, always) but there are many possible explanations. Perhaps Tiger
is correct in concluding that male bonding for hunting purposes reinforced
male aggression and thus made men dominant. Perhaps in societies where
physical strength is essential for survival, superior status attaches to those
who demonstrate it, usually men. Possibly, as Justice Brewer suggested,
women, sensing their own weakness, submitted to male dominance for
their own protection in a kind of exchange. My own suspicion is that we
have here an enormously complex chain of causation, in which all of these
factors, as well as others which may operate far below the level of consciousness,[43] interact. I am not an anthropologist or a psychoanalyst—however reliable members of those two professions have been in this area—and
any observations I make here are tentative. To explain male dominance
solely in terms of differences in reproductive function would probably be
a gross oversimplification. But reproductive function gets us a very long
way in explaining division of labor, which is the most solid basis remaining for the kind of legislation I have examined. Furthermore, it provides
the most frequently offered justification for the status quo.

Identifying explanation is, however, precisely the error that we must
avoid. The fact that a situation developed in response to genuine social
needs does not make the situation fair or just, especially if the needs satisfied by the situation no longer exist. We no longer live in a primitive, mar-

ginally viable society in which pregnancy and childbirth are frequent and debilitating and breast-feeding is a necessity. Modern societies have an opportunity to think about what they are doing and how they want to develop, and to exert control over their own futures in ways that were impossible before. Thinking about questions of morality is a luxury we can afford.

The traditionalist argument has usually gone something like this: From the fact that women bear and can nurse children, it follows that women have the primary responsibility for child care. From women's primary responsibility for child care, which takes place in the home, follows the conclusion that homemaking is also her responsibility. From the assignment of these responsibilities follows the conclusion that all else in a woman's life must be subordinate to this. And from that follows the necessity for restrictions. Anatomy is destiny, as Freud said.

At the end of the previous chapter, I raised some questions which are provoked by these assumptions. One of these questions was whether the fact of childbearing capacity entailed the assignment of domestic tasks to women as their primary function. On one level, this is a question about logic, and as such can be readily answered in the negative. But on a deeper level, this is a question not about logic but about psychology. Rephrased, the question might read something like this: Is a woman's personality constructed around "the fact that her somatic design harbors an 'inner space' destined to bear . . . offspring," and does this fact carry "with it, a biological and ethical commitment to take care of human infancy?"[44] In other words, does childbearing capacity set a certain psychological makeup which produces this commitment? Answering this question will involve exploring some of the literature on the psychology of men and women, weighing the available data against the standards I have set up: the insistence that the status assignment must fulfill the interests, independently determined, of women themselves.

NOTES

1. With apologies to John Schaar. See "Some Ways of Thinking About Equality," *Journal of Politics* 26 (November 1964): 867.

2. See, e.g., Helene Deutsch, *The Psychology of Women*, 2 vols. (New York: Grune & Stratton, 1944); Sigmund Freud, "Femininity," in *New Introductory Lectures in Psychoanalysis*, trans. by James Strachey (New York: W. W. Norton & Co., 1964), pp. 112-35; "Some Psychological Consequences of the Anatomical Distinc-

tion Between the Sexes," *International Journal of Psychoanalysis* 7 (January 1927): 133-42; Ferdinand Lundberg and Marynia F. Farnham, *Modern Woman: the Lost Sex* (New York: Grosset & Dunlap, 1947).

3. See Katharina Dalton, *The Menstrual Cycle* (New York: Warner Paperback Library, 1969); Estelle Ramey, "Men's Cycles (They Have Them Too, You Know)," *Ms.*, preview issue (Spring 1972), pp. 8-15.

4. See William H. Masters and Virginia E. Johnson, *Human Sexual Response* (Boston: Little, Brown & Co., 1966); Mary Jane Sherfey, "Female Sexuality," in Morgan, ed., *Sisterhood Is Powerful*, pp. 220-30; Barbara Seaman, *Free and Female*, chs. 1-4.

5. Therese Benedek, *Psychosexual Functions in Women*, quoted in Marie N. Robinson, *The Power of Sexual Surrender* (Garden City, N.Y.: Doubleday & Co., 1959), p. 24.

6. See, e.g., Erik H. Erikson, *Identity: Youth and Crisis* (New York: W. W. Norton & Co., 1968); A. H. Maslow, *Motivation and Personality* (2nd ed.; New York: Harper & Row, 1954).

7. *The Second Sex*, trans. by H. M. Parshley (New York: Alfred A. Knopf & Co., 1952), pp. xv-xvi.

8. *Economics and the Public Purpose* (Boston: Houghton Mifflin & Co., 1973), p. 33.

9. John R. Commons, *Documentary History*, 7: 212.

10. Ibid., pp. 213, 215.

11. *Man's World, Woman's Place*, pp. 40-42, 45-46.

12. *New York Times* (April 8, 1973), 6: 72ff.

13. See, e.g., Betty Friedan, *The Feminine Mystique* (New York: W. W. Norton & Co., 1963), passim, Even Friedan did not expose and question this assumption, but argued it on the traditionalists' grounds by presenting evidence that children were not harmed by maternal employment.

14. *Child Care and the Growth of Love*, arr. & ed. by Margery Fry (London: Penguin Books, 1953), p. 11.

15. See Margaret Mead, "Some Theoretical Considerations on the Problem of Mother-Child Separation," *American Journal of Orthopsychiatry* 24 (July 1954): 471-83.

16. *Child Care*, p. 17.

17. *Civilization and Its Discontents*, tr. & ed. by James Strachey (New York: W. W. Norton & Co., 1961).

18. *Political Life* (New York: Free Press, 1959), p. 355.

19. *Democracy in America*, trans. by George Lawrence, ed. by J. P. Mayer (Garden City, N.Y.: Doubleday & Co., 1969), p. 601.

20. Ibid.

21. Bradwell v. State, 16 Wall. (83 U.S.) 130, 141-42 (1872).

22. (Chicago: Aldine-Atherton, 1971).

23. Ibid., p. 88.

24. Ibid., pp. 88-101.

25. Ibid., p. 163.

26. *The Politics,* Book I. v. Secs. 6-9, trans. by Ernest Barker (New York: Oxford University Press, 1958), p. 13. Interpolations in the original. Emphasis supplied.

27. For an interesting discussion of this point, see Mary Ellman, *Thinking About Women* (New York: Harcourt Brace Jovanovich, 1968), pp. 62-64.

28. *The Pursuit of Loneliness* (Boston: Beacon Press, 1970), p. 68.

29. "Speaking for the Working-Class Wife," *Harper's* 225 (October 1962): 129-33. See also Lillian Breslow Rubin, *Worlds of Pain* (New York: Basic Books, 1976), ch. 9.

30. See, e.g., Friedan, *Feminine Mystique,* ch. 7; Mirra Komarovsky, *Women in the Modern World* (Boston: Little, Brown & Co., 1953), ch. 3.

31. Judith Bardwick and Elizabeth Douvan, "Ambivalence: the Socialization of Women," in Vivian Gornick and Barbara K. Moran, eds., *Woman in Sexist Society,* pp. 225-41.

32. Janeway, *Man's World,* ch. 8.

33. Deutsch, *Psychology of Women,* I: 290.

34. See, e.g., David T. Hamburg and Donald T. Lunde, "Sex Hormones in the Development of Sex Differences in Human Behavior," in Eleanor E. Maccoby, ed., *The Development of Sex Differences* (Stanford, Calif.: Stanford University Press, 1966), pp. 1-24; Walter Mischel, "A Social-Learning View of Sex Differences in Behavior," ibid., pp. 56-81.

35. *The Republic,* Book IV, tr. by W. H. D. Rouse in *Great Dialogues,* pp. 217-46.

36. See, e.g., Lionel Tiger, *Men in Groups* (New York: Random House, 1969).

37. Ibid.

38. New York: William Morrow & Co., 1973.

39. *Men,* p. 190.

40. Ibid., p. 182.

41. *Patriarchy,* chs. 2-4.

42. *Social Structure* (New York: Macmillan Co., 1949), p. 7. Cf., Tiger, *Men,* pp. 44-45.

43. See, e.g., H. R. Hays, *The Dangerous Sex: The Myth of Feminine Evil* (New York: G. P. Putnam's Sons, 1964); Karen Horney, "The Flight from Womanhood: the Masculinity Complex in Women, as Viewed by Men, and by Women," *International Journal of Psychoanalysis* (July 1926): 324-39.

44. Erikson, *Identity,* "Womanhood and the Inner Space," p. 266.

7

EQUALITY AND SEXUAL DIFFERENCES: RESOLVING THE CONTRADICTIONS

Any social scientist could easily derive a lifetime's work from the literature on sexual differences. Students of medicine, biology, psychology, sociology, anthropology, philosophy, and literature have all dealt extensively with this subject, producing some valuable material and much that is less valuable. I could not possibly wade through this mass, as diverting as it might be. Some telling criticisms of many of these works have yet to be made. But even if a critique of all this literature were manageable in one chapter, it would be superfluous for my purposes.

The preceding chapter has suggested that any form of sex-based discrimination (with the possible exception of compensatory treatment) is legitimate only if it is acceptable and beneficial to whatever sex is disfavored by it. The types of discrimination with which I have been concerned—employment restrictions based on women's physical structure and the assignment of family responsibilities to women as their primary task—could be justified if it were shown that women were psychologically so constructed that their interests were indeed identifiable with those of their families, and this role would indeed be best for them. In considering this possibility, two problems immediately arise. First, traditionalists have frequently produced versions of this argument which are blatantly unsound. Secondly, there is ample evidence that all women do not agree on which policies they will accept, or on what will benefit them. Some women apparently do want to be primarily wives and mothers, but clearly, not all women feel that way. This disparity leads very naturally into a consideration of the logical consistency of traditionalist efforts to deal with it.

ODDBALLS AND FREAKS: A SHORT ESSAY ON LOGIC

Logic soundness and consistency are not qualities which distinguish typical traditionalist arguments. Nancy Reeves had written an essay in which she exposes various types of logical fallacies in a series of typical antifeminist statements.[1] My discussion here is an adaptation of hers.

The first fallacy she discusses, *secundum quid,* includes the error of founding a sweeping generalization on the basis of a few examples. Arguing that the sexes are inherently different in character because one's own male and female children (or, in extreme cases, only son and only daughter) have behaved differently from one another since birth, or arguing that homemaking makes women happy on the basis of happy housewives one knows personally, are examples of this fallacy, as are most statements beginning, "Woman is . . . ." Reeves has no trouble finding her own examples of this fallacy. Certainly, it is well illustrated by Freud and subsequent psychoanalytic theorists.

A second fallacy is one I have already discussed, *ignoratio elenchi,* supposing a point proved or disproved by irrelevant argument. This fallacy has three subdivisions. *Ad hominem (feminam?)* is an attack on the character of the person making the statement: "The suffragists were neurotic old maids," "They're all a bunch of dykes," etc. *Ad populum* is an appeal to the crowd "through the tug of the great abstractions": love, motherhood, and the like. Many vocal opponents of the Equal Rights Amendment are extremely adept at employing this kind of fallacy. *Ad baculum* is an appeal to fear, common in those statements which introduce a parade of imaginary horribles such as universal impotence, test-tube babies, and the death of the nuclear family as probable consequences of change.

The third fallacy is *petitio principii,* or begging the question: i.e., assuming the truth of a proposition which needs to be proved. One example of this fallacy, which I have discussed at, I feel, sufficient length, is the assumption that women's interests are identical with, or subordinate to, those of others. Another example of question-begging is that shown in Erikson's assumption that childbearing capacity carries with it a general ethical commitment to care for human infancy. The related argument that homemaking and child care are primarily women's responsibilities, and women's primary responsibilities, has had such a

powerful hold on our society that until the last decade virtually no one
—not even Betty Friedan in *The Feminine Mystique*—questioned it.

Fourth, Reeves discusses the fallacy *post hoc, ergo propter hoc:* in
this context, the practice of blaming social evils on changes in sex roles.
The classic example of this is, perhaps, Philip Wylie's attribution of the
Teapot Dome scandal to women's suffrage.

Reeves has performed an invaluable service by exposing the fallacies
in many of the arguments I am concerned with. I would like to take logic
a step further to discuss the ways in which antifeminists resolve the apparent contradictions between their arguments and the way many women
actually conduct their lives. An elementary logical device, the syllogism, is a useful tool for analyzing these arguments. Consider statements like "Women want to marry" or "Women want children" or "As
much as women want to be good scientists or engineers, they want even
more to be womanly companions of men and to be mothers"[2] or "I believe the female's need to establish herself in a loving, intimate relationship, to love and be loved, is dominant. I also believe that the gratification of maternal needs are necessary for feelings of well-being. And I
think that for most women in our society gratification of these needs,
at home or at work . . . are dominant motives."[3] A combination of the
thoughts in the preceding statements might read: "Women want close,
loving personal relationships, primarily as wives and mothers, more than
they want professional success." Suppose we make this the major premise
of a syllogism. "X is a woman" could become the minor premise. It should
follow, then, as the conclusion, that "X wants marriage and motherhood
more than she wants professional success."

But suppose X's behavior and her reports of her own feelings indicate
that she wants professional success more than she wants a family, or values
both goals equally, or wants a profession and does not want a family at
all, or wants a profession and a husband, but no children. On any university campus, for example, each of these cells is filled by large numbers of
women; we do not need to hunt around for cases. There is an abundance
of evidence which directly contradicts the above conclusion.

At this point, there are several possible resolutions of the contradiction.
At least one of the three parts of the above syllogism must be false. If this
were only a problem in logic, the best resolution would probably be to
discard the major premise. As a generalization, it is far more vulnerable
to attack than either the minor premise, which seems incontrovertible,

or the conclusion about X, based on empirical observation of a single
case. But this is the last step anyone has been willing to take. Instead,
both in everyday life and in social science, people have concentrated on
the other two parts of the syllogism.

The conclusion that X's desires depart from conventional expectations
is subject to attack. People have denied in such cases that X knows what
she "really" wants, or have suggested that her priorities will change in the
future. If X has any ambivalence about what she wants—as most people
have, at least some of the time—chipping away at the conclusion (and X's
ambition) is not difficult. Even if she is unambivalent, we know—too well,
I sometimes think—that people can misperceive their own interests. We
have all been sensitized, if not oversensitized, to the difference between
false and real consciousness. However, we can go only so far in denying
that people know what they want and insisting that *we,* on the other
hand, know what they *really* want until our assumption of superior wisdom mades us ludicrous. So, eventually, people began attacking the minor
premise.

To deny that a person was the sex she or he appeared to be might seem
to be impossible, or to degenerate into a biological horror story. After all,
X must be either a woman or a man, and in the overwhelming majority of
cases even the casual observer can tell which. But one can chip away at
X's sexual identity by denying that she is a "real" woman, or a "normal"
one. This device was not invented by modern psychology, but it has been
encouraged by the psychological concepts which have been trickling down
from the scholarly journals to the Sunday supplements since the 1920s.
If X does not suffer from false consciousness, these arguments have suggested, she is "abnormal" or "sick" (usually without quotation marks),
like the heroine of the 1944 musical comedy *Lady in the Dark,* a successful but neurotic career woman who is psychoanalyzed into domesticity.
The psychiatric profession has saturated the public, both as patients and as
readers, with this kind of reasoning. From Freud, who saw female resent-
ment of or ambition for the statuses enjoyed by males as unresolved penis
envy,[4] to Helene Deutsch, who wrote, "All observations point to the fact
that the intellectual woman is masculinized,"[5] to Ferdinand Lundberg
and Marynia Farnham, who would forbid unmarried women to teach children "on the basis of theoretical (usually real) emotional incompetence,"[6]
to Joseph Rheingold, who wrote, "when women grow up without dread of
their biological functions and without subversion by feminist doctrine and

. . . enter upon motherhood with a sense of fulfillment and altruistic senti-
ment, we shall attain the goal of a good life and a secure world in which to
live it"[7] —the most influential writers in this discipline have interpreted
deviance from the domestic pattern as evidence of psychopathology.

Members of the profession have never been unanimous on this point.
Freud's own conclusions were tentative, although he sometimes sounded
very sure of himself indeed, as when he developed an extremely intricate
theory of superego development in both sexes, resting on several abstract
assumptions, and appeared to find its truth obvious.[8] That was uncharac-
teristic, as his frequently quoted query, "What does a woman want?" suggests. And not all subsequent psychoanalysts agreed with his tentative
conclusions. Both Karen Horney[9] and Clara Thompson,[10] for instance,
repudiated his theories of male and female psychology, but their writings
have not been picked up by the culture as much as have those of Deutsch
and Farnham, to name only the best known, who went even farther than
Freud in an antifeminist direction.[11]

With the help of modern differential psychology, the major premises
have been qualified somewhat. Now we get statements like Judith Bardwick's "In the reality of current socializations and expectations, I regard
women who are not motivated to achieve the affiliative role with husband
and children as not normal."[12]

But this kind of reasoning does not depend mainly on the deviants' being
in the minority, as the statement just quoted appears to do. The psychological theorists do not usually conclude from the fact that most women become wives and mothers that women are generally suited best for these
roles. They can be interpreted as arguing that no matter how most people
behave, this is the right or the healthy way to conduct one's life. Of course,
the fact that the majority of women have fitted the stereotype, at least
superficially, has helped give credence to these arguments. As de Tocqueville observed long ago, we have nearly always been very majoritarian in
the United States. Since his time, the functional school of sociology,
trickling down from the scholarly journals, has helped reinforce this
trend. Americans are strongly inclined to believe that "what 51% of the
population does today, 100% should do tomorrow."[13]

The effect of all of this on public policy considerations has apparently
been something like this. If the major premise I have identified is correct,
as most people have assumed, public policy should be developed with it
in mind: shortened working days, exclusion from jury duty, and alimony

for divorced wives are advisable, and employment discrimination and inferior pay may not be undesirable. If we protest that the Xs are damaged by these policies, two answers to the objection are possible, along the lines I suggested above. First, one can argue that women who deviate from the stereotype have misinterpreted their own interests. If that is the case, public policy based on the wife-mother role does benefit the Xs ultimately.

Alternatively (or concurrently, for that matter), one can argue that the Xs are not normal or healthy women. At best, they are exceptions, and at worst, they are oddballs and freaks. And public policy, it is assumed, need not respond to the needs of oddballs and freaks.

Even before the development of psychoanalytic theory, this kind of understanding enabled Justice Bradley to argue, in the opinion quoted in Chapter 6, that despite individual exceptions, the general destiny of women was to fulfill the wife-mother role. The fact that the appellant was a *married* woman who had so far departed from her natural timidity and delicacy of character to seek bar admission did not cause Bradley to reexamine his stereotype. Instead, he rejected the claim as unnatural and improper, which is tantamount to rejecting the claimant as an oddball.

CONFLICT, ACCEPTABILITY, AND ADVANTAGE

The claim of many women that the status quo is not acceptable to them—and their departure from expected behavior—has led to the dismissal of these women as atypical, and, therefore, to the dismissal of their claims. The conclusion which has been drawn is that the status quo is acceptable to "real" or "normal" women. Even if one refuses to accept, without more evidence than has been forthcoming, this resolution of the conflict among the wishes of different women, the conflict remains. And if we conclude that this conflict is unresolvable, how can we use the criterion of acceptability? If inequalities based on fixed natural characteristics are justified only if they are acceptable and beneficial to the disadvantaged group, and that group is divided on the issue of acceptability, then either of two conclusions is possible. The first is that when such disagreement exists among a group, *no* inequalities are justifiable because of the permanency of the characteristics which set the group apart and the inescapability of the unequal status for all members of the group. The second, more moderate, possible conclusion is that one must discard the criterion of acceptability as unworkable, and focus on the criterion of advantage.

At first glance, it seems easier to challenge a person's perception of her own interests than her report of her wants. We may begin to sound ludicrous when we argue that people do not know what they really want, but, considering the prevalence of self-destructive behavior in our society, one can assert that people frequently do not know what they need. To take an extreme example, an argument that someone who has repeatedly attempted suicide does not really *want* to die might sound ridiculous, but an argument that death is not to her *advantage* would be taken seriously. One could make similar arguments about less blatant forms of self-destruction. But when we examine the wide range of human behavior which is not evidently self-destructive—like rejection of the usual sex roles—assertions that this behavior is not to the real advantage of the people observed are harder to defend. One can, of course, search for neurotic symptoms in anyone, and a thorough enough search will probably reveal some. Most people, after all, at least occasionally act in ways that can be interpreted as neurotic by observers who are sufficiently eager to see these tendencies. Once the neurotic behavior has been observed, it is an easy matter to attribute the symptoms to any particular cause, such as rejection of what society considers the roles appropriate to one's sex. But observers who engage in this process are very vulnerable to accusations of selective perception: seeing what they want to see, and making the causal connections they want to make. Eventually, the criterion of advantage leaves us with the same problem as does the criterion of acceptability. No single answer is possible to the question of whether inequalities are to the advantage of women.

This whole discussion produces a feeling of dissatisfaction. Must we, as policy-makers, discard this criterion too? Is the whole question unanswerable in these terms? Or should we insist that, because there is no single answer to the question of advantage, no sex-based discrimination is possible? If we do not resolve conflicts among women by arbitrarily dismissing the claims of some of them, is it still possible to make a case for favoring some women at the expense of others?

Such a case has frequently rested on the assertion that a majority of women are psychologically so constructed that they are advantaged by channelling into the domestic role, and that their interests are harmonious, not to say identical, with those of their actual or potential families. But suppose that were true, one is tempted to ask, so what? Even if most women fit the Bardwick and Bettelheim descriptions,[14] does public policy have to be based on this? Is it not possible for the law simply to leave men and women free to order their own priorities within a framework of *equal* rights, benefits, and responsibilities? If both men and women can get leaves from work to care for their infants, would it matter if most of the people who took such leaves were women? Do we want or need a system in which millions of people are classified as oddballs and freaks? What good or harm is done by so classifying people? *Should* 100 percent of the people do tomorrow what 51 percent do today? As I said earlier, the law in many instances makes no discrimination among many people who are very different indeed from one another, and it is at least arguable that sexual differences should be treated in the same way. One who insists that sexual differences must *not* be treated in the same way would have the burden of proving at least one of two propositions. First, she or he might have to show that there is a causal connection between sex and certain personality traits, to the extent that not only most women, but virtually all women, are psychologically so constructed; that this is true because of physiological distinctions and not because of differential socialization; that women are best served by traditional policies; and that they cannot be left free to work out their own destinies without legal channelling into sex roles. If such a determination were to be made, it would permit rejection of the claims of atypical women (if there were any), but the truth about female human nature would have to be proved, not assumed. And any argument which favored traditional role assignment would have to deal adequately with the observable differences among women. Or, alternatively, the traditionalist would have to prove that, however polymorphous and malleable the human personality is, women, men, children, and society in general are best served by channelling into these sex roles. Throughout the examination of psychological data, I shall be concerned with questions suggested partly by these two formulations: first, evaluating the validity of the conclusions, and, second, assuming that people really are as described, and asking, so what? These approaches are not entirely compatible and, on occasion, may produce confusion.

THE FEMININE PERSONALITY: PORTRAIT OF THE WOMAN AS A HAPPY CRYPTO-SLAVE

Examining the data on sex differences can be made much easier if I describe a hypothetical personality for which traditional policies would be beneficial, and then ask if the literature indicates that this is, indeed, the typical, or ideal, female personality. What sort of personality would the woman served by traditional expectations have? This hypothetical woman would not be just any woman who derived satisfaction from serving others and frequently subordinated her own interests to those of others. It is to be hoped that all of us, men and women, serve others and get satisfaction from such service. But we may perform such service in the pursuance of our own independently determined goals as much as we do in self-sacrifice. Sometimes, of course, most of us have to sub-ordinate our own interests to those of others, but our motives need not always be primarily altruistic. Furthermore, service to others does not always take place in a domestic context. A woman who derived her great-est satisfaction and benefit from the domestic role would have to be a person who was centered on others rather than herself, to such an extent that the gains she reaped from these relationships compensated for the isolated performance of repetitious tasks. Her gratification would have to come primarily from relationships with others whom she nurtured rather than from her own achievement.

One's first impulse may be to recoil from such a description. But I think it is a measure of the extent to which both men and women have been taught to devalue nurturant roles (at the same time that women have been channelled into them) that we do so. If one examines it, that paragraph does not describe so unattractive a personality. It does not strike me as the *ideal* to which we should all aspire, but it is *one* model worthy of emulation. A life centered on others need not be dehumanizing or degrading.

Perhaps our unease with this stereotype reflects a recognition that many of the women who perform traditional roles do not, in fact, fit it: instead, they appear to have channelled unacknowledged aggressive drives into modes of behavior which are very destructive to their families, and to be beset by frustrated ambition. C. S. Lewis once described this type of woman as "the woman who lives for others . . . and you can tell the others by their hunted expression."[15] Another souce of dissatisfaction with this formulation is just the opposite phenomenon: people who fit the stereotype who flourish in some role other than the domestic one. I am thinking here, for example, of Eleanor Roosevelt, as she emerges in Joseph Lash's two-volume biography.[16] Although she is revealed in these books as the supreme altruist, Mrs. Roosevelt apparently was not, for a variety of reasons, very happy and successful as a wife and mother.

However, she performed superbly as a teacher, politician, and diplomat —and clearly derived great satisfaction from these activities.

If women are indeed nurturant, supportive, and altruistic, a very good case can be made against relegating them to domestic life and for encouraging their participation in public activities. As Erik Erikson writes:

> Do we and can we really know what will happen to science or any other field if and when women are truly represented in it—not by a few glorious exceptions, but in the rank and file of the scientific elite? . . . My main point is that where the confinements are broken, woman may yet be expected to cultivate the implications of what is biologically and anatomically given. She may, in new areas of activity, balance man's indiscriminate endeavor to perfect his dominion over the outer spaces of national and technological expansion (at the cost of hazarding the annihilation of the species) with the determination to emphasize such varieties of caring and caretaking as would take responsibility for each individual child born in a planned humanity. There will be many difficulties in a new joint adjustment of the sexes to changing conditions, but they do not justify prejudices which keep half of mankind from participating in planning and decision making, especially at a time when the other half, by its competitive escalation and acceleration of technical progress, has brought us and our children to the gigantic brink on which we live, with all our affluence. . . . Mankind now obviously depends on new kinds of social inventions and on institutions which guard and cultivate that which nurses and nourishes, cares and tolerates, includes and preserves.[17]

As critical as I am prepared to be of Erikson's conception of female personality,[18] I cannot quarrel with his conclusions about women's role in public life. Even if he and his colleagues are right and I am wrong, we need not disagree very much in our conclusions about public policy. As scholars, business executives, or politicians, women might behave very differently from men, if allowed to, but these activities might well be improved by such performance, as Erikson has suggested.

These reservations imply that more than altruism or nurturance is required to fit a woman mainly for the domestic role. Altruism and nurturance can be channelled in other directions. One is almost reduced to the tautology that the woman who is best suited for the wife-mother role is the one who likes that sort of thing, but I think I can be more definite than this. Not only would the domestic woman need to be motivated to subordinate her own needs to those of others, but to do so in a particular way, involving personal care for their domestic and emotional needs. And this motivation would have to be strong enough to counterbalance aggressive and ambitious tendencies. One is almost tempted to conclude that such a woman would have to display the passivity and masochism which Deutsch attributes to women.

At this point, three questions arise. First, do female personalities really correspond to this revised stereotype? The formulation has a certain plausibility; in everyday life, women do seem generally to be more concerned with others than men are, and to be more aware of people's feelings. Secor should women be channelled into this personality model? And third, what should the role of public policy and law be in this area?

Many, if not most, of the scholarly treatments of this issue suggest that women do indeed conform to this stereotype. Two interesting treatments of this issue, one by a physician and one by a philosopher-theologian, reach compatible conclusions. Writing in 1923, the former, Gina Lombroso, provides a description which would neatly fit my hypothetical one. She concludes, as "the result of spontaneous and frank observation of woman and of long reflections on [her] problems"[19] that:

> woman is alterocentrist, that is to say, *she centers her feelings, her enjoyment, her ambition in something outside herself; she makes not herself but another person, or even things around her, the center of her emotions; and usually this person is someone whom she loves and by whom she wants to be loved, husband, son, father, friend, etc.*[20]

Man, on the other hand, is "*egocentrist,* that is to say, *he makes himself and his pleasures and activities the center of the world in which he lives.*"[21]

Lombroso's formulation is fascinating, but it is unsatisfactory as scholarship. She advances no concrete evidence for these propositions. Throughout her book, she writes about "woman" and "man," nowhere telling the reader who the people are she has been observing or, outside of a few references to Bible stories and fiction, providing support for these sweeping generalizations.

David Bakan, the philosopher-theologian, has written a book called *The Duality of Human Existence*,[22] in which he posits

> two fundamental modalities in the existence of living forms, agency for the existence of the organism as in individual, and communion for the participation of the individual in some larger organism of which the individual is a part. Agency manifests itself in self-protection, self-assertion, and self-expansion; communion manifests itself in the sense of being at one with other organisms. Agency manifests itself in the formation of separations; communion in the lack of separations. Agency manifests itself in isolation, alienation, and aloneness; communion in contact, openness, and union. Agency manifests itself in the urge to master; communion in noncontractual cooperation. Agency manifests itself in the repression of thought, feeling, and impulse; communion in the lack and removal of repression.[23]

Bakan yields to a temptation which must be nearly irresistible with bimodal metaphors: to apply it to the sexes. He reaches the unsurprising conclusion that women are predominantly communitarian, men primarily agentic. In addition to the Lombroso book he reviews two fruitful sources of data in this area: psychoanlaytic theory and differential psychology, the study of personality differences in human beings through psychological testing.

Naomi Weisstein has accurately summarized the conclusions of the psychoanalysts by remarking that they "have set about describing the true natures of women with an enthusiasm and absolute certainty which is rather disquieting."[24] Reviewing much of the material I have mentioned —Freud, Bettelheim, Rheingold, and Erikson (who arrives at this theory through methods more typical of differential psychology) get particular scrutiny—Weisstein illustrates their near unanimity in viewing mentally healthy women as altruistic, nurturant, and passive. Weisstein quite properly criticizes these clinicians for reaching their conclusions on the basis of evidence "which violated the most minimal conditions of scientific rigor,"[25] and castigates their colleagues and successors for accepting these theories on the basis of such evidence without testing and confirmation. At worst, the psychiatric writers have been guilty of constructing dogmatic theories on the basis of data drawn from their own limited clinical experience. At best, their conclusions rest, as Erikson's do, on experiments with a small group of subjects who are already old enough to have learned what society expects of them. Drawing conclusions about inherent human nature from data about very few adults and fewer children, all of whom have been subject to socialization and, in the case of patients, are usually self-selected, is clearly unacceptable, and Weisstein is entirely justified in rejecting the conclusions.

What has differential psychology contributed to our knowledge about sexual differences? Bakan explores the major studies: the works of Lewis Terman and Catharine Cox Miles,[26] Anne Anastasi,[27] David McClelland,[28] and Leona Tyler,[29] among a few others. Their findings, he discovers, are compatible with one another and with his own personality theory.

McClelland, for example, found that the women he tested usually were motivated by social acceptability, while the men valued leadership capacity and intelligence.[30] In a review of the literature up to 1949, Anastasi concluded that it suggested that females were significantly more interested than males in children, family life, and people in general.[31] Tyler, studying much of the same literature, suggested that females enjoyed sentimental and domestic stories and were apt to concern themselves with "personal attractiveness, etiquette, and getting along with people" whereas males preferred action stories and were more interested in "money, health, safety, study, recreation, and civic affairs."[32] My summary of these sometimes massive works by no means covers all of the findings on sexual differences which they contain, but it does cover those most relevant to my problem here. Even investigations performed according to the usual standards of scientific investigation turn up a composite picture of women as motivated by affiliative needs, communitarian rather than agentic, and primarily interested in personal matters and social relationships.

But even these studies do not prove that "woman is alterocentrist." For one thing, these investigators reported what Anastasi termed "the wide individual differences within each sex, with the consequent overlapping between their distribution. Since in any psychological trait women differ widely from each other, and men also vary widely among themselves, any relationship found between group averages will not necessarily hold for individual cases."[33] None of the data provides any support for generalizations beginning, "Woman is. . . ." The most one can say is "Most women seem to be . . . ." And then we are right back to the old questions: So what? Does the fact that some generalizations hold about the majority of women or men entitle us to dismiss the minority from policy considerations? For another thing, evidence that women are more nurturant and altruistic than men does not prove that women are primarily nurturant and altruistic.

A third problem with these studies is that—as the investigators themselves admit—they cannot resolve the "nature vs. nurture" controversy. They cannot separate natural from environmental factors in causation. It is not surprising that females turn out to be concerned with domestic life, children, and personal attractiveness, and take a lively interest in other people. After all, that is what they have been raised to be like. But it is also true that even from birth, many children display personalities that differ from one another; probably there is something in human character that is innate. Both nature and nurture are significant, and in looking at individual personalities it is probably impossible to separate one from the other. If some features of personality are inherent, then sexual differences might to some extent be among these features.

But the influence of environment and socialization is evident. Anthropologists like Margaret Mead and Ruth Benedict who have done cross-cultural studies have shown that different cultures have very different prevailing male and female personalities.[34] These differences can be found, interestingly enough, even though the division of labor according to sex follows similar patterns across almost all cultures.[35] Beyond reasonable doubt, environmental factors affect personality development. If most girls grow up alterocentrist and boys egocentrist at the present time, it is nonetheless possible that at some later time this may not happen.

It is impossible to avoid the conclusion that we lack the kind of psychological evidence we would need to justify assigning women to a restricted status, and basing public policy on this, and the principles of equality and justice dictate that we cannot assign any group a certain status because it benefits others. Exploration of the problem might reveal that men and children are in fact hurt rather than benefitted by the status quo, but those are not the grounds on which the issue should be argued.

IF PERSONALITIES ARE MALLEABLE, THEN WHAT?
THE MORALITY OF CHANNELLING

The analysis cannot stop here, however, The lack of evidence that women are best suited for the role of crypto-slave does not prove the opposite, or deal with the other questions I have raised. Public policy shapes reality as well as responding to it; law has an effect on society as well as being affected by it. If personality is, as Mead argues, malleable, it is malleable to these effects. Policies based on the domestic role will help channel women into that role, from which they will be forced to derive their primary satisfactions. This role, like any other role people play, would affect women's personalities, presumably influencing them to become the kind of person I have described. And after all, one might ask, what is wrong with that? The nurturant, altruistic personality is not, after all, without value. The second question I raised earlier must be considered: whether channelling women into this sort of personality is healthy.

The kind of observation which Herbert Simon called "casual empiricism" might well favor a negative answer. We find many women wreaking havoc in the domestic role, and many functioning beautifully outside of it. Personality may be malleable, but it appears that it is not infinitely so; people, even women, seem to have aggressive drives which cannot be totally submerged and are going to come out somehow. If women do not have impersonal outlets for this aggression, their families may become the foci of these drives, to their detriment.[36]

Even Gina Lombroso recognized other possible effects of such channelling, and the inherent tragedy of alterocentrism: "As a woman makes something outside herself—not her own person—the center of her joys and ambitions, she is absolutely powerless to attain happiness by her own means. Because of her fatal love for others, woman inevitably depends on others."[37] But these others will not always behave in ways that will gratify her, and she will be relatively powerless to correct this.

Furthermore, if women's personalities develop in a particular way, what happens to men's personalities? Someone has to be aggressive, agentic, and egocentric if problems are to be solved and the environment is to be mastered; with women channelled into passivity, nurturance, and altruism, who is left? If certain aspects of women's personalities become predominant, then almost inevitably opposite aspects of male personalities will become predominant. What we seem to have now are women who are too passive, nurturant, and alterocentrist, and men who are not passive, nurturant, and alterocentrist enough. In a discussion of race and sex, Eldridge Cleaver makes a similar argument: that people are channelled into four opposite roles, which become "two sets of competing images,"[38] on the basis of race and sex. These roles, he concludes, permit the expression and development of only selected and highly limited aspects of each personality.

Leaving the racial question aside, the generalization about the sexes seems profoundly true. The sexual differences in personality whose development our culture encourages to such an extent frequently seem to produce women who are too deeply attuned to the feelings of others, and men who are not attuned enough. We have all encountered women whose intuition could be an embarrassment to all, and men who are utterly insensitive to others' emotions. (Incidentally, I have always wondered why writers like Helene Deutsch never seem to realize that intuition is a two-edged sword: understanding gained in this way can be used to wound others as easily as to nurture them.) For another example, the fact that men find it impossible to cry even in situations where tears are appropriate is frequently, and quite rightly, bemoaned. But it is also true that many women resort to tears rather too quickly, using them as a means of social control. In these areas as well as in others, each sex would do well to emulate the other to an extent. This would not result in everyone's developing like personalities; people would still differ, but there would be more disparity within each sex.

The personality I have described has serious defects as a model for all female personalities. And my final question remains: whether we are justified in using the law to so narrow the range of opportunities available to each sex as to channel people into particular roles, life styles, and personalities. The foregoing discussion has not necessarily answered this in the negative. Even if the channelling I have described can have unfortunate results, it might be the best possible choice. But I have said enough to case doubt on this possibility. If we refuse to assign women automatically to crypto-slave status, it is hard to justify assigning them to the domestic role. The burden of proof on those who would argue for it is considerable, and it has not been met.

PUBLIC POLICY AND SEXUAL ROLES: THE PLACE OF LAW IN SHAPING LIVES

The foregoing critique of psychological studies of sex differences has indicated the impossibility of proving the first proposition which I suggested would justify the status quo. All that I have said in these last two chapters points to the conclusion that there is no demonstrable connection between sex, capacities, and character, and that, therefore, sex satisfies all the criteria for a suspect classification. But in spite of all of this, could one argue in favor of my second proposition: that the need to assign women to a certain status is so compelling that it outweighs all the considerations on the other side? I think not. Even if women and society are best served by female domesticity, we must remember that people have considerable leeway in arranging their own lives without coercion. No matter what the law says, women who want to be self-sacrificers can do so. They can immolate themselves, if that is what they really want, and so, in spite of contrary expectations, can men. Public policy which is neutral on the question of women's priorities will increase freedom of choice and therefore make life more complicated for everyone, but it will not force any woman to take advantage of new opportunities. But the converse is not true: public policy based on traditional assumptions does close off possibilities to women. And it does not even benefit wives and mothers very much; it just gives them claims, like those to support, which they have about as much chance of successfully activating as nineteenth-century workers did of exercising their freedom of contract. When policy does benefit homemakers, this result could be achieved as well by restrictions of narrower scope, such as those permitting jury-duty exemptions for anyone responsible for the care of young children.

But if it is unjust to base public policy on traditional assumptions, are all laws which discriminate between the sexes unjust? What about policies based on physical functions which do not impose restrictions on all women? I remember hearing as late as 1970 arguments, made in all seriousness, that support for the Equal Rights Amendment was inconsistent with support for maternity leaves from work, but that argument is not very convincing. The late stages of pregnancy and the period of convalescence after childbirth can be viewed simply as temporary disabilities; giving women such leave with pay is not more discriminatory than giving men leave for prostate surgery.

Furthermore, because these laws, like those against rape, apply by definition to only one sex, they can be phrased in terms of persons.[39] *Compulsory* maternity leaves (when no other kind of sick leave was compulsory), *childrearing* leaves which are offered only to women, or benefit plans like General Electric's are discriminatory and violate the principles of equal treatment I have set forth. In these discussions, social attitudes about the appropriate relationship of mothers and infants clearly play a part; childbirth is not viewed only as a medical phenomenon. But there is no reason why it, or rape, has to throw a wrench into an egalitarian doctrine. After all, it is not the law which says that women cannot commit rape, or that men cannot bear children.

A final problem must be dealt with here. On the basis of a lengthy analysis of philosophical and psychological materials, I have concluded that the relationship between sex and capacity is so problematical and tenuous that even in the absence of antidiscrimination laws or a constitutional amendment, sex must be assigned to the category of suspect classification under the Equal Protection Clause of the Fourteenth Amendment in constitutional adjudication. The reader might well question whether it is the role of appellate court judges, who have to decide cases dealing with sex discrimination, to wade through and evaluate this type of material. Any thoughtful scholar would hesitate before adding to the burdens of judges by insisting that they become psychologists. But I do not think this kind of investigation would be necessary for judges. We all know enough about sexual differences to conclude that sex satisfies the test set out in *Sail'er Inn* for suspect classification: a relationship between it and capacity is *frequently* lacking. Perhaps, in the absence of extensive psychological investigation, it is only casual empiricism which provides such knowledge—but, after all, that is the only kind of research which has enabled courts to conclude that such a relationship is *frequently* lacking with race, ethnicity, or social class. Stereotypes based on these factors may, as I have suggested, frequently be valid, but courts have not thoroughly investigated them before rejecting them as a basis for discrimination. I would suggest that on the face of it, sex should be treated the same way: "Everybody knows" a predictable relationship between sex and capacity is lacking in the same way that "everybody knows" that such a relationship is lacking with race or ethnicity. The sort of investigation I have done would be necessary not to prove that sex is a suspect classification, but to prove the very opposite.

CONCLUSION

My purpose here has been to approach the moral questions surrounding the position of men and women in society through the study of a kind of public policy based on an identifiable set of assumptions about

the sexes. In my examination of the history of special labor legislation,
I discovered, first, that policies whose primary effect initially was to
provide protection eventually imposed restrictions of dubious necessity.
I also found that laws which seemed desirable because of temporary situations in which working women found themselves frequently were adopted and defended on the basis of permanent or quasi-permanent conditions.

In my analysis of the judicial response to this legislation, I found that,
through a series of simple and complex accidents, early decisions emphasized permanent rather than temporary conditions. Partly because of
further historical accidents, later judges uncritically accepted these decisions as binding. I discovered further that these precedents, which arose
from laws enacted for the noble (if misguided) purpose, and sometimes
with the effect, of protecting the disadvantaged from exploitation by the
advantaged, later were used to uphold laws enacted with the mean purpose,
and with the effect, of protecting the advantaged in their superior position
from competition from the disadvantaged.

This conclusion was supported by an examination of the decisions
which finally invalidated protective legislation: cases decided under the
Equal Pay Act of 1963 and Title VII of the Civil Rights Act of 1964.
This litigation reveals the ubiquity in American industry of sex discrimination which works to the benefit of men and the detriment of women,
and the fact that much of this discrimination originated in, and was intertwined with, laws which purported to protect women. Once the courts
were confronted with a statutory commitment to sexual equality, they
could not avoid perceiving the connection between protection and restriction.

Some aspects of the history of protective legislation may be unique to
this area of public policy, but its history indicates the ease with which
protection can become restriction, and the ways in which the presence
of permanent sexual differences can obscure the impact of changing social
conditions. Furthermore, the arguments which recurred in the opinions
over the years echoed many of the familiar defenses of the status quo.
The assumption that certain duties follow from the fact that women can
bear children, and the position that all women must be protected from
things that might harm some of them, but are not forced on any of them,
are two prominent examples. A third, more subtle implication which
emerges from the material studied is the assumption that the interests of
women are properly subordinate to those of others. This implicit inferior
status assignment has encouraged the conducting of public controversy

on the issue primarily in terms of the interests of men and children. Once we refuse to accept these assumptions, the traditional arguments begin to crumble, and efforts to reconstruct them on a more secure basis fail.

In a society in which workers have a considerable degree of choice of occupation, in which no one is forced to take dangerous jobs, and in which the physical characteristics of females do not produce burdensome disabilities, the only plausible justification which remains for this kind of treatment is the assignment of the domestic role to women as their primary task in society. Exposing this role assignment as unfair and unjust —no matter how efficient or functional it is, and no matter how easy it is to understand how it happened—destroys the base on which special legislation rests. There is an alternative purpose which it can serve—the protection of men from competition—but that purpose is as clear a bit of illegitimate preference of one group over another that I can imagine.

This study does not claim to have answered all of the moral questions which could be raised about sex equality. In a sense, the goal I began with has not been achieved; I have really dealt only with moral questions relevant to protective labor legislation. But I think that exploration of this limited judicial topic has provided a basis for exploring some profoundly important questions about the ways in which society and law should respond to the presence of two sexes.

NOTES

1. "The Identity of Woman as Woman," in Leo Kanowitz, ed., *Sex Roles in Law and Society: Cases and Materials* (Albuquerque: University of New Mexico Press, 1973), pp. 15-25.

2. Bruno Bettelheim, "The Commitment Required of a Woman Entering a Scientific Profession in Present Day American Society," *Woman and the Scientific Professions* (Cambridge, Mass.: MIT Symposium on American Women in Science and Engineering, 1965), p. 15.

3. Judith Bardwick, *Psychology of Women*, pp. 158-59.

4. "Femininity"; "Some Psychological Consequences of the Anatomical Distinction Between the Sexes."

5. *Psychology of Women*, I: 291.

6. *Modern Woman: the Lost Sex*, pp. 304-05.

7. *The Fear of Being a Woman* (New York: Grune and Stratton, 1964), p. 714.

8. "Anatomical Distinction," p. 142.

9. *Feminine Psychology*, ed. by Harold Kelman (New York: W. W. Norton & Co., 1967).

10. "Cultural Pressures in the Psychology of Women," *Psychiatry* 5 (August 1942): 331-39.

11. See Naomi Weisstein, "Kinder, Kuche, Kirche as Scientific Law: Psychology Constructs the Female," in Robin Morgan, ed., *Sisterhood Is Powerful*, pp. 205-20.

12. *Psychology of Women*, p. 162.

13. Friedan, *Feminine Mystique*, p. 170.

14. "Commitment"; *Psychology of Women*, pp. 158-59.

15. *The Screwtape Letters* (New York: Macmillan Co., 1943), p. 135.

16. *Eleanor and Franklin* (New York: W. W. Norton & Co., 1971); *Eleanor: The Years Alone* (New York: W. W. Norton & Co., 1972).

17. "Womanhood and the Inner Space," in *Identity*, pp. 292-93.

18. For an example of inadvertent *reductio ad absurdam* of this sort of argument, see Jerome Frank, *Courts on Trial* (Princeton, N.J.: Princeton University Press, 1949), ch. 28. Frank's discussion illustrates the dangers inherent in theses like Erikson's.

19. *The Soul of Woman* (New York: E. P. Dutton & Co., 1923).

20. Ibid., p. 5. Emphasis in the original.

21. Ibid., p. 6. Emphasis in the original.

22. (New York: Rand-McNally, 1966).

23. Ibid., pp. 14-15.

24. "Kinder, Kuche, Kirche," p. 206.

25. Ibid., p. 209.

26. *Sex and Personality* (New York: McGraw-Hill, 1936), pp. 257-59.

27. *Revised Differential Psychology* (New York: Macmillan Co., 1949).

28. *The Achievement Motive* (New York: Appleton-Century-Crofts, 1953).

29. *The Psychology of Human Differences* (New York: D. Appleton-Century, 1947).

30. *Achievement Motive*, pp. 173-81.

31. *Differential Psychology*, ch. 19.

32. *Human Differences*, p. 82.

33. *Differential Psychology*, p. 618.

34. Mead, *Male and Female*; Ruth Benedict, *Patterns of Culture* (2nd ed.; Boston: Houghton Mifflin Co., 1961). An even earlier study, reaching similar conclusions but weakened by conceptual defects, is Mathilde Vaerting and Mathias Vaerting, *The Dominant Sex* (New York: George H. Doran Co., 1923).

35. G. P. Murdock, *Social Structure*, p. 7.

36. See, e.g., Slater, *The Pursuit of Loneliness*, ch. 3, "Women and Children First," pp. 53-80.

37. *Soul of Woman*, p. 15.

38. "The Primeval Mitosis," in *Soul on Ice* (New York: McGraw-Hill, 1968), pp. 176-90.

39. Murray and Eastwood, "Jane Crow and the Law," pp. 239-40. See also Comment, "Love's Labors Lost: New Conceptions of Maternity Leaves," *Harvard Civil Rights-Civil Liberties Law Review* 7 (January 1972): 260-97.

BIBLIOGRAPHY

Abbott, Edith. *Women in Industry,* New York: Appleton & Co., 1909.

Academy of Political Science, ed. *The Economic Position of Women,* New York: Academy of Political Science, Columbia Univ., 1910.

Adams, Mildred. *The Right to Be People,* New York: J. B. Lippincott, 1967.

Anastasi, Anne. *Revised Differential Psychology,* New York: Macmillan, 1949.

Aries, Philippe. *Centuries of Childhood,* trans. by Robert Baldwick, London: Jonathan Cape, 1962.

Aristotle. *The Politics,* trans. by Ernest Barker, New York: Oxford Univ. Press, 1958.

Avins, Alfred, ed. *The Reconstruction Amendments' Debates,* Richmond: Virginia Commission on Constitutional Government, 1967.

Babcock, Barbara et al., eds. *Sex Discrimination and the Law: Cases and Remedies,* Boston: Little, Brown & Co., 1975.

Bakan, David. *The Duality of Human Existence,* New York: Rand McNally, 1966.

Baker, Elizabeth Faulkner. *Protective Labor Legislation,* rev. ed., New York: AMS Press, 1969.

———. *Technology and Women's Work,* rev. ed., New York: Columbia Univ. Press, 1964.

Banfied, Edward. *The Unheavenly City,* Boston: Little, Brown & Co., 1970.

Bardwick, Judith M. *Psychology of Women,* New York: Harper & Row, 1971.

Beard, Mary. *On Understanding Women,* New York: Longmans, Green, & Co., 1931.

———. *Woman as Force in History,* New York: Macmillan, 1949.

Bell, Norman W., and Ezra F. Vogel, eds. *A Modern Introduction to the Family,* Glencoe, Ill.: Free Press, 1960.

Benedict, Ruth. *Patterns of Culture,* 2nd ed., Boston: Houghton Mifflin Co., 1961.

Bernard, Jessie. *Women and the Public Interest,* Chicago: Aldine-Atherton, 1971.

Bickel, Alexander. *The Least Dangerous Branch,* New York: Bobbs-Merrill Co., 1962.

Bird, Caroline. *Born Female,* New York: David McKay Co., 1968.

Blackstone's Commentaries on the Law, ed. by Bernard C. Gavit, Washington, D.C.: Washington Law Book Co., 1941.

Boston Women's Health Collective, *Our Bodies, Ourselves,* New York: Simon & Schuster, 1973.

Bowden, Witt. *The Industrial Revolution*, New York: F. S. Crofts & Co., 1928.

Bowlby, John. *Child Care and the Growth of Love*, arr. & ed. by Margery Fry, London: Penguin Books, 1953.

Brenner, Y. S. *A Short History of Economic Progress*, New York: Augustus M. Kelley, 1969.

Briffault, Robert. *The Mothers*, 3 vols., London: Allen & Unwin, 1927.

Brownmiller, Susan. *Against Our Will: Men, Women, and Rape*, New York: Simon & Schuster, 1975.

Cahill, Marion Cotter. *Shorter Hours: A Study of the Movement Since the Civil War*, rev. ed., New York: AMS Press, 1968.

Chesler, Phyllis. *Women and Madness*, New York: Doubleday & Co., 1972.

Chesler, Phyllis, and Emily Jane Goodman. *Women, Money and Power*, New York: William Morrow & Co., 1976.

Cleaver, Eldridge. *Soul on Ice*, New York: McGraw-Hill, 1968.

Commons, John R., and John B. Andrews. *Principles of Labor Legislation*, 4th rev. ed., New York: Harper & Brothers, 1936.

Commons, John R. et al. *History of Labor in the United States*, 4 vols., New York: Macmillan, 1936.

Commons, John R. et al., eds. *Documentary History of American Industrial Society* 10 vols., New York: Macmillan, 1910-1936.

Cooley, Thomas M. *Constitutional Limitations*, 8th ed., Boston: Little, Brown, & Co., 1927.

Cott, Nancy F., ed. *Root of Bitterness: Documents of the Social History of American Women*, New York: E. P. Dutton & Co., 1972.

Crosskey, William W. *Politics and the Constitution*, 2 vols., Chicago: Univ. of Chicago Press, 1953.

Dalton, Katharina. *The Menstrual Cycle*, New York: Warner Paperback Library, 1969.

de Beauvoir, Simone. *The Second Sex*, trans. and ed. by H. M. Parshley, New York: Alfred A. Knopf, 1952.

De Crow, Karen. *Sexist Justice*, New York: Random House, 1974.

de Tocqueville, Alexis. *Democracy in America*, trans. by George Lawrence, ed. by J. P. Mayer, Garden City, N.Y.: Doubleday & Co., 1969.

Decter, Midge. *The New Chastity*, New York: Coward-McCann & Geoghegan, Inc., 1972.

Deutsch, Helene. *The Psychology of Women*, 2 vols., New York: Grune & Stratton, 1944.

Dexter, Elizabeth Anthony. *Career Women in America, 1776-1840*, Francestown, N.H.: Marshall Jones Co., 1950.

Dulles, Foster Rhea. *Labor in America*, 3rd ed., New York: Thomas Y. Crowell & Co., 1966.

Ehrlich, Eugen. *Fundamental Principles in the Sociology of Law*, Cambridge, Mass.: Harvard Univ. Press, 1936.

Eidelberg, Paul. *The Philosophy of the American Constitution*, New York: Free Press, 1968.

Ellmann, Mary. *Thinking About Women,* New York: Harcourt Brace Jovanovich, 1968.

Ely, Richard T. *The Labor Movement in America,* rev. ed., New York: Thomas Y. Crowell & Co., 1890.

————. *Studies in the Evolution of Industrial Society,* New York: Macmillan, 1936.

Epstein, Cynthia Fuchs. *Woman's Place: Options and Limits in Professional Careers,* Berkeley: Univ. of California Press, 1970.

Erikson, Erik H. *Identity: Youth and Crisis,* New York: W. W. Norton & Co., 1968.

Faulkner, Harold U. *American Economic History,* 8th ed., New York: Harper & Row, 1959.

————. *The Quest for Social Justice,* New York: Macmillan Co., 1931.

Figes, Eva. *Patriarchal Attitudes,* New York: Stein & Day, 1970.

Fine, Sidney. *Laissez-Faire and the General-Welfare State,* Ann Arbor: Univ. of Michigan Press, 1956.

Firestone, Shulamith. *The Dialectic of Sex,* New York: Bantam Books, 1970.

Flexner, Eleanor. *Century of Struggle,* New York: Atheneum, 1971.

Frank, Jerome. *Courts on Trial,* Princeton, N.J.: Princeton Univ. Press, 1949.

Frankfort, Ellen. *Vaginal Politics,* New York: Bantam Books, 1973.

Frankfurter, Felix, Mary W. Dewson, and John R. Commons. *State Minimum-Wage Laws in Practice,* New York: National Consumers' League, 1924.

Freeman, Jo. *The Politics of Women's Liberation,* New York: David McKay Co., 1975.

Freud, Sigmund. *Civilization and its Discontents,* tr. & ed. by James Strachey, New York: W. W. Norton & Co., 1961.

Freund, Ernst. *The Police Power,* Chicago: Callaghan & Co., 1904.

Friedan, Betty. *The Feminine Mystique,* New York: W. W. Norton & Co., 1963.

Friedrich, Carl J., and John W. Chapman, eds. *Nomos VI: Justice,* New York: Atherton Press, 1963.

Fuller, Lon L. *The Morality of Law,* New Haven: Yale Univ. Press, 1964.

Galbraith, John Kenneth. *Economics and the Public Purpose,* Boston: Houghton Mifflin & Co., 1973.

Garraty, John A., ed. *Quarrels That Have Shaped the Constitution,* New York: Harper & Row, 1964.

Gilder, George. *Sexual Suicide,* New York: Quadrangle Books, 1973.

Gilman, Charlotte Perkins. *Women and Economics,* ed. by Carl Degler, New York: Harper & Row, 1966.

Glass, David C., ed. *Biology and Behavior,* New York: Russell Sage Foundation, 1968.

Goldberg, Stephen. *The Inevitability of Patriarchy,* New York: William Morrow & Co., 1973.

Goldmark, Josephine. *Fatigue and Efficiency,* New York: Charities Publications Industries, 1912.

Gornick, Vivian, and Barbara K. Moran, eds. *Woman in Sexist Society,* New York: Basic Books, 1971.

Groat, George Gorham. *Attitude of American Courts in Labor Cases: A Study in Social Legislation,* Columbia Univ. Studies in Political Science, vol. XLII, New York: Longmans, Green, & Co., 1911.

Harris, Robert J. *The Quest for Equality,* Baton Rouge: Louisiana State Univ. Press, 1960.

Hays, H. R. *The Dangerous Sex: The Myth of Feminine Evil,* New York: G. P. Putnam's Sons, 1964.

Henry, Alice. *Women in the Labor Movement,* New York: George H. Doran Co., 1923.

Horney, Karen. *Feminine Psychology,* ed. by Harold Kelman, New York: W. W. Norton & Co., 1967.

Hunt, Morton M. *Her Infinite Variety,* New York: Harper & Row, 1962.

Janeway, Elizabeth. *Between Myth and Morning: Woman Awakening,* New York: William Morrow & Co., 1974.

——. *Man's World, Woman's Place: A Study in Social Mythology,* New York: William Morrow & Co., 1971.

Kanowitz, Leo. *Women and the Law: The Unfinished Revolution,* Albuquerque: Univ. of New Mexico Press, 1967.

Kanowitz, Leo, ed. *Sex Roles in Law and Society: Cases and Materials,* Albuquerque: Univ. of New Mexico Press, 1973.

Kelley, Florence. *Some Ethical Gains Through Legislation,* 2nd ed., New York: Macmillan, 1910.

Klein, Viola. *The Feminine Character,* London: Kegan Paul, Trench, Trubner, & Co., 1946.

Kingsbury, Susan. *Labor Laws and Their Enforcement,* New York: Longmans, Green, & Co., 1911.

Komarovsky, Mirra. *Women in the Modern World,* Boston: Little, Brown, & Co., 1953.

Konefsky, Samuel. *The Legacy of Holmes and Brandeis,* New York: Macmillan, 1956.

Kreps, Juanita. *Sex in the Marketplace: American Women at Work,* Baltimore: John Hopkins Press, 1971.

Lane, Robert. *Political Life,* New York: Free Press, 1959.

Lash, Joseph. *Eleanor and Franklin,* New York: W. W. Norton & Co., 1971.

——. *Eleanor: The Years Alone,* New York: W. W. Norton & Co., 1972.

Lemons, J. Stanley. *The Woman Citizen: Social Feminism in the 1920s,* Urbana: Univ. of Illinois Press, 1973.

Lewis, C. S. *The Screwtape Letters,* New York: Macmillan Co., 1943.

Lombroso, Gina. *The Soul of Woman,* New York: E. P. Dutton & Co., 1923.

Longford, Elizabeth. *Queen Victoria: Born to Succeed,* New York: Harper & Row, 1965.

Lundberg, Ferdinand, and Marynia F. Farnham, *Modern Woman: The Lost Sex,* New York: Grosset & Dunlap, 1947.

Maccoby, Eleanor E., ed. *The Development of Sex Differences,* Stanford, Calif.: Stanford Univ. Press, 1966.

MacLean, Annie. *Wage-Earning Women,* New York: Macmillan, 1910.

Mailer, Norman. *The Prisoner of Sex,* Boston: Little, Brown, & Co., 1971.

Malinowski, Bronislaw. *Sex and Repression in Savage Society*, London: Routledge & Kegan Paul, 1927.

Maslow, A. H. *Motivation and Personality*, New York: Harper & Brothers, 1954.

Mason, Alpheus Thomas. *Brandeis: A Free Man's Life*, New York: Viking Press, 1946.

Masters, William H., and Virginia E. Johnson. *Human Sexual Response*, Boston: Little, Brown, & Co., 1966.

McClelland, David C. et al. *The Achievement Motive*, New York: Appleton-Century-Crofts, 1953.

McCloskey, Robert G. *American Conservatism in the Age of Enterprise, 1865-1910*, 2nd ed., New York: Harper & Row, 1964.

McGinley, Phyllis. *The Province of the Heart*, New York: Viking Press, 1959.

———. *Sixpence in Her Shoe*, New York: Macmillan Co., 1964.

McNeill, George E., ed. *The Labor Movement*, Boston: A. M. Bridgman & Co., 1887.

Mead, Margaret. *Male and Female*, New York: William Morrow & Co., 1949.

Millett, Kate. *Sexual Politics*, New York: Doubleday & Co., 1970.

Mitchell, Juliet. *Psychoanalysis and Feminism*, New York: Pantheon Books, 1974.

Montagu, Ashley. *The Natural Superiority of Women*, rev. ed., New York: Macmillan, 1968.

Morgan, Robin, ed. *Sisterhood Is Powerful*, New York: Random House, 1970.

Murdock, G. P. *Social Structure*, New York: Macmillan Co., 1949.

Myrdal, Alva, and Viola Klein. *Women's Two Roles*, 2nd ed., London: Routledge & Kegan Paul Ltd., 1968.

National Consumers' League. *Women in Industry*, New York: National Consumers' League, 1908 (*Muller v. Oregon*, 208 U.S. 412, Brief for Appellees).

Olafson, Frederick A., ed. *Justice and Social Policy*, Englewood Cliffs, N.J.: Prentice-Hall, 1961.

O'Neill, William L., ed. *Women at Work*, Chicago: Quadrangle Books, 1972.

Osgood, Ellen L. *A History of Industry*, rev. ed., Boston: Ginn & Co., 1935.

Paul, Arnold M. *Conservative Crisis and the Rule of Law*, rev. ed., New York: Harper & Row, 1969.

Pennock, J. Roland, and John W. Chapman, eds. *Nomos IX: Equality*, New York: Atherton, 1967.

Piersall, Ronald. *The Worm in the Bud*, London: Weidenfeld & Nicolson, 1969.

Plato. *The Republic. Great Dialogues of Plato*, trans. by W. D. Rouse, New York: Mentor Books, 1956.

Pogrebin, Letty Cotton. *Getting Yours*, New York: David McKay Co., 1975.

Rainwater, Lee, Richard P. Coleman, and Gerald Handel. *Workingman's Wife*, New York: Oceana Publications, Inc., 1959.

Rawls, John. *A Theory of Justice*, Cambridge, Mass.: Belknap Press of Harvard Univ. Press, 1971.

Rheingold, Joseph. *The Fear of Being a Woman*, New York: Grune & Stratton, 1964.

Riegel, Robert. *American Feminists*, Lawrence: Univ. of Kansas Press, 1963.

——. *American Women,* Rutherford, N.J.: Fairleigh Dickinson Univ. Press, 1963.

Robinson, Marie N. *The Power of Sexual Surrender,* Garden City, N.Y.: Doubleday & Co., 1959.

Rossi, Alice S., ed. *Essays on Sex Equality: John Stuart Mill and Harriet Taylor Mill,* Chicago: Univ. of Chicago Press, 1970.

Rubin, Lillian Breslow. *Worlds of Pain,* New York: Basic Books, 1976.

Sampson, Ronald V. *The Psychology of Power,* New York: Pantheon Books, 1965.

Schattschneider, E. E. *The Semisovereign People,* New York: Holt, Rinehart, & Winston, 1960.

Scott, Anne Firor, *The Southern Lady,* Chicago: Univ. of Chicago Press, 1970.

Seaman, Barbara. *Free and Female,* New York: Coward-McCann & Geoghegan, Inc., 1972.

Selznick, Philip. *Law, Society, and Industrial Justice,* New York: Russell Sage Foundation, 1969.

Slater, Philip. *The Pursuit of Loneliness,* Boston: Beacon Press, 1970.

Smuts, Robert W. *Women and Work in America,* New York: Columbia Univ. Press, 1959.

Stumpf, Samuel E. *Morality and the Law,* Nashville: Vanderbilt Univ. Press, 1966.

Terman, Lewis W., and Catherine Cox Miles. *Sex and Personality,* New York: McGraw-Hill, 1936.

Thomas, W. I. *Sex and Society,* Boston: Gorham Press, 1907.

Thompson, E. P. *The Making of the English Working Class,* New York: Random House, 1964.

Thompson, Helen. *The Mental Traits of Sex,* Chicago: Univ. of Chicago Press, 1902.

Tiedeman, Christopher G. *State and Federal Control of Persons and Property,* St. Louis: F. H. Thomas Law Book Co., 1900.

——. *A Treatise on the Limitations of the Police Power in the United States,* rev. ed., New York: Da Capo Press, 1971.

Tiger, Lionel. *Men in Groups,* New York: Random House, 1969.

Timasheff, N. S. *An Introduction to the Sociology of Law,* Cambridge: Harvard Univ. Press, 1939.

Twiss, Benjamin R. *Lawyers and the Constitution,* Princeton, N.J.: Princeton Univ. Press, 1942.

Tyler, Leona E. *The Psychology of Human Differences,* New York: D. Appleton-Century, 1947.

Urofsky, Melvin I. *A Mind of One Piece: Brandeis and American Reform,* New York: Charles Scribner's Sons, 1971.

Urofsky, Melvin I., and David W. Levy, eds. *Letters of Louis D. Brandeis, Volume II, 1907-1912,* Albany: State University of New York Press, 1972.

Vaerting, Mathilde, and Mathias Vaerting. *The Dominant Sex: A Study in the Sociology of Sex Differentiation,* New York: George H. Doran Co., 1923.

Westermarck, Edward. *The History of Human Marriage,* London: Macmillan & Co., 1911.

Willoughby, W. F. *State Activities in Relation to Labor in the United States*, Johns Hopkins University Studies in Historical and Political Science, vol. 19, nos. 4-5, Baltimore: Johns Hopkins Press, 1910.

Wood, Stephen B. *Constitutional Politics in the Progressive Era*, Chicago: University of Chicago Press, 1968.

ARTICLES AND PERIODICALS

Avins, Alfred. "The Equal 'Protection' of the Laws: The Original Understanding," *New York Law Forum* 12 (Fall 1966): 385-429.

———. "Social Equality and the Fourteenth Amendment: The Original Understanding," *Houston Law Review* 7 (Spring 1967): 640-656.

Baer, Judith A. "Equality Under the Constitution: The Limits of Equal Protection," prepared for delivery at the annual meeting of the Western Political Science Association, San Francisco, Calif., April 1-3, 1976.

———. "*Griswold v. Connecticut:* The Zone of Privacy and Freedom," unpublished, Univ. of Chicago, 1970.

———. "Sexual Equality and the Burger Court," prepared for delivery at the annual meeting of the American Political Science Association, San Francisco, Calif., September 2-5, 1975.

Ballantine, Henry W. "Labor Legislation and the Recall of the 'Judicial Veto,' " *Case and Comment* 19 (September 1912): 225-232.

Binder, Denis. "Sex Discrimination in the Airline Industry: Title VII Flying High," *California Law Review* 59 (September 1971): 1091-1112.

Breckenridge, Sophonisba P. "Legislative Control of Women's Work," *Journal of Political Economy* 14 (January 1906): 107-118.

Brown, Barbara A. et al. "The Equal Rights Amendment: A Constitutional Basis for Equal Rights for Women," *Yale Law Journal* 80 (April 1971): 871-986.

Bruce, Andrew Alexander. "The Illinois Ten-Hour Labor Law for Women," *Michigan Law Review* 8 (November 1909): 1-24.

———. "Statutory Regulations of the Employment of Women," *Central Law Journal* 58 (February 12, 1904): 123-128.

Cheadle, J. Kennard. "The Parrish Case: Minimum Wages for Women and, Perhaps, for Men," *University of Cincinnati Law Review* 11 (May 1937): 307-326.

Cohen, Harry. "Minimum Wage Legislation and the Adkins Case," *New York University Law Review* 2 (March 1925): 48-56.

Comment. "Constitutional Law: Police Power: Minimum Wage for Women," *California Law Review* 11 (July 1923): 353-362.

Comment. "Constitutionality of the New York Minimum Wage Law," *Yale Law Journal* 42 (June 1933): 1250-1259.

Comment. " 'A Little Dearer Than His Horse': Legal Stereotypes and the Feminine Personality," *Harvard Civil Rights-Civil Liberties Law Review* 6 (March 1971): 260-287.

Comment. "Love's Labors Lost: New Conceptions of Maternity Leaves," *Harvard Civil Rights-Civil Liberties Law Review* 7 (January 1972): 260-297.

Comment. "The Mandate of Title VII of the Civil Rights Act of 1964: To Treat Women as Individuals," *Georgetown Law Journal* 59 (October 1970): 221-239.

Comment. "Sex Discrimination in Hiring Practices of Private Employers: Recent Legal Developments," *Tulane Law Review* 48 (December 1973): 125-148.

Corwin, Edward S. "The Supreme Court and the Fourteenth Amendment," *Michigan Law Review* 7 (June 1909): 643-672.

Crozier, Blanche. "Constitutionality of Discrimination Based on Sex," *Boston University Law Review* 15 (November 1935): 723-756.

———. "Marital Support," *Boston University Law Review* 15 (January 1935): 28-58.

Daniel, Anna S. "Conditions of the Labor of Women and Children, Observed by a Dispensary Physician in New York," *Journal of Social Science* 30 (September 1892): 73-85.

de Graffenreid, Clare. "The Condition of Wage-Earning Women," *Forum* 15 (March 1893): 68-71.

"Developments in the Law: Employment Discrimination and Title VII of the Civil Rights Act of 1964," *Harvard Law Review* 84 (March 1971): 1109-1316.

"Developments in the Law: Equal Protection," *Harvard Law Review* 82 (March 1969): 1065-1192.

Edwards, Percy L. "Constitutional Interpretation and Limitations as Applied to Laws Limiting the Hours of Labor," *Central Law Journal* 74 (March 22, 1912): 226-228.

Ely, Richard T. " The Report of the Industrial Commission: Labor," *Yale Review* 11 (November 1902): 229-250.

Frank, John P., and Robert F. Munro. "The Original Understanding of 'Equal Protection of the Laws,' " *Columbia Law Review* 50 (February 1950): 131-169.

Frankfurter, Felix. "Hours of Labor and Realism in Constitutional Law," *Harvard Law Review* 29 (February 1916): 353-373.

Freud, Sigmund. "Femininity," *New Introductory Lectures in Psychoanalysis,* trans. by James Strachey, New York: W. W. Norton & Co., 1964.

———. "Some Psychological Consequences of the Anatomical Distinction Between the Sexes," *International Journal of Psychoanalysis* 7 (January 1927): 133-142.

Freund, Ernst. "Constitutional Limitations and Labor Legislation," *Illinois Law Review* 4 (April 1910): 609-623.

———. "Limitation of Hours of Labor and the Federal Supreme Court," *Green Bag* 17 (July 1905): 411-417.

Gleason, Caroline J. "For Working Women in Oregon," *The Survey* 36 (September 9, 1916): 585-586.

Goble, George W. "The Minimum Wage Decision," *Kentucky Law Journal* 12 (November 1923): 1-9.

Gouldner, Joseph C. Review of Paul Hoffman's *Lions in the Street,* in *New York Times Book Review* (July 8, 1973), p. 10.

Greeley, Louis M. "The Changing Attitude of the Courts Toward Social Legislation," *Illinois Law Review* 5 (November 1910): 222-232.

Green, B. A. "The Legal Aspects of the Labor Movement," *Oregon Law Review* 15 (December 1935): 13-38.

Green, John B. "Labor's Fighting Legionnaries on the Legal Field," *Case and Comment* 19 (September 1912): 233-239.

Groat, George Gorham. "The Courts and the Labor Question," *Case and Comment* 19 (September 1912): 261-264.

Gunther, Gerald. "In Search of Evolving Doctrine on a Changing Court: a Model for a Newer Equal Protection," *Harvard Law Review* 86 (November 1972): 1-48.

Hale, Robert L. "Minimum Wages and the Constitution," *Columbia Law Review* 36 (April 1936): 629-633.

Hand, Learned. "Due Process of Law and the Eight-Hour Day," *Harvard Law Review* 21 (May 1908): 495-509.

Harper, Fowler V. "Due Process of Law and State Labor Legislation," *Michigan Law Review* 26 (April-June 1928): 599-630, 773-789, 888-905.

"Height Standards in Police Employment and the Question of Sex Discrimination: The Availability of Two Defenses for a Neutral Employment Policy Found Discriminatory under Title VII," *Southern California Law Review* 47 (February 1974): 585-640.

Holcombe, A. N. "The Legal Minimum Wage in the United States," *American Economic Review* 2 (March 1912): 21-37.

Horney, Karen. "The Flight from Womanhood: the Masculinity Complex in Women, as Viewed by Men, and by Women," *International Journal of Psychoanalysis* 7 (July 1926): 324-329.

Johnston, John D., Jr. "Sex Discrimination and the Supreme Court," *New York University Law Review* 49 (November 1974): 617-692.

——. "Sex Discrimination and the Supreme Court—1975," *University of California at Los Angeles Law Review* 23 (December 1975): 235-265.

Johnston, John D., Jr., and Charles D. Knapp. "Sex Discrimination by Law: A Study in Judicial Perspective," *New York University Law Review* 46 (October 1971): 675-747.

Jones, Dana T. "Does the United States Constitution Inhibit State Laws Limiting Hours of Private Daily Employment?" *Central Law Journal* 52 (November 15, 1901): 384-390.

Kagan, Jerome. "Check One: Male: Female," *Psychology Today* 3 (July 1969): 39-41.

Kelley, Florence. "Minimum Wage Laws," *Journal of Political Economy* 20 (December 1912): 999-1010.

Kennedy, Joseph P. "Sex Discrimination: State Protective Laws Since Title VII," *Notre Dame Lawyer* 47 (February 1972): 514-549.

Kurland, Philip B. "The New Supreme Court," *John Marshall Journal* 7 (Fall 1973): 1-14.

Landau, Eliot A., and Kermit L. Dunahoo. "Sex Discrimination in Employment: A Survey of State and Federal Remedies," *Drake Law Review* 20 (June 1971): 417-527.

"Legal Interference with the Hours of Labor," *Lippincott's Magazine* 2 (November 1868): 527-533.

Lukens, Edward C. "Shall Women Throw Away Their Privileges?" *American Bar Association Journal* 11 (October 1925): 645-646.

Marshino, Ora L., and Lawrence J. O'Malley. "Wage and Hour Legislation in the Courts," *George Washington Law Review* 5 (May 1937): 865-878.

Mason, Alpheus Thomas. "Labor, the Courts, and Section 7a," *American Political Science Review* 28 (December 1934): 999-1015.

Mathews, Burnita Sheldon. "Women Should Have Equal Rights with Men: A Reply," *American Bar Association Journal* 12 (February 1926): 117-120.

McCloskey, Robert. "Economic Due Process and the Supreme Court," *Supreme Court Review* (1962): 34-62.

Mead, Margaret. "Some Theoretical Considerations on the Problem of Mother-Child Separation," *American Journal of Orthopsychiatry* 24 (July 1954): 471-483.

Mendelson, Wallace. "From Warren to Burger: The Rise and Decline of Substantive Equal Protection," *American Political Science Review* 66 (December 1972): 1226-1233.

Moewe, Parke W. "The Case for Benign Sex Discrimination," *Los Angeles Bar Bulletin* 44 (June 1969): 337-349, 359-360.

Murray, Pauli, and Mary Eastwood. "Jane Crow and the Law: Sex Discrimination and Title VII," *George Washington Law Review* 34 (December 1965): 232-256.

Myrick, O. H. "Hours of Labor," *Central Law Journal* 63 (August 21, 1906): 147-150.

National Consumers' League. "The Eight Hours Day for Wage Earning Women," *Women in Industry* series, no. 14, December 1916.

Note. "The Adkins Case Reconsidered," *Yale Law Journal* 45 (June 1936): 1490-1494.

Note. "Classification on the Basis of Sex and the 1964 Civil Rights Act," *Iowa Law Review* 50 (Spring 1965): 778-798.

Note. "Holden v. Hardy," *Central Law Journal* 46 (April 1, 1898): 355-356.

Note. "Present Status of the Adkins Case," *Kentucky Law Journal* 24 (November 1935): 59-68.

Note. "Sex Discrimination and Equal Protection: Do We Need a Constitutional Amendment?" *Harvard Law Review* 84 (April 1971): 1499-1524.

Oldham, James C. "Sex Discrimination and State Protective Laws," *Denver Law Journal* 44 (Summer 1967): 344-376.

Parkinson, Thomas I. "Minimum Wage and the Constitution," *American Labor Legislation Review* 13 (June 1923): 131-136.

Parsons, Talcott. "Age and Sex in the Social Structure of the United States," *Essays in Sociological Theory,* rev. ed., Glencoe, Ill.: Free Press, 1954.

Persons, C. E. "Women's Work and Wages in the United States," *Quarterly Journal of Economics* 29 (February 1915): 201-234.

Pound, Roscoe. "Liberty of Contract," *Yale Law Journal* 18 (May 1909): 454-487.

Powell, Thomas Reed. "The Judiciality of Minimum-Wage Legislation," *Harvard Law Review* 37 (March 1924): 545-573.

"Progress in the Minimum-Wage Struggle," *Iowa Law Review* 22 (March 1937): 565-579.

Puller, Edwin S. "When Equal Rights are Unequal," *Virginia Law Review* 13 (June 1927): 619-631.

Ramey, Estelle. "Men's Cycles (They Have Them Too, You Know)," *ms.*, preview issue (Spring 1972): 8-15.

Robinson, F. Mabel. "Our Working Women and Their Earnings," *Fortnightly Review* 47 (July 1, 1887): 50-63.

Rogers, William P. "Constitutionality of Minimum Wage Statutes for Women and Minors," *Cornell Law Quarterly* 21 (April 1936): 501-504.

Sangerman, Harry. "A Look at the Equal Pay Act in Practice," *Labor Law Journal* 22 (May 1971): 259-265.

Sape, George P., and Thomas J. Hart. "Title VII Reconsidered: The Equal Employment Opportunity Act of 1972," *George Washington Law Review* 40 (July 1972): 824-889.

Schaar, John. "Some Ways of Thinking About Equality," *Journal of Politics* 26 (November 1964): 867-895.

Seager, Henry R. "The Attitude of American Courts Towards Restrictive Labor Laws," *Political Science Quarterly* 19 (December 1904): 589-611.

———. "The Theory of the Minimum Wage," *American Economic Review* 3 (February 1913): 81-91.

Selznick, Philip. "The Sociology of Law," *International Encyclopedia of the Social Sciences* 9 (1966): 50-59.

Sexton, Patricia Cayo. "Speaking for the Working-Class Wife," *Harper's* 225 (October 1962): 129-133.

Sturgis, Robert F. "Demands of Labor and the Fourteenth Amendment," *American Law Review* 41 (July-August 1907): 481-497.

Symposium. "Women and the Law," *Valparaiso University Law Review* 5, no. 2 (1971).

Thompson, Clara. "Cultural Pressures in the Psychology of Women," *Psychiatry* 5 (August 1942): 331-339.

Thompson, W. D. "The Development of Women's Rights in the Law," *Marquette Law Review* 8 (April 1924): 152-167.

Tussman, Joseph, and Jacobus ten Broek. "The Equal Protection of the Laws," *California Law Review* 37 (September 1949): 341-381.

Wallach, Aleta, and Larry Rubin. "The Premenstrual Syndrome and Criminal Responsibility," *UCLA Law Review* 19 (December 1971): 210-312.

Webb, Sidney. "The Economic Theory of a Legal Minimum Wage," *Journal of Political Economy* 20 (December 1912): 973-998.

Wilcox, Jonathan J. "The Sex Discrimination Provisions of Title VII: A Maturing Controversy," *Pacific Law Journal* 3 (January 1972): 37-62.

Willoughby, W. F. "The Philosophy of Labor Legislation," *American Political Science Review* 8 (March 1914): 14-24.

"Women and the Law: A Symposium." *Rutgers Law Review* 25 (Fall 1970).

Zilboorg, Gregory. "Masculine and Feminine: Some Biological and Cultural Aspects," *Psychiatry* 7 (August 1944): 257-296.

GOVERNMENT PUBLICATIONS

United States. Bureau of the Census. Monograph no. 9, *Women in Gainful Occupations, 1870 to 1920,* Washington, D.C.: U.S. Government Printing Office, 1929.

——. *1950 Census of Population,* vol. 1, Washington, D.C.: U.S. Government Printing Office, 1952.

United States. Congress. Senate. *Report on the Condition of Women and Child Wage-Earners in the United States,* 61st Cong., 2nd Sess.; 62nd Cong., 1st and 2nd Sess.; 63rd Cong., 1st Sess., 19 vols., Washington, D.C.: Government Printing Office, 1910-1915.

United States. Women's Bureau. Bulletin no. 61. *The Development of Minimum-Wage Laws in the United States, 1912 to 1927,* Washington, D.C.: Government Printing Office, 1928.

——. Bulletin no. 65. *Effects of Labor Legislation on the Employment of Women,* Washington, D.C.: Government Printing Office, 1928.

——. Bulletin no. 66. *History of Labor Legislation in Three States and Chronological Development of Labor Legislation for Women in the United States,* rev. ed., Washington, D.C.: Government Printing Office, 1935.

——. Bulletin no. 294. *Handbook of Women Workers,* Washington, D.C.: Government Printing Office, 1969.

INDEX OF CASES

SUBJECT INDEX

Abbott, Edith, 19, 22
Age, as basis for discrimination, 127-29, 179
Alienage, as basis for discrimination, 126-27, 129
American Federation of Labor (AFL), 33-34, 89
Anastasi, Anne, 210-11
Aristotle, 184-86, 190-91

Bakan, David, 209, 210
Banfield, Edward, 75
Bardwick, Judith, 202, 204
Benedict, Ruth, 211
Bernard, Jessie, 184
Bettelheim, Bruno, 204, 209
Bickel, Alexander, 119, 124
Bird, Caroline, 72
Black, Hugo L., 115
Bowlby, John, 181-84
Bradley, Joseph P., 64, 183, 203
Brandeis, Louis D., 78-79, 89; appointed to Supreme Court, 76, 89; as counsel in Muller, 57-61; as Supreme Court Justice, 90, 92, 93, 99. *See also* Brandeis briefs
Brandeis briefs, 5, 76, 110, 166-67; in Bunting v. Oregon, 89-90; in cases on hours after Muller v. Oregon, 78-80; in cases on men's and women's hours, compared, 89-90; and minimum wage, 75, 95; in Muller, 57-61; in night work cases, 76-77, 84-85; and U.S.

Senate report on women and child workers, 73
Breckenridge, Sophonisba Preston, 38-39
Brennan, William J., Jr., 161-62
Brewer, David, and Muller opinion, 27, 57, 62-67, 94-96, 110, 131, 194
Burger, Warren, 157
Butler, Pierce, 98

Cardozo, Benjamin N., 99
Childbearing, 23-25, 27, 28, 65, 175, 193-95. *See also* Family
Choate, Joseph H., 9
Civil Rights Act of 1964, Title VII, 4, 5, 108, 109, 141, 148, 216; and bona fide occupational qualification (BFOQ), 150, 154-55, 162-69; and Equal Employment Opportunity Commission, 149; and facially neutral policies, 156-59; legislative history of, 136, 149; and pregnancy, 159-62; procedures under, 150; and "sex plus" discrimination, 152-56; and women's labor legislation, 138-39, 162-69. *See also* Equal Employment Opportunity Commission; Race discrimination; Sex discrimination
"Class legislation," 45, 48
Cleaver, Eldridge, 213
Commons, John R., 19, 25, 32, 92-93

ABOUT THE AUTHOR

Judith A. Baer, Assistant Professor of Political Science at the State University of New York, Albany, previously taught at the University of Hawaii. She specializes in public law and political philosophy. This is her first book-length work.

DATE DUE